BUSINESS COMMUNICATION

BUSINESS COMMUNICATION

C. R. Reddy
UGC Emeritus
Department of Commerce
Sri Krishnadevaraya University
Anantapur (AP), India

TECHSAR™
NEW DELHI

Published and Printed by
Techsar Pvt. Ltd.
4435-36/7,AnsariRoad,Daryaganj
NewDelhi-110002(India)
E-mail:tech_info@techsarworld.com
Website:www.techsarworld.com

ISBN: 978-93-84588-63-2

Reprint2025

Dedication

to

the Lotus Feet of

ALMIGHTY VENKATESWARA SWAMY

and

HIS CONSORTS

Preface

Communication constitutes the lifeline of every organization, be it a business, service institution, governance of government and nation, group of individuals and alike particularly in the context of global reach finding an expression for problems. In other words, to make a continuous success of business, avoiding fear and doubt which are the major enemies of success and achievement, the students should have a clear insight into frame of message, clarity in sending it to the recipient being influencing perception to the message thought of the sender is possible through one measure called **communication**. Today, communication is a dynamic skill in managing the competency and capacity. Because of this feature, communication has become a part in the life of human beings.

Communication is a fascinating study with challenging field of interaction of people through means of exchanging facts, feelings, emotions, ideas, opinions either in the written, oral or non-verbal form. Proficiency in all segments of communication is the need of the day and, in fact, the demand of the society. The students are challenged to exhibit skills of their own in terms of thinking, writing, observing and speaking effectively and also about right perception, use of information, analysis of situation and logical findings for making a decision. Hence, in developing skills, knowledge of communication is a must.

Communication, which now is recognized as an important and interesting discipline, need to all the students irrespective of their academic background undergraduation and postgraduation of both conventional and distance mode institutions.

This book is a comprehensive coverage of concepts and cardinal canons of communication to acquire a good understanding of all relevant and rational facets of communication highlighting the formats and modalities in current use. The subject matter is supported by thought provoking ideas given in exhibits. It is conscious and comprehensive coverage of all the topics of business communication prescribed for students of Commerce, Management and professional courses. Students of Business Communication stand to benefit substantially from this book.

More than three decades of teaching experience to the postgraduate students of Commerce and research students in Commerce; and exposure to varied forms of students has gone into making this book. I express my indebtedness to the Department of Commerce and Sri Krishnadevaraya University, Anantapur, Andhra Pradesh. I also express my gratitude to the authors whose thoughtful ideas encouraged me and many of which quoted in this book.

It is sincere and bounden duty of mine to express indebtedness to my beloved parents, late Sri C. Gurivi Reddy and late Smt. C. Munemma for showering their blessings. I gracefully express my feelings to my lovely granddaughter, S. Nirvi Reddy daughter of Mr & Mrs. Ravali Sai Krishna, M. Tech Software Engineers, Bangalore, and grandson, L. Avyan Reddy son of Lahari Sudheer Reddy, software engineers, Bangalore for showing their everlasting smiling face. I welcome comments and suggestions on the subject for improvement of this book.

C. R. Reddy

Contents

Preface *vii*

1. Basics of Communication **1**

1.1 Communication and Knowledge Management 1
1.2 Time in Communication 4
1.3 Evolution of Communication 4
1.4 Communication and Mankind 5
1.5 Meaning of Communication 6
1.6 Definition of Communication 7
1.7 Nature and Scope of Communication 8
1.8 Features of Communication 9
1.9 Principles of Communication 9
1.10 Objectives of Communication 10
1.11 Effects of Communication 11
1.12 Importance of Communication 12
1.13 Functions of Communication 12
1.14 Is Communication a Discipline? 15
1.15 How to Improve Communication? 16
1.16 Guidelines Governing Effective Communication 25
1.17 Policy of Communication 25
1.18 Communication Barriers 26
Questions 32

2. Business Communication Management **34**

2.1 Communication 34
2.2 Interface of Business Communication and Management 36
2.3 Foundation 38
2.4 Management Tool 39
2.5 Is Communication a Managerial Role? 40

2.6 Communication Approach 46
2.7 Does Business Need Communication? 49
2.8 Governance and Communication 50
Questions *51*

3. Classification of Business Communication **52**
3.1 Classification of Communication 53
3.2 Verbal Communication 54
3.3 Oral Communication 65
3.4 Interactive Communication 73
3.5 Importance of Non-Verbal Communication 95
3.6 New Dimensions to Visual Communication 103
Questions *108*

4. Channels of Communication **110**
4.1 Channels of Communication 110
4.2 Formal Communication 111
4.3 Anonymous Communication 117
4.4 Personal Communication 117
4.5 Three-Phase Communication 118
4.6 Consensus 118
4.7 Informal Communication 118
4.8 Grapevine 119
Questions *122*

5. Corporate and Mass Communication **123**
5.1 Corporate Communication 123
5.2 Interface of Media and Business 147
5.3 Trends in Business Communication 149
5.4 Mass Communication and Its Types 153
5.5 Interpersonal Communication 156
Questions *157*

6. Business Report Writing **158**
6.1 Meaning of Report 159
6.2 Purpose of Report 159
6.3 Functions of a Good Report 160
6.4 Types of Business Report 160
6.5 Structure of Business Report 165
6.6 Documentation of Report 168
6.7 Qualities of Good Business Report 170

6.8 Specimen Reports	171
Questions	*176*
7. Marketing Service Communication	**177**
7.1 Marketing Communication Process	178
7.2 Communication Model	187
7.3 Message Development	187
7.4 E-Marketing	188
Questions	*194*
8. Communication and Listening and Speaking Skills	**195**
8.1 Corporate Education	196
8.2 Communication Skills	197
8.3 Soft Skills	198
8.4 Listening Skills	200
8.5 Types of Listening	203
8.6 Public Speaking	205
Questions	*211*
9. Electronic Communication	**212**
9.1 Evolution of Modern Network	213
9.2 Classification of Communication	214
9.3 Social Networking	228
9.4 Classification of Social Media	233
Questions	*245*
10. Resume Writing and Career Opportunity	**246**
10.1 Basics in Career Planning	246
10.2 Curriculum Vitae	247
10.3 Preparation of Job Application	248
10.4 Preparation of Resume	250
10.5 Specimen	253
10.6 Group Discussion	256
10.7 Job Interviews	263
10.8 Moving Towards a Career	264
Questions	*265*

11. Analysis of Case Studies **266**

11.1 Effective Top-down Communication 266
11.2 Clarity of Thought 267
11.3 Career Recognition 268
11.4 Social Advertising 269
11.5 Effective Listening 269
11.6 Effect of Understanding 270
11.7 Understanding Message 270
11.8 Effects of Television 271
11.9 Open-door Policy 271
11.10 Memo Preparation 272
11.11 Advertisement 273
11.12 Understanding of Communication 273
11.13 Financial Aid for Peace Progress 274
11.14 Knowledge Management 275
Questions *275*

Objective Questions **277**

Glossary **283**

Bibliography **288**

Index **289**

1 CHAPTER

Basics of Communication

The world is changing, communication is wireless, business is cashless, cooking is fireless, telephone is cordless and food is fatless. Success of business is twines of communication and human relations.

LEARNING OBJECTIVE

This chapter will enable you to

- understand knowledge management;
- know evolution of communication;
- understand meaning and definition of communication;
- know features, principles, objectives, effects, functions and importance of communication;
- identify determinants and process of communication;
- know essentials of communication; and
- understand ethics and communication.

INTRODUCTION

The basic need to mankind for peace, progress and good life is communication. Communication occurs with words and without words – senses, sound, sight, touch, smell and taste. Business operations are being done by different workers in the process of management of an organization.

Communication and decision are common parameters to all functions of effective management of business. Therefore, communication has all-pervasive in management.

1.1 COMMUNICATION AND KNOWLEDGE MANAGEMENT

Educational institute place emphasis on acquisition of knowledge. It is a universal fact that not enough importance is given to the practical implications of whatever is acquired as knowledge in the classrooms. What is needed is **application-oriented knowledge** to meet the ever changing environmental challenges of change and growth in the context of globalization. Individuals can create knowledge only. Business organizations need to support these creative individuals and provide a context for them to create knowledge. Therefore, knowledge of business organization is a process of identifying, creating and supporting creative individuals and amplification and crystallization of their knowledge as a part of knowledge network of the organization. Economists realized the role of knowledge long back and, in fact, it is the interest of the economists in knowledge which led to the new management thought of knowledge management (KM). Alfred Marshall, the noted economist, has stated explicitly the importance of knowledge in economic affairs. Knowledge management deals with knowledge as a 'strategic' resource in every firm's success and improvement of the whole range of man. Education and advances in knowledge are as important as capital and natural resources to the economic growth of a nation. Integration of knowledge management and customer relation management (CRM) helps the business to satisfy customers in an efficient and flexible manner. Thus, knowledge management aims at 3 'K's, namely: (i) knowledge generation, (ii) knowledge dissemination, and (iii) knowledge development. Hence, knowledge management is the brain which is key to sustainable economic growth.

The application orientation of this knowledge is a powerful tool and a resource to business organizations. In other words, education is the basic foundation which depends upon the progressiveness of human beings with two aspects of (i) peace and (ii) economy of a nation with sound and energetic role of business organizations aiding to improve knowledge management. In this context, it is viewed that 'language is a tool and communication is an art.' Albert Einstein once said: "Education is the progressive realization of our ignorance." The application of knowledge for progress of nation's economy and quality life of human beings as well as peace in the society depends upon the development of human resources which, in turn, depends upon the following five components given below. Promotion of skills is essential for meaningful decision-making which includes the ability to think analytically and inferentially synthesizing information from various sources.

Knowledge management has emerged as a powerful concept to provide a business firm with the sustained competitive advantage. It deals with knowledge as a corporate resource and works around establishing the corporate policy and practices for creating and deploying the firm's intellectual assets for optimum benefit. Alfred Marshall, the noted economist, was the first to state explicitly the importance of knowledge in economic affairs as: "Capital consists in a great part of knowledge and organization. Knowledge is our most powerful engine of production and organization aids in knowledge."

The good old-fashioned art of reading books helps cultivate discerning minds which are most essential for making sound decisions in the information age of to-day. According to the noted educationist, David Olson, reading changes the cognitive landscape of the reader and makes him/her more observant. Shortage of skills has been preventing large segments of human resource from being part of economic growth of a nation. The abbreviated word, 'SKILLS' stands as:

S is for skills
K is for knowledge
I is for improvement
L is for livelihood

L is for living
S is for standards

The acronym, SKILLS bears the promise of becoming part of the growth story. Therefore, acquisition of skills will meet the match of supply-side demand with demand-side strategy. In the process of human resources development, there are five essential components which are as follows.

1. **Self-development:** Learning is what one does in education and, perhaps, for the rest of life. It is a much more active experience than being taught; one must learn himself using what the teachers say, what the other students contribute, and what they read in the library to understand and improve the capacity for thought. A Chinese proverb says, "A journey of a thousand miles begins with a single step." Hence, one must plan a career for self-development and work hard to achieve lifetime goals. One should always keep in mind the worst enemy to creativity is self-doubt. Here the word, SMART is appropriate instilling confidence among the students. The acrimony of the word SMART stands as:

   S is for specific (specific study say, commerce)

   M is for measurable (measurable say, the achieved progress)

   A is for attainable (review previous progress and complete associate exercise if any)

   R is for realistic (say be in top five or ten)

   T is for timely (next task)

   With the above goal, one can become a good entrepreneur with vision through mission in visualizing and actualizing the efficiency of enterprising nature. When one who visualizes, he will certainly reap the results. An entrepreneur, like liquid, tends to take the shape of its container.

2. **Study Skills:** Knowing how to study is like knowing how to fish. It is a set of skills that lasts a lifetime and brings many rewards. Like learning how to fish, there are many ways to develop the study skills competency. One has to select the way that suits him/her best rather than look for the best way. "The function of education is to help you from childhood not to imitate anybody, but be yourself all the time." (J. Krishnamurty)

3. **Communication Skills:** Reading is a basic source of knowledge. Listening and discussion supplement reading in the pursuit of acquiring knowledge. Through writing, knowledge can be more precisely and effectively developed than through either reading or discussion alone. Indeed, an individual's whole experience is built upon the plan of his/her language. To demonstrate knowledge, one needs to speak, make presentation and write an examination or assignment or report on fieldwork. This would help him master language and communication skills. It is worth to quote Bacon on communication skills, "Reading makes a full man, conference a ready man and writing an exact man."

4. **Thinking Skills:** Thinking is a skill that must be learnt. Creative thinking is not a talent; but it is a skill that can be learnt. It empowers the learner by adding the strength in his natural abilities to improve teamwork, productivity and appropriate

profits. Like a knife, if one keeps mind sharper, it will work more effectively. Edward de Bono remarked: "Intelligence is something we are born with." Hence, continuously working aids in increasing the quality of thinking and attaining the intended goals. It is most appropriate to quote the words of Confucius who said: "Learning without thought is labour lost; thought without learning is perilous."

5. **Interpersonal Skills:** Integration is the buzzword in the scenario of globalization. So, consider the ideas of two people even if they are different in their nature of living together, which leads to creative and effective approaches for finding means to the problems/situations and solving them. Two heads are better than one, as no man is an island even though accustomed doing things on his own. By discussing a subject with others, one can develop interpersonal skills such as assertiveness, debate, thinking, critical and diligent examination, time management, decision-making, etc. Quoting Henry Ford's observation is worth. He said: "Coming together is a beginning. Keeping together is progress. Working together is success." Therefore, widening one's horizons is the greatest benefit from attending college in addition to gaining a degree.

1.2 TIME IN COMMUNICATION

People need quality education for self-reliance and also utilizing fully nature's gifted resources such as land, water, minerals, metals, manpower, forest wealth, crop, animal husbandry, etc., for sustaining the economic growth and development of a nation. To be self-reliant, one should possess skills along with knowledge to tackle the multifaceted situations/problems as harnessing the potential of human genome, developing sustaining energy and economic system, and dealing with far reaching issues like global warming and green global. These tasks need innovative knowledge with skills of managerial communication in the disciplines of art, science, entrepreneurship, business, and information technology, crossing the boundaries of nations. John Adair expressed: "If you get the results of working with other people, it is essential that you should develop your abilities and skills in three interrelated areas of leadership, decision-making and communication." See Exhibit 1.1 for research results showing how much time is spent in communication to acquire skills.

EXHIBIT 1.1 **Time Spent in Communication**

Research findings made that 50 to 80 per cent of working hours are spent in communicating; of which about 45 per cent in listening, 15 per cent in reading, 30 per cent in speaking and 10 per cent in writing.

1.3 EVOLUTION OF COMMUNICATION

The art of communication has evolved over the centuries. It goes back to the Biblical era, mythological times and pre-historic period. The pre-historic man produced sounds and made gestures to convey his feelings of joy, fear and sorrow. He sent smoke signals over long distances by lighting fire.

People need to learn to communicate with themselves much before they fully evolve into the present state of speaking, reading and writing. From sounds, grunts, actions, signs, gestures and gesticulations to spoken words; and thereafter to the world of reading and writing with modern sophisticated methods of communication. In the process of fascinating journey of communication, people learned to convey messages by interpreting or adopting sounds, understanding actions, and using signs and signals. Sages and saints of yore learnt to pass on the sacred verses and holy texts through word-of-mouth. People, thereafter, learned to use symbols and pictures to convey messages. Early writings were on stones and leaves. Then, the communication system progressed and revolutionized with the invention of printing. The results of inventions and innovations were affected in modern days which have been diffused to the target-audience in the society.

With the invention of recording of spoken words and their transmission; and the emergence of new media technology enabled storage and retrieval of oral words and written records in an effective time-saving and cost-conscious manner. Communication abounds its reach of messages which shrunk the world into a village and made globalization a reality. The reach of communication, therefore, is worldwide and is truly pervasive human life in all its facets. Communication becomes fruitful and successful only when it reaches the destination. Hence, communication is described as a link between 'people' and 'purposes'. Today, communication encompasses all the human beings and pervades the animal world too. The president of a nation, the chief executive and managers of corporate sector, the scientists in invention or investigation, the parent-child, the teacher-taught, the government-public, the wife-husband and alike are more concerned to achieve the intended goal by using effective communication. In a nutshell, communication, thus, in modern times, can be described as a 'pervasive' and 'fascinating' journey through time. The success or failure of efforts is the result of the ability to communicate effectively with others.

1.4 COMMUNICATION AND MANKIND

Breathing and wanting are part of life of human beings, so also communication has become the basic need of mankind for peace of the society, good economic progress and good life. A person may be the president, prime minister, chairman, executive, officer, salesman, scientist, teacher, student, technician, worker, husband, wife, child, etc., distinguishing himself from the rest of creation on the earth from the point of expressing message in words. Therefore, communication has become an important link that connects all human beings and serves the intended purpose to achieve. Sensory communication with physical and biological surroundings to find food, get protection and reproduce the species can, perhaps, be traced to the evolution of man. Simply, sensory communication was not enough for mankind to survive and progress. Hence, aroused the need for discovery of symbolic communication called **language**.

Communication occurs with words and sense of audio, visual, touch and smell. It is the act of imparting information in the form of verbal, written and printed words and is a dynamic and continuous process. The success of every venture of human beings lies in the ability and style of effective communication across the barriers and beyond the boundaries involving interactions in the environment. Intelligent and right communication skills will certainly help to make the lives of human beings richer and better. Communication, therefore, is the lifeline contributing to the development of 'personality' of people. The word, PERSONALITY stands as:

P is for positive attitude
E is for effective communication
R is for role model
S is for strength measurement
O is for originality
N is for national integrity
A is for avoiding conflict
L is for leadership quality
I is for inter-personal relationship
T is for time management
Y is for yearning

1.5 MEANING OF COMMUNICATION

The term, communication derives from the French word "*communis*" and Latin word, *communicare* which means 'common' and 'to share' respectively. Literally, communication means to inform, to tell, to show or to spread information with the meaning. It creates confidence among human beings and enhances good relations for accomplishing the things meant for. The essential motto of communication is that the communicated message should be understood correctly and transferred in the right direction. Let us take an example: organization is a group of human beings constituted for some specified objectives. Any achievement of these depends upon the human efforts which are needed to be coordinated and integrated. In an organization, the individuals performing different activities are functionally interrelated. The working and maintenance of this relationship is possible through communication, which provides for exchange of information and sharing of ideas. It also performs energizing of function in the organization by transmitting information, facts, feelings and ideas thereby making all possible coordinated efforts. Therefore, communication is regarded as a basic to the functioning of an organization, and in its absence, the organization ceases to exist.

Communication in the context of modern competitive and complex organization has a greater role. To achieve the designed and defined results in an organization on the basis of 3 'D's, namely, departmentalization, divisionalisation and decentralization with specialization need coordination requiring the mutual understanding of the objectives of organization. This can be achieved through communication only. Communication is an essential ingredient in any human grouping. Hence, communication is a prerequisite in business, government, military organization, hospitals, schools, homes, communities, foreign relations and in all such functions wherein human beings exist.

1.6 DEFINITION OF COMMUNICATION

Communication has been defined by many theorists; some of the definitions quoted here bring out different facets of communication and together facilitate an understanding of the expanse of the concept.

"Communication is the broad field of human interchange of facts and opinions." This definition focuses on the fact that communication is an interchange or exchange of facts and opinions of social or commercial intercourse.

— Newman and Summer

"Communication is the process of conveying messages (facts, ideas, attitudes and opinions) from one person to another so that they are understood." It delineates that communication is used to send messages between persons for what they want to inform to each other.

— Cunning M.W.

"Communication encompasses all forms of expression which serve the purpose of mutual understanding." This definition highlights the encompassing nature and has a purpose to achieve.

— Revesz

"Communication is a process which involves the transmission and accurate replication of ideas ensured by a feedback for the purposes of eliciting actions and accomplishing organizational goals." This definition describes that communication is transmitting messages and provide feedback with a purpose to achieve the goal of organization.

— William Scott

"Communication is an intercourse by words, letters, symbols or messages and is a way that one organization member shares meaning and understanding with another." It underlines that communication is sharing feelings or experiences by organizations among themselves using the course of words, letter and symbols.

— Koontz and O'Donnell

"Communication maintains and animates life. It creates a common pool of ideas, strengthens the feelings of togetherness through exchange of messages and translates thought into action." This definition touches what communication strives to achieve, especially through information sharing, relationship building and action orientation.

— UNESCO Many Voices One World

"Communication is the sum of all the things one person does when he wants to create understanding in the mind of another. It involves a systematic and continuous process of telling, listening and understanding." This definition pinpoints that communication is the total of achieving the indented ones through a meaningful process of telling and listening.

— Louis A. Allen

"Communication involves transmission and reception of messages. As communicators, people use symbols to create messages. They cannot literally communicate to other individuals a meaning, attitude, perception, belief or feeling. Rather, they use a message or messages to represent what they see or experience. Just as an artist uses brush and paint to depict a beautiful sunset or landscape, so too, do communicators use messages to represent their perceptions, thought and feelings."

— Donald D. White and David A. Bednar

"Communication is the process of meaningful interaction among human beings. More specifically, it is the process by which meanings are perceived and understandings are reached among human beings."

— McFarland, D.E.

"Communication is the transfer of information from one person to another person. It is a way of reaching others by transmitting ideas, facts, thoughts, feelings and values." This definition is more useful in management.

— Newstrom and Davis

It is understood that communication is seen as an interchange, an expression, a transmission, a dynamic process, a connecting link, a means to power and a force that maintains and animates sending the messages to the intended persons sharing the commonness in understanding keeping in touch with words and music, pictures and print, nods and backs, postures and plumages. It means that communication is the 'ground' of meeting and the 'foundation' of linking people and purposes.

1.7 NATURE AND SCOPE OF COMMUNICATION

Communication is an integrative process of exchange of information between the individuals, groups of individuals, organizations and subsystems of an organization with a view to interact as well as interface for accomplishing the desired goals. Achieving goals is concerned with human behaviour and human relationship dealing with the multiple aspects of social sciences as economics, politics, sociology, commerce, management, history, anthropology, sociology and so on pertaining to the aspects of linguistic and psychology of human beings. In other words, it is a two-way process involving both transmission and reception of exchange of facts, ideas, feelings, attitudes, opinions, interactions and figures with others through using a set of symbols, words, action, pictures, etc.

Communication is both internal and external. Internal communication may be formal and informal which flows in different directions say, vertical, horizontal, diagonal and across the organizational structure. External communication is concerned with the transmission of messages outside the organization to the customers, dealers, shareholders inter-corporate bodies, investors, general public, government and its departments. Internal communication helps to discharge the managerial functions like planning, direction, coordination, motivation, staffing and controlling while external communication promotes goodwill with the stakeholders.

The broad policies and objectives of a business organization flow downward from the top management to the lower level through either written and oral or verbal media. Written media consists of instructions, orders, letters, memos, house journals, posters, bulletins, boards, manuals, annual reports, etc., whereas verbal media consists of face-to-face conversation, lectures, conferences, meetings, interviews, counsel, public address system, telephone, grapevine, etc.

Every business organization has an interface between the subsystems; and transmits the information and data to the subsystem as well as to the total system for achieving its goals. Gathering information and data of both past and present, and keeping storage, processing and monitoring are vital measures in information system to be said effective management in business organizations. Therefore, communication is a human process with the nature of universal application.

1.8 FEATURES OF COMMUNICATION

Effective communication has the following six features.

- Initiates message
- Sender picks up idea and encodes it
- Transmits encoded message through appropriate channel
- Receiver receives message and decodes it
- Receiver acts upon the decoded message
- Feeds back upon received message to the sender

The phenomena of communication has been widened as well as deepened in the modern time on availability of technology. Hence, the message should be framed well and attractive with possible good contents for achieving the intended purpose.

1.9 PRINCIPLES OF COMMUNICATION

An organization is a body of persons formed to bring together both human and physical resources and arrange them in an orderly and coordinated manner for accomplishing the planned goal. Communication focuses a thrust of enlivening the employees of an organization to cross safely the river of misunderstanding. The more effective is the listening, more is the effective talking. Failure leads to confusion and chaos which hampers what the message is intended to achieve.

Communication is *sine-qua-non* of an organization, particularly in a business organization, where the impetus is for the improved production and productivity; and the increased morale and motivation depend upon the principles governing communication. The management of organization would need to take care and caution about the integrated principles of sound communication to govern business in a healthy atmosphere.

The principles of communication are in the nature of universal application to the social, religious, charitable, formal and informal organizations including non-profitable ones but not necessarily and exclusively applicable to any of them. The principle of universality of communication is one of the features pertaining to the nature of communication. In fact, the problem of effective communication is present in all the interpersonal groups and organizational activities. The problems are present everywhere whether it is family, school, department of state and central governments, undertakings, corporation sector, trade unions and in all joint activities; the governance of national and international affairs. The principles of governing an effective communication are given below.

Integral Part of Process: Decisions of the managers or concerned heads of business organization convey to their subordinates down the rank and file. It means work performance in terms of coordination becomes a part and parcel of the function in any organization. Therefore, communication integrates the integral and inseparable part of the process for achieving the expected results. "The first executive function is to develop and maintain a system of communication"

Control and Supervision: Receiving feedback makes one understand the response or reply of the receiver of communication. Personal involvement of all managers in the process and their interaction help them for making appropriate decisions. The managers who perform the management functions through communication and managerial positions become the communication centres to receive information from various sources.

Two-way Approach: The completeness and effectiveness of communication fulfils only when it is a two-way traffic, i.e., means of transmission and reception.

Adequacy: Message communication contains all the relevant information facilitating fair assessment of the state of affairs.

Formal and Informal: Communication is both formal and informal. While the formal has authority and official backing, the latter does not.

Internal and External: Transmitting matters say, giving policy matters, orders, instructions, directions, suggestions, or public notice to the people working inside the organization either upward or downward or diagonal communication is referred to as internal communication. Transacting with outside public like customers, shareholders, dealers, government departments, investors, complaints, etc., are referred to as external communication.

Honesty: Honest (sense of morality and obligation) and rightness (sense of intuition) of purposes are the hallmarks of communication for good governance.

1.10 OBJECTIVES OF COMMUNICATION

A business organization would need to ensure the optimum use of its resources of time, and money. The communication system puts in place all resources in the organization and addresses to meet its objectives. Information and persuasion are the main objectives of communication. The specific objectives of communication for the success of an organization are:

- Communicating right information to the concerned persons
- Coordinating various multi-complex functions of management for better results
- Ensuring better understanding of communicated ideas
- Understanding of peoples' action and attitude which aid in skill development
- Improving the effectiveness of policy implementation
- Enhancing corporate image
- Helping in decision-making

1.11 EFFECTS OF COMMUNICATION

The very motto of communication is to bring in some changes in the attitude, behaviour and actions of the receiver. They are:

- If the receiver receives the message with purpose of it being sent, it refers to **successful on effective communication.** This communication brings desirable effects (See Exhibit 1.2).

Exhibit 1.2 **How a Gift Becomes a Good Communication**

Noticing nothing can replace effective communication, an individual would do better than mere words in conveying 'feelings.' A gift can do wonders on such occasions provided it is chosen carefully. Gift speaks language of affection with better chances of being heard as compared to the other messages. All of us are familiar with the wonderful feeling when we receive someone who sends flowers as a gift. The universality of sending flowers as gift, in fact, gives rise to the organizations like 'inter-flora' and the adage 'say it with flowers.'

- If communication does not bring any changes in the attitude and action of the receiver, it is said to be **no communication.**
- If there is an undesirable change contrary to the sender's expectations in the receiver's action and attitude, it is said to be **miscommunication** or **insufficient communication**. This communication may produce adverse effects.

Illustrations are examined through the consumers who form their own assumptions which solidify into beliefs and myths when communication is insufficient. Some examples are given in Exhibit 1.3.

Exhibit 1.3 **Communication and Effects**

Communication	Effect
Price and quality are directly related	Low-priced products which may not have good quality
The products of a big company are costlier per se	Consumers are made to pay for high overheads
New products are always costly	Patient waiting can result in prices coming down
Synthetic products are low in quality	Products are of high quality if made with natural material
Large quantities of same product presented	Packages are always economical
If the sale is at clearance, closing down sales, etc	Must be a good bargain
Advertised goods are costly	Must have paid more for advertisement cost

To rationalize these beliefs, communication has to be made worthwhile by the marketer through advertisement or presentation specifically in the content, and not by the general or vague assurances. For this, the marketer needs to inform his consumers with regards to the product(s) which they assumed as low because of low quality. The marketer must say that due to the economic scale of production and the basic economy in design or raw material or economy of distribution, he is a clever manufacturer or distributor and passes on his benefit to his customers.

1.12 IMPORTANCE OF COMMUNICATION

The management experts consider communication as a unifying link and drive in the modern-day environment. Perhaps, this could make them say, that the modern day is called the age of communication and information. Because of the emphasis on building a mutual and amicable atmosphere of cooperation in the enterprise, growth of business in size and volume, complexity of organizing inputs and finding market for goods or services, technical development, good deal of social responsibility obligations to the society, i.e., stakeholders, effective communication is a prime factor. Among the management problems, communication stands out as 'number one.'

With the passage of time, the business and the industrial community have become more complex with challenging tasks particularly in the context of global scenario. It works as life-blood of business enterprise like the veins and arteries to sustain the flow of blood to the vital organs of human body. A good instance is how an organization's image is reflected by information broadcasting through communication channel is that of tsunami on December 25, 2004, havoc caused by floods in Andhra Pradesh on October 2, 2009, terrorists attack in Mumbai on November 26, 2009, etc.

1.13 FUNCTIONS OF COMMUNICATION

Communication is understood from its meaning and definition that it performs a dual function of transmitting thoughts or ideas, and understanding thoughts or ideas. Transmitting information implies that there must be a sender and a receiver of communication. The sender of message has to send message to the receiver with meaning and purpose from the point of understanding its contents.

Achieving the end-result of activity or activities framed on vision and mission of an organization for which it came into being is called function. As an agent, communication is affected in getting or giving information or message for accomplishing the intended motto. Thus, communication has objectives depending upon the group say classroom, seminar, conference, boardroom, war field, etc., and the context in which one is addressing with the intended motto in his mind.

Business connotes production and commercial motive which is distinct from a charitable or religious organization. In meeting the specific needs of society, communication in every business enterprise irrespective of its primary function, has a common purpose. Business institution functions effectively by using its resources of finance, manpower, raw material, capital, know-how and also target-group as the specific clients and markets within and outside the organization requiring to act, interact, reach, share, exchange and get across each other so that the specific objectives are accomplished in an effective manner.

The business enterprise, in liberalized economy, is multidisciplinary in nature with competence and competitiveness with focus on business relationships, business dynamics, business values and business ethics for sustainable results with profit which would need communication in an interdisciplinary approach to be said effective. The network of large business enterprises with objectives, activities and interrelationship is interdependent which necessitates communication to subserve its diverse functions. The functions of communication are explained below.

1. **Dissemination of Information:** Informing the right message is the first and foremost function of any communication. In today's world of globalization, communication brings power or disseminates covering a wide range of areas both internal as well as external. Internally, organization should inform about its working towards objectives – planning, policies, procedures, rules, priorities, processes, systems; and strategies about product-mix, client-mix, market-segmentation, and employee-employer relationship management including generic services. Externally, it has to inform the customers, competitors, suppliers and public about services and alike. Thus, information helps to plan for achieving the defined goal.
2. **Educating and Training:** Educating the workers about know-how and do-how, and familiarizing them with the system, procedure and process is a prerequisite. Product literature, publicity, presentation of data analysis and demonstration are right modes in the process of education. In instruction or training to improve skills and enhance capacities and capabilities of an individual, communication, thus, is indispensable to upgrade their 'do-how' skills. Business organizations need to train their workers to achieve proficiency and efficiency at working for better result, for which, communication is an integral part of training sessions involving teaching, instructing, demonstrating and discussing. All education and training take place by means of communication.
3. **Motivation:** Actuating behaviour or energizing an individual towards a particular goal is called **motivation**. Many studies proved that moulding and bringing a desirable and positive change in the attitudes and actions of employees for achieving the intended results if the information and ideas of one firm's objectives, its policies, plans, procedures and its problems are shared with all the concerned ones in the organization. In other words, all these provide a great stimulus; instill a great confidence and belongingness with oneness in the minds of employees. "Communication with mechanism of talks, lectures, films, meetings, workshops and non-verbal messages motivates workers which are prerequisites to ensure and insure higher productivity and efficiency. Communication is, thus, used to raise morale, confidence and courage.
4. **Integration:** Communication is vital in every sphere of organization like business, factories, hospitals, corporate bodies, religious bodies, military services, educational institutes, political institutions, etc. This is so particular in the large sized organization with departmentalization and decentralization in pursuing

objectives and sub-objectives. Workers working in different functional and geographical areas need to integrate themselves in pursuit of organization's objectives. Communication as an interaction process in the organization brings about togetherness of workers for common objectives and helps in team-building. Therefore, communication integrates all the concerned ones in building a team force.

5. **Smooth Working:** The continued success of any business operation depends upon good communication. A good communication facility provides better means for building and nurturing mutually beneficial relationship between the employees, supervisory staff, top management and the outside business relating to customers, suppliers, press and other players. Organization's existence and its continuing life heavily depend on communication. G. R. Terry has stated: "Communication serves as a lubricant fostering for smooth operations of the management."

   An example is Air India with its operations department for its flights. Placing an order is an operation as to purchase or sale across the counter. Thus, the operations of departments of a business concern on the availability of coordination being explained by the operational efficiency. The key to the success of operations research and operational efficiency is the result of a good communication system.

6. **Unifying Link:** In a business organization, there are many employees working under the line and staff; and branching system with specialization and division of work. There is a need for coordination among such workers/ officers to attain the purpose of organization. The coordination is obtained through communication. May Curling said, "good communication is essential for coordination. These are necessary to upward, downward and sideways, through all the levels of authority and advice for transmission, interpretation and adoption of policies for sharing of knowledge and information and for the more subtle needs of good morale and mutual understanding. Daub and Lord said, "communication is a basic process of organization and makes it coherent to permit its members to cooperate and coordinate." Hence, communication is an all-unifying link and a binding force.

7. **Promotion:** Survival and sustenance of business enterprises depend upon a sound product-mix. One of the 'P's of marketing is promotion. It relates to various activities like advertising, publicity, public relations and communication aiming at customers' satisfaction, education, communication and retention. Development of effective demand for products hinges on the customers' awareness of the need for products, their knowledge and their preference. It is here that the promotional aspect of service is relevant to inform, educate, persuade and actualize the market. Communication forms the basic plank on which promotional strategy is built.

8. **Persuasion:** Persuasion means convincing. It is an effort to change the behaviour or to convince another person through transmission of messages. It is through communication, that persuasion takes place. A manager persuades his subordinates in drawing their special knowledge rather than commanding; and politician persuades voters to vote for him. Persuasion is a subtle part of communication which will encourage the continuance of favourable behaviour of the existing stakeholders in the business.

9. **Entertainment:** It is one of the features of business enterprise. Lighter moments are necessary in releasing tension, fostering camaraderie and getting rid of negative feelings. Communication with humour plays an important role in fostering positive behaviour of business enterprise. In entertainment industry (cinema), communication with humour play an important role to achieve its purposeful objective.
10. **Decision-making:** Knowing the prospects of current variable is referred to as the function of decision-making. The respect of top management's command in organization depends upon timely decision-making ability across all the functional areas, i.e., finance, production, inventory, marketing, personnel, quality products and accounts on the availability of adequate and timely information. It calls for facts, figures, analysis, deliberations, classification, confirmation and evaluation. Chester Barnard said: "The first executive function is to develop and maintain a system of communication."

    Dynamic and ever-changing objectives of communication, thus, depend upon the nature and functions of business organization involving dimensions of caution, counsel, persuasion, clarification, elicit support, reprimand, appraisal, evaluation and alike. In the dynamic context, nothing ever remains the same for long and the business development with paperless offices and flexible work hours have had their impact on the approach of organizational communication.
11. **Saves Time and Cost:** Saving of time and cost of communication are the fundamental aspects of efficient communication. If the message is transmitted through a channel quickly as well as more inexpensively, it is considered efficient. For example, the quality control manager intends to communicate the grades of quality products to the concerned employees; for, he wrote such grades on a sheet of paper and fixed it on the notice board. Another approach is that of calling all the concerned employees at one place and discussing about the grades. This is efficient and effective in terms of learning and developing relationship between the manager and the workers. It is learnt that sending and receiving accurate information with full comprehensiveness are efficient and cost effective. "Our costliest expenditure is time" (Theophrastus).

To sum up, the use of communication skills intelligently and rightly can certainly help to make our lives as we wish to be. What degree of important role has to be attached to the communication can be understood from this phrase. "Building a city needs more communication than concrete." In the context of business which has become more complex with challenging tasks, communication has become inevitable tool.

1.14 IS COMMUNICATION A DISCIPLINE?

Communication is applicable universally; the problem of effective communication is presented in interpersonal (chairman, managing director, managers of functional areas and subordinates), group (social, religious, charitable, formal, non-formal, non-profit) and organization (activities of family, school, state and central government departments, corporations, trade unions, and in all joint activities). The techniques and principles of communication are universal in application but not necessarily and exclusively applicable to only business. Universality implies that all the people have to follow the same principles and the same skills regardless of their position in communication.

Science explains the phenomena of relationship between cause and effect while art explains the ability or creative skill approach in the best way of doing things. Like, theoretically acquired knowledge is accompanied with practical work to perform a phenomenon, so also theoretically acquired communication is accompanied with skills that help in sending a message. Thus, the art of communication deals with the application of skills and efforts for achieving the desired results of sending messages effectively. To sum up, communication is a science as well as a social science with creativeness and universality with interrelated phenomena of both science and art. It concerns more with social sciences influencing each other like (i) psychology, (ii) linguistics, (iii) etymology, (iv) semantics, (v) accounting, (vi) economics (vii) auditing, (viii) sociology, (ix) English and (x) philosophy. Hence, communication is an interdisciplinary and an independent body of knowledge like the disciplines of management, commerce, economics, accounting, engineering, sociology, life-science, anthropology, etc.

In ancient times, business was done through the barter system. The trade continued to grow both in size and competition; and became a more multi-complex proposition nationally as well as globally. Under these circumstances, the business communicator had perforce to sharpen his techniques avoiding mistakes. Mistakes could mean loss and obviously losing business to the competitors in the market. In modern era, business environment is liable to frequency changes. Hence, business communication is considered an absolute felt need for making decisions in an ever changing competitive environment in order to achieve efficiency and effectiveness with desired goals.

1.15 HOW TO IMPROVE COMMUNICATION?

The passing of a message from sender's mind to receiver's mind may seem to be simple and straightforward. Essential measures to improve communication effectively within the organization depends on two fundamental requisites to improve communication which manager's must improve their messages – ideas or information intended to be transmitted and seek to improve their understanding of what the employees intend to communicate to them.

The managers should use subordinates' language and avoid faulty translations so that the messages to their subordinates reach promptly and accurately for their immediate understanding and action. In brief, the business managers and executives would need to become better encoders and decoders of messages. Growth and development of commerce and industry, thus, depends upon the skills of effective communication without barriers. The following are some measures to improve the communication network; and also to remove or improve barriers to communication.

- A free and fair two-way flow of communication.
- Open mind and willingness to perceive messages. It means ability to put oneself in other person's role and assume individual viewpoints and emotions of the individual. Simply, it means empathy.
- Use a communication language for an complete message.

- Trusting one's appropriate action is the first step towards credibility.
- Listen carefully with concentration.
- Use of words to convey message should be precise and accurate in meaning.
- Avoid ambiguity in verbal language, terms with abstract and multiple meanings.
- Adhere to time and timeliness in communication.

1.15.1 Determinants of Communication

Effective communication is successful communication. Hence, the management should take the responsibility of sending messages effectively to the concerned people for necessary action and implementation to accomplish the intended goals or purposes. The factors that influence selection of a communication program are:

- Cost and utility of communication program
- Secrecy of message. Absence of secrecy is nothing but a pot with holes; nobody can fill it
- Need of accurate message as 'no communication' or 'miscommunication' results in nothing
- Speed of message; it is ineffective if not delivered on time.
- Convenience to handle
- Choose appropriate communication programme meeting the needs of the target group as one programme cannot be suitable at all times
- Record properly the communicated message for future reference or strategic decision
- Communicated message creates a good impression in receiver's mind when it is expressive serving the purpose

1.15.2 Process of Communication

Communication is the process by which information is passed between the individuals and/or organizations by means of previously agreed symbols. Communication is exchange of thoughts or ideas between two individuals or organizations. Communication process involves nine elements:

- Sender
- Receiver
- Message
- Media (major communication tools)
- Encoding
- Decoding
- Response
- Feedback (major functions)
- Noise

Impact of a message depends on the personality of the sender also. For example, a message from an officer known for his fair play will be listened to and believed much more than an officer who is known for his corrupt or litigant nature. A sensitive sender will look at the communication. The elements of communication are explained below.

1. **Message:** Information put forth in speech form, writing and body movement (such as gestures, facial expressions, silence, etc.) is referred to as **message**. The originator or sender of a message has to transmit it in a language familiar to the receiver.
2. **Encoding:** The process of putting thoughts into symbolic form is known as **encoding**. An advertising agency assembles words and illustrations into an advertisement that conveys the intended message. Speech, written documents and facial expressions constitute a message. How poor English hampers growth can be seen in Exhibit 1.4.

Exhibit 1.4 Poor English Hampers e-commerce Growth in China

Incorrect spellings of brand names in English and mistrust of the internet are hampering electronic commerce according to the study published. Some Chinese especially those with little exposure to the English language, spell famous brands like Boeing and Mercedes Benz wrongly which can hamper transactions in cyberspace. The report said Boeing which is translated into Bo-yin and Mercedes Benz translated as Bian-shi, were households names in China but less than ten per cent of Chinese can spell them correctly.

This language handicap severely affects the international business development strategy of these companies for the Chinese market, warned the report.

3. **Media:** The communication channels through which the message moves from the sender to the receiver is referred as **media**. It is the medium by which a message moves between the sender and the receiver. The television, print media, face-to-face communication, newspapers, films, audio-video, etc., are the important channels in communication. The print media enjoys the highest credibility while television is the lowest. Among the lower socio-economic classes, television has a good credibility. Face-to-face communication, from the point of view of involvement, offers the greatest possibility whereas print media is the least. The choice of channel depends upon the purpose of communication. The written media is used to deal with the matters of business which require a written record while face-to-face conversation is used when the communicator wants to discuss informal, private and confidential matters. Various purposes that include communication are to:

- Buy
- Sell
- Inform
- Prevent
- Affirm
- Clarify
- Learn
- Disclose

- Conceal
- Cause
- Compliment
- Criticize
- Disseminate
- Learn
- Send information
- Reach
- Teach
- Confirm

4. **Decoding:** The process by which the receiver assigns meaning to the symbols encoded by the sender is called **decoding**.
5. **Receiver:** The party receiving the message sent by another party is known as **receiver**. The receiver like the sender has his own frame of reference and has the responsibility for decoding. Decoding is the process by which the symbols are interpreted by the receiver. His attitude, opinion, prejudice and relationship with the sender besides the type of message, the type of channel used, the manner of its reception, etc., will play a greater role in receiving effective message. Equally important is the interpretation i.e., organization of ideas for suitable decoding of the message on the receiver's frame of mind. In the words of John Newstrom and Keith Davis communication is "what the receiver understands, not what the sender says."
6. **Response:** The reaction or response of the receiver after being exposed to the message is known as **response**.
7. **Feedback:** Sending back the information about the message to the message sender is called **feedback**. It enables the source to know whether the message has been received and interpreted correctly. In other words, it is receiver's response to a message. For completion of the circuit between the sender and the receiver so as to increase the accuracy as well as confidence; and to reduce the doubts and misgivings in the relationship, the feedback is essential. This feedback provides a better understanding for both the parties. Douglas G. Curley calls this two-way communication as feedback loop or communication loop. Feedback is the last step and the important essential in a single cycle of two-way communication for an effective communication. If the sender got feedback, then the cycle of communication is complete. Feedback is used to improve understanding and avoid faulty communication as the sender and the receiver interact for getting clarity about a question or doubt, if any, in oral communication. In written communication, an instant feedback is not possible. The incident of feedback is illustrated in Exhibit 1.5.

Exhibit 1.5 Incident of Feedback

On August 1, 2016 Mr. Ram, the Manager told his subordinate, Mr. Rao. "The report you submitted on July 20, 2016 contains some mistakes. I want to talk to you about it. Please meet me on August 4, 2016 at 11 o'clock. "Mr. Rao was sensitive, intelligent and due for promotion. At 11 a.m. on August 4, 2014, Mr. Rao entered Mr. Ram's office with no records, in no position to discuss the report or correct the mistakes. The Manager spent his valuable time reassuring Mr. Rao and has to set another time to discuss the report.

Was the manager's feedback to Mr. Rao about the report successful?

How could the situation have been avoided if both had feedback skill?

It is known that communication is really a dynamic process and does not end with one cycle. The description of the process is only the purpose of understanding its elements and how it works.

Merits of Feedback: The merits of feedback are:

- Feedback provides better understanding
- Reduces frustration
- Generates favourable feelings
- Improves accuracy

Demerits of Feedback: Until there is a two-way communication (a) strong disagreement may, and (b) cognitive dissonant may arise.

Noise: The unpleasant static or distortion during the communication process which results in the receiver getting a different message than the one the sender sent. In other words, the receiver may not often receive the transmitted message in original form due to distortions arising out of channel noise and psychological selectivity which the receiver exercises to listen to the message.

1.15.3 Ways of Communication

Communication is of two ways, viz., (i) one-way communication and (ii) two-way communication. The sender communicates without expecting a feedback from the receiver; it is called **one-way communication** or **one-way traffic**. This communication is associated with formal communication with the characteristic feature of one-way communication and transmits information downward only. Information concerning all matters of policy, procedure, rules, etc., travels with message load of orders as well as instructions downward from the top management through the middle level managers. It implies that one-way communication provides superiors with a route for conveying information to their subordinates.

The purposes are to (a) give specific job instructions; (b) understand organization structure and interrelationship; (c) provide procedures and policies, etc. As such, there is no provision for feedback, interaction, etc., and hence the management of organization does not recognize the receiver's point of view. The organization structure establishes route for this one-way communication as 'through proper channel.'

If the receiver provides feedback to the sender's message, then it is known as **two-way communication**. Its features are both transmission of information and reception of feedback. No feedback means that the receiver may not have understood or has not reacted. Management and workers are giving and receiving information; passing it up and down respectively. Hence, the management when conveying any message should focus knowing its response, reaction, acceptance or rejection of the message for taking final decision; indeed need all to work together in an organization. George Terry said, "the sender must get through the receiver if the communication is to be completed and satisfactory." Graphically, the ways of communication process is shown in Exhibit 1.6.

Exhibit 1.6 **Ways of Communication Process**

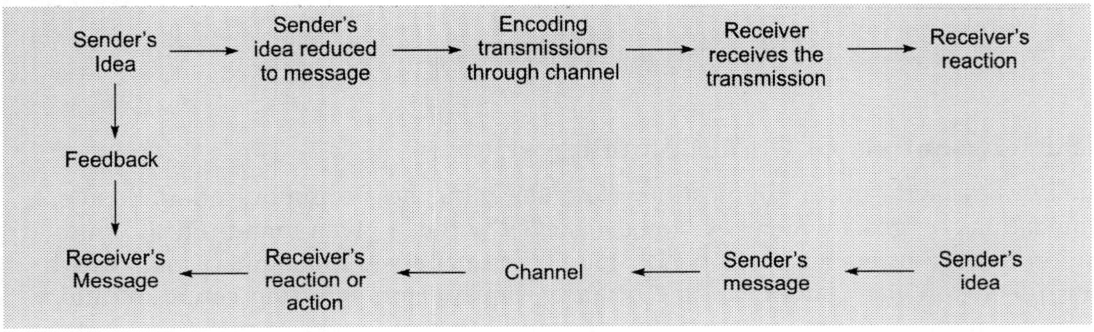

The receiver got the message and interpreted, i.e., decoded the message, and replied (feedback). The sender, now the receiver, received the message and interpreted favourably. Here is an example of a two-way communication. Reddy and Ram are faculty members in the Commerce Department of a University College. The former asks the latter to take class in the first period instead of third period. The latter replies okay. Here, Reddy is sender and Ram is receiver in the first communication while Ram is sender and Reddy is receiver in feedback. This communication is effective. This is more relevant in interpersonal communication. But, hardly a need is felt of sending or providing information of general nature. For example, communicating to the employees of an organization about holiday on a specific day or menu contents in a canteen is one-way communication which does not require feedback.

1.15.4 Loss of Message

Soon after receiving the message, the receiver has to interpret the idea of the sender. The accurate interpretation will depend upon past experience, knowledge, beliefs, attitudes, etc. When the idea passes through the mind, some pieces of information are subject to the cognitive structure. It means a set of values, attitudes, knowledge and expectation which, in turn, cause rejection or acceptance of the bits of information. In practice, there are more filter messages at various stages in business organization which lost some information at those stages. See Exhibit 1.7.

Exhibit 1.7 Loss of Message

Understanding 100 per cent Top Management
Understanding 66 per cent Vice-president
Understanding 56 per cent General Manager
Understanding 40 per cent Plant Manager
Understanding 30 per cent Foreman
Understanding 20 per cent Production Line

(*Source:* Hellreigel D., et al., Management, 1982)

1.15.5 Essentials Of Good Communication

Time is a key factor in communication, particularly business communication. Business organizations set goals which have to be achieved within a given time-frame. Communication concerning such goals depends upon good and effective communication which, in turn, helps in clear understanding of: (a) various factors affecting communication, (b) the essentials of communication, (c) the significance of language, and (d) the manner in which people read meaning into messages. Feedback is the last and important component of communication process. The sender calls for feedback to assure him that the message has reached the target group as envisaged. Such feedback helps assess the time of reaching, quality and understanding of message, the efficacy and reliability of the type, method and channel of communication used.

All the essential qualities of a good communication begin with the letter 'C'; hence collectively called 9 'C's of communication. These are: clarity, correctness, conciseness, courtesy, consistent, cost-consciousness, credibility, continuity and channel. These are discussed below.

1. **Clarity:** Existence of an idea gets translated into a message what the sender wants to convey and gets it transmitted to the intended receiver through a letter, a speech, a film or a presentation. Clarity of concept is, thus, a very important factor giving proper shape to the thought developing into a message meaningfully. If one is not clear about his thoughts and ideas, to whom to send (i.e., right person), the message will end in a futile exercise. Therefore, the message must be clear for a good communication beginning the process and about the right intended receiver. Perhaps, this explains why the conceptual skills like reading, writing, listening, speaking, body language, presentation, etc., are given importance in modern-day business organizations. An appreciable letter is one which takes very little time to read and understand but makes clear the meaning of message. Clearly, the written messages avoid misunderstanding and save time. Clarity of a letter depends upon:
   - Simple and familiar words
   - Short and simple sentences
   - Proper punctuation

- Definite and concrete details with figures and names (phrases like "in two weeks" or "within two weeks" instead of phrases likes "in due course" or "at your earliest convenience") convey clarity
- Logical sequence of ideas
- Indefinite words like about, nearly, almost, etc., and negative expressions must be avoided.

Well conceived thoughts make a good beginning of the communication process simple in conveying the true meaning of message. The motto of communication is to bring down two minds together. This can be possible only when how the sender's message is understood by the receiver in the same true sense that the sender intends to convey.

2. **Correctness:** If the message conforms the purpose of it to the sender in addition to precise, accurate and up-to-date information it is known as **correctness**. The correctness demands no error at all – in grammar, idiom, diction, spelling and punctuation (appearance and form layout, appropriate tone) and presenting full information on a situation. Wrong or incomplete information is the most harmful thing which causes goodwill loss and business loss.

3. **Conciseness:** Expressing more in a few words and writing it to the point is known as **conciseness**. It does not necessarily mean being brief. Clear and definite details often reduce the length of a sentence if conciseness and clarity are closely related. The features of conciseness are: (i) planning and organizing thoughts thoroughly, (ii) including only relevant material avoiding irrelevant, (iii) avoiding rambling sentences and repetition of the same ideas in different words, and (iv) condensing the unimportant ideas. The sentences can be condensed by:

    - Substituting simple words for phrase, i.e., soon or early, for at an early date
    - Substituting phrases for clauses, i.e., thank you, for thanking you in anticipation
    - Avoiding phrases, i.e., in view of the fact, for instead of viewpoint or standpoint
    - Do away with clumsy beginnings and endings:
        - 'I wish to apply for the post of a sales distributor advertised in the Hindu' instead 'with reference to your advertisement in the Hindu of .... I wish to apply for the post of sales distributor.'
        - 'I wish to inform you' instead 'in answer to your enquiry of...'
        - 'We have received your application' instead 'we beg to acknowledge receipt of your application'
        - 'To discuss the matter' instead 'with a view to a discussion of the matter'
        - We would appreciate if you send the goods as early as possible since arrangements have to be made for exporting them so that they reach our foreign office within the required time. This can be phrased as: "Please dispatch the goods so as to reach us by 10th January since we have to ship them to Japan by 18th."

4. **Courtesy:** Considering other people's feelings is called **courtesy**. A well-mannered and courteous person shows consideration and thought for others. The style, the manner and the choice of words reflect courtesy of the writer. The simple rules for courtesy are:
   - Use please, thank you or sorry as per the situation
   - Express appropriate feeling to the situation accordingly (sympathy when someone suffers, good wishes when someone secures award or reward)
   - Make the other person feel comfortable (use words like thank you, or sorry appropriate to the situation)
   - Promptness in responding
   - Tone, choice of words and style of message reflect your consideration for the feeling and needs of the reader
5. **Consistency:** Communication is a continuous process either in personal dealings or organizational settings or business conduct; and takes place all the time involving the parties quite often the same. Hence, communication should be consistent with correction if required but not contracted. Oral message should be in tandem with the body language.
6. **Cost-Conscious:** Message sending involves both direct and indirect costs; and varies depending upon the method of communication and the means of transmission. Such cost should justify the achieved results. If not, there is no effectiveness in such communication. Organizations particularly business firms should make conscious efforts to make their communication system not only efficient but also cost effective.
7. **Credibility:** Effective communication always depends upon the degree of honesty and sincerity of both the sender and the receiver. If the process of communication suffers in terms of credibility, the receiver of the message loses faith in the communicator. Therefore, effective communication presupposes credibility with bolstering. For example, if an automobile manufacturer communicates message that a particular model gives best mileage, it remains only a claim. If the claim is bolstered with a proven test result published by a neutral testing authority or an editorial comment in a special magazine, then the instant credibility will accrue.
8. **Continuity:** Communication is an unending process until the style of achieving the target goals. It requires reception and penetration.
9. **Channel:** Modes and channels which vary from situation to situation determine the degree of effective communication. There are instances that (a) a written communication cannot convey as forcefully as oral communication, (b) telephone call can convey messages appropriately than a letter, and (c) fax is better than regular mail. Hence, the right choice of mode and channel is important.

If the sender gets intended results from the receiver, it is referred to as **effective communication**. In effective communication, the sender achieves his goal of influencing the receiver's attitude, action or behaviour. If the receiver correctly understands the sender's message in the spirit of what it means, it is called **good communication**.

Receiver's understanding about the message is the goal. For understanding business communication, one has to have a fair knowledge of the business world.

1.16 GUIDELINES GOVERNING EFFECTIVE COMMUNICATION

In communication process, the speaker and the listener both are important because their effectiveness depends on effective communication. The need and importance of speaking and listening in industry and commerce or organization increase the efficiency so that messages are paid attention to in transmitting and receiving. Then only the receiver understands the message what the sender understood. Guidelines for speaking and listening are given in Exhibit 1.8.

Exhibit 1.8 **Guidelines Governing Effective Communication**

Speaking	Listening
Prepare speech	Show keen interest in the speaker by looking at him and watching his gesture, facial expressions, posture, etc.
Underline keywords or phrases	Listen to his words and observe feelings being conveyed
Maintain eye contact with the audience	Observe pitch, tone and pauses in speaker's words
Properly enunciate and articulate words or phrases with voice and right movements	Minimize distraction to listening process
Focus attention	Follow trend of discussion to make response when your turn comes
Speak with enthusiasm and vitality which convinces listeners	Take notes but not too many
Give rhythmic movement to your speech	Clarify the meaning of words or phrases

1.17 POLICY OF COMMUNICATION

Communication focuses on (i) set of objectives to achieve through communication, (ii) directives to be applied for making decision, and (iii) a combination of both. The communication policy is either formally expressed or informally understood. Hence, it is desirable to draw up a document policy concerning various aspects of communication. A policy is a guideline to action. So, a well drawn up policy document covering adequacy, transparency and consistency would certainly ensure clarity and effectiveness in sending the intended information and having interactions with the concerned ones in the society. Fraud, damaging press reports and other such adverse developments is a matter of policy; for which swift action is initiated. See exhibit 1.9 for corrective advertisement for impressing the consumer.

Exhibit 1.9 How Corrective Advertisement Helps Business Progress

A company advertises untruthful, misleading or false claims which cause damage to the consumers who see the advertisement and believe it in good faith. Subsequently, a regulatory agency came into operation on complaint lodged by the consumer or competitor to make a corrective advertisement. It serves a purpose that the prospective consumers at least are warned against wrong inferences, but the damage already done to the existing consumers cannot be repaired. There is also a minor satisfaction that some damage is inflicted on the company which erred. Perhaps, the very fear of being humiliated in this fashion would prevent wrong claims being made by the companies. In fact, this preventive effect alone makes all regulations worthy.

Volvo USA ran an advertisement in 1990s showing a demonstration car-crushing. In the demonstration, a giant truck goes about crushing various brands of cars and only the Volvo comes out unscathed. It was discovered later that the company specially strengthened its car used for the test. The regulatory body stepped in and the company was compelled to run corrective advertisements which showed a letter "To all interested consumers from the President of the Company." It admitted "... the earlier advertisement inaccurately characterized the vent as car crushing exhibition was only a dramatization....etc."

1.18 COMMUNICATION BARRIERS

"All forms of social progress......physical barriers to communication are rapidly disappearing but the psychological ones remain. These psychological difficulties are, in part of function of the very nature of language; they are due to the emotional characters and mental limitations of human beings" (Daniel Katz). Organizational communication is a complex process with certain characteristic features. First, the organization and the environment influence each other. Second, a communication network which consists of tools for problem-solving, workflow and information. Third, the basic purpose of communication is (i) furnishing information for decision-making and control and (ii) motivating people for organization development. Third is compatibility. The success of communication depends upon the matrix of all these issues.

Communication is a process involving the measures of encoding, transmission and decoding among the others which hinder or dilute the objective in getting the intended message to the recipient. An obstacle or a difficulty in transmitting information is known as **barrier**. A barrier to communication is called **noise**. The barriers to communication in an organizational context may crop up due to authority structure, status difference, reporting relationship, socio-psychological, cross-cultural and physical factors (spelling, handwriting, legibility, accent, speed of delivery and appropriateness of language). Misunderstanding, misinformation, misconception, unfavourable attitudes, conflicts and enemity are often the results of communication barriers. All this is costly and burdensome to the organization in terms of money. For the progress and well-being of an organization, it is the utmost duty of the management to locate, identify and analyze the barriers of communication and take concrete measures to remove them.

1.18.1 Semantic Barriers

Semantics is the science of meaning while phonetics is the science of sounds. Expression of words and language is the most important and powerful tool of communication and determines the quality of message to be communicated. In other words, semantic means the systematic study of meaning of words. For effective communication, the idea of message is to develop properly as well as it should be structured appropriately with the words making the concept clear. A skill in handling is an utmost need. For instance:

1. Use of 'verb' and 'noun' with no difference in spelling. The words like (i) charge, spring, check, suit, ring, etc., have different meanings; (ii) current, minute and wind pronounced in different ways mean different things, and (iii) present, transfer, record, sound, etc. Similar sounding words like access and excess, miss and mess, flour and floor, cite, site and sight, no and know, kite and knight, not and knot, etc., can cause misunderstanding in speech.
2. Nouns like, table conveys a writing table, a dining table, a statistical table to different persons. Phrases like 'a red and a blue carpet' and 'a red and blue carpet signify thus: one red and one blue carpets in the former and one carpet in two (red and blue) colours in the latter. Persons who are not familiar with computers may take a different meaning to the word, 'mouse' as an animal. Words mean different things to different persons. It is thus said: meaning is in people but not in words. Either avoid use of technical words or explain them clearly while using them to persons who are of different occupation.
3. Person who uses mixed language is referred to **pidgin**. The use of words and forms is simple and spoken by a person who does not speak the language well or when he is not talking to someone who does not know the language, say a person speaking Kannada and an Andraite communicating with each other in pidgin Hindi.
4. Poor expression of thought and ideas without appropriate words results in improper organization of ideas. Coherence-less and clarity-less messages leads to incorrect meanings. This would cause unavoidable errors and need clarifications which not only cost but also delay communication. Great speakers master the skill of using the right words at the right time; and refrain from using words which may have scope for misunderstanding. Touching of an elder's feet is the mark of respect in India while it is a mark of humiliation in other countries/cultures.
5. Sometimes, meanings exist not in words themselves but in the minds of people who use them. Simple words like love, freedom, happiness, tragedy carry numerous associations depending upon the situation of people. For instance, take the word profit. It is good and essential for the sustenance and building up of future business adding further installation of plant and machinery. It means expansion of business and opening for new jobs. However, employees interpret it as extra gains obtained by squeezing their salaries and wages. An illustration is explained in Exhibit 1.10.

Exhibit 1.10 Plan of Speaking

An officer along with his assistant was travelling in countryside. Suddenly, they noticed that they had lost their way. The officer told his assistant, when you see a person on the road, stop the car and ask him where we are. On finding a person on the road, the assistance stopped the car and asked him, where they were? He (passerby) replied, you are in your car. Now, the officer observed that the truth does not tell anything more than what we know.

1.18.2 Physical/Technical Barriers

In transmitting messages many channels, instruments and gadgets (like photocopying, microphone, projector, printing, telex, fax, radio, films cassette, floppy and alike) are in use. In these situations, availability and smooth functioning of channels serves the purpose. If it fails to perform efficiently and timely, then it acts like a barrier and as a result communication fails to reach the intended recipients. Barriers to communication arise when:

- There is noise in transmitting the message.
- There are differences among people in terms of language groups, cultural background, rural-urban origin, hierarchical level (work structure, authority, status and relationship) etc.
- There is a disturbed organizational climate with dissenting voices cropping up.

1.18.3 Cross-cultural Barriers

A shared set of values and attributes of a person or a group of persons is called **culture**. In other words, it is the sum total of the ways of living built up in talking, behaving, sharing and thinking of a person or a group of persons and transmitted from one generation to another. If the relationship between two groups or countries are not friendly for historical or political reasons, the problem of communication may emerge. This is so in the context of globalization of business too. Skill in communicating across cultures provides a good foundation to avoid the cross-cultural barriers in communication. The most significant differences between cross-cultures are:

- Language (when the Japanese say 'yes' they mean 'yes' while Americans say 'yes' when they 'agree')
- National character (every nation has its own character)
- Behaviour values (value culture differs from country to country say, western culture differs from eastern, south Indian culture differs from north Indian culture)
- Social relationship (grouping in the society say, Indian family relationship reflects elaborate and precise relationship between two persons indicating descent of three or four generations)
- Concept of time (punctuality and scheduling of activities depends upon the concept of time say, non-punctuality and non-functioning to schedule is normal in India while it is disciplined in advanced countries like Japan as they separate work time from personal time)

- Thinking process (some are strictly logical and rotational while others are holistic and emotional)
- Non-verbal communication (body language say, reacting unconsciously to physical appearance, colour and texture of skin, hairstyle, shape and colour of eyes, stature and body structure, style of dress and grooming, etc)
- Perception (smell of good or bad perceived differently, belief in the Almighty perceived differently by different groups of people, etc)

1.18.4 Socio-psychological Barriers

Problem in understanding, interpretation and response to communication arises either partly from socially-learnt attributes or partly from personal attributes. A kind of window through which we look out at the people, at the words, at the events and at the situations is known as **socio-psychological barrier;** also called **personal barrier**. People tend to look at the things and hear only in terms of their personality and experience. The receiver with his mind free from any pre-conceived bias or prejudice with kind disposition and being forward looking are likely to receive and interpret the messages more objectively as well as accurately. If he, on the other hand is influenced by some reason or the other by any sort of anxiety, emotion, etc., will probably interpret it more subjectively.

Hence, skills in communication are said to be the means of sound communication. People have personal feelings, desires, fears and hopes, likes and dislikes, attitudes, views and opinions; some are formed by family background and social environment while some others by individual's own intelligence, inherited qualities, education and personal experiences. The socio-psychological barriers are:

- Self-centred attitude (paying attention to those which are useful personally)
- Improper perception distorts messages. Surgical doctor's idea of cleanliness may not be the same as that of a worker in factory. Full stop (.) in telegraphic message is spelt out as 'stop.' If the receiver has same perception as to what the sender has, then the communication is perfect. Instead, the receiver perceived it as word, rather than full stop, then it becomes a great barrier.
- Trust, confidence and faith play a dominant role in understanding message by the receiver and credibility of the sender too. The typical example is: The management with honesty and sincerity gives statements like "promotion from within", changes likely to be affected in wage structure and so forth. This may not convince employees enough. The past experience of employees with regard to similar statements made by the manager may influence them not to believe in the present context.
- Group identification (every person belongs to a group like family, locality, religion, language, age, nationality, economic and alike) tends to reject any ideas which go against the interests of his group. For example, parents and children in age, women and men in gender, etc.
- Self-image (difficult to give and take feedback in the case of a self-centred image).

- Selective perception (selectively seeing, reading and hearing according to one's own needs, interests and experience).
- Defensiveness (threat messages become defensive and respond in preventing understanding)
- Filtering (reducing or colouring a message according to one's own understanding of the situation).
- Status block (senior positions often develop a feeling that they know everything about how to make business successful and may not agree with some good ideas of subordinates).
- Knowing everything. For example, businessmen have no ethics and honesty, women are more intelligent, rural people are worthless, politicians are corrupt, etc.
- Resistance to change (some people avoid new ideas because they feel insecure or afraid of changes in the situations).
- Poor communication skills (lack of skill in writing affects language use, nervousness in facing audience affects a person's clarity in speaking, excitement about an achievement or a new idea may make a person's speech incoherent, etc.).
- Half-listening or selective listening or non-empathetic listening arises in the process of communication. Suppose, the manager has informed to his subordinates including his PA that he is going to Delhi tomorrow. Later, he informed his PA through phone that his family is not going to Delhi and inform this to others in the office. The employees who are supposed to be in office are not there. Suddenly, the manager enters the office and finds no one in office. Half-listening is like racing scooter with gears in neutral.

In personal communication, a constant effort and training in effective communication along with periodical review and reorganization of communication network ensure the information reaches people. Cultivate and develop all communication skills including getting feedback and non-verbal communication. Maintenance of channels and systems in good working condition, keeping up the working conditions, intercoms, notice-boards and information meetings, etc., are the responsibility of management. Before communicating, try to feel yourself in the other's role, values and frame of reference which make success of communication with the target goal.

1.18.5 Sender's Responsibility

Being the initiator of communication, the sender has the following responsibilities:

1. **Set Goal of Communication:** The sender must set purpose clearly in communicating the message. A well organized talk or written communication will serve the purpose if the information is properly disseminated. A skillful communication is very much needed if the purpose is to change the opinion of the receiver.
2. **Use Appropriate Language:** Language is a major barrier in communication. So, the sender of communication must structure messages in clear, simple and understandable words to the receiver and avoid the use of jargon.

3. **Emphatic Communication**: The sender understands the receiver's approach to appreciate and how he will receive and interpret the sent message. It will solve many problems associated with communication. Hence, the need of the sender is to place himself in receiver's frame of reference.
4. **Improve Credibility**: Expertise (mastery over the topic under discussion) and trustworthiness (quality of action what one preaches) are the credibility of the sender. This can be improved by means of mastering the subject of communication and building up trustworthiness.
5. **Encourage Feedback**: Effective communication ends with feedback. It enables the sender to know whether the receiver has understood the message exactly in true sense what he intended to convey.
6. **Use Correct Redundancy**: If the message is so important or complicated, it is necessary to repeat it in several different ways so that the receiver understands it. Overuse of cliché or redundancy will spoil or dull the message. In written, redundancy is not necessary than in oral communication.
7. **Develop Climate of Trust**: An effective communication can take place and serve the purpose only if trust exists between the sender and the receiver.

1.18.6 Receiver's Responsibility

In making communication effective, the receiver plays a greater role on the following lines:

1. **Effective Listening:** Listening is a primary requirement for effective communication. Effective listening does not just happen but it requires much hard work and effort. See exhibit 1.11 for principles of effective communication.

Exhibit 1.11 Principles of Effective Listening

Principle	Good Listener	Bad Listener
Look at areas of interest	Seeks personal enlightenment or information, entertains new topics as potentially interesting	Turns out dry subjects, defines narrowly what is interesting
Overlooks errors directly	Attends to meaning and content; ignores delivery errors while being sensitive to any message in them	Ignores if delivery is poor, misses messages because of personal attributes of the communicator
Judgement	Avoids quick judgement, waits until comprehensiveness of the core	Quickly evaluates and passes judgement
Listen to ideas	Listens to ideas and themes	Listens to only facts and details

Takes notes	Takes careful notes and uses a variety of note taking or recording schemes depending on the speaker	Takes incomplete notes using one system
Active response	Responds with body state	Passive or no response
Changes mind	Uses material, stimulates the mind and seeks to enlarge understanding	Does not seek to broaden knowledge base
Encourages speaker	Asks for clarification of information or examples which help to rephrase the idea	Interrupts, asks trivial questions, makes distracting comments

2. **Avoid Premature Judgement:** The receiver must avoid making premature judgements (either positive or negative) about the sender and his message, thus distorting communication. Instead, the receiver needs to create a climate which fosters acceptance, trust and understanding.
3. **Provide Responsive Feedback:** Understanding of the message by the receiver what he feels about the message is known as **responsive feedback**. The motto of responsive feedback is to engage in constructive dialogue and achieve common ground in communication.

   The following aspects are to be kept in mind to overcome communication barriers:

   - A free and fair two-way flow of communication is encouraged.
   - Open mind and willingness to perceive messages through the eyes of others.
   - Use an understandable language.
   - Mental trust and confidence must be built among all.
   - Follow effective listening.
   - Both the sender and the receiver are familiar with dictionary meaning of words.
   - Avoid ambiguity in language.
   - Regulate information flow.
   - Adhere to the time and timeliness in communication.
   - Adopt feedback and playback by asking questions from the listener and by requesting the listener to repeat the message respectively.

QUESTIONS

1. What is knowledge management? Explain the components of human resource development.
2. What is communication? Discuss its evolution.
3. State the nature and scope of communication.
4. State the principles and objectives of communication.
5. Define communication. Explain the effects of communication.

6. Explain the importance of communication.
7. Is communication a discipline? Substantiate.
8. Discuss the process of communication with an example.
9. What are the essentials of good communication?
10. What are the barriers in communication? Explain semantic barriers to communication with an illustration.
11. Discuss the physical and cross-cultural communication barriers citing examples.
12. What are socio-psychological barriers? Illustrate some of them.
13. Explain the following:
    (a) Feedback
    (b) Guidelines governing effective communication
    (c) Communication policy
    (d) Effective communication and good communication

CHAPTER 2

Business Communication Management

"Commerce links all mankind in one common brotherhood of mutual dependence and interest"

— James A. Garfield

LEARNING OBJECTIVES

This chapter will enable you to

- understand the relevance and rationale of communication in business; and
- know the need of communication in managerial performance.

INTRODUCTION

An organization is involved with personnel, for marketing of goods or services covering large number of persons/institutions for recruitment and for performing various services in the functional areas of business. In simple words, the management is always involved in carrying out its functions by communicating with others. Every step of management begins with communication. Therefore, the communication in any organization is considered and recognized as an area of prudent management function. Thus, management and communication are intertwined, and hence management's functions cannot be accomplished without communication. More aptly said that 'communication is with words we govern men' and communicate forget not 'to do well.' Essentially, communication is, thus, the basic process of organization which has come to be identified as a life-line of commerce.

2.1 COMMUNICATION

Business development has a primary multiplier effect and is an indispensable and inescapable adjunct to creation of wealth in the society. It is the process of making efforts to bring in the resources of economy together, putting them together systematically and coordinating their activities for production or services and supply of them in the process creates job opportunities, offers better quality of life and contributes to the economic growth. Thus, business is understood as an institution or organization in the society which performs an exchange function and helps in value-creation, value-addition and value-consumption in the process of supplying goods and services for satisfaction of human-beings with motto of making suitable profit. Thus, business creates clear-cut lines of authority and responsibility to effects in improving the activating function, and controlling function of business management. Interaction with each other function in an organization in exchanging ideas and knowledge on coordination and cooperation approach safely with no misunderstanding to attune the effectiveness and efficiency is the end result. As a unifying link, communication finds a prime place in enlivening of business organization. Thus, the establishment of a sound organization and a healthy communication policy to promote effective communication is an inevitable requisite by all means before any kind of human activity. Communication is of two types: internal and external.

2.1.1 Internal Communication

If communication takes place between employees and/or among them, between employers and employees with motto of informing, instructing, educating, developing, motivating, persuading, entertaining, directing, controlling and cautioning, it is known as **internal communication.** In other words, flow of information concerns to the operating level and required by all who work together in an organization to achieve common goal. It may be oral or written, visual or audio-visual, formal or informal; and upward or downward. The subject matters that address in the internal communication are knowledge, skills, corporate concerns, review and monitoring, performance appraisal, counseling and training. Thus, managing communication internally of pure official matter, moving with files is termed indoor management.

In small organizations, internal communication poses no serious problem; the office with little effort can communicate with each other effectively. Big business organization, with a large group of people is a difficult task. In such cases, an effective internal communication is a real problem which compels a certain amount of care and scientific way of communication. An effective internal communication keeps informed all the employees and the management influencing the behaviour and attitude towards higher efficiency for better productivity. In fact, efficient employee communication is the difference between unlocking and blocking the full potential of the organization.

A professional approach and careful management with active and deliberate measures to build, manage, enhance and protect the company brand, both internally and externally is a must as it necessitated strategically to the initiatives of 'corporate communication professionals'. Hence, dedicated staff with the use of sophisticated approaches in communication initiation to create a strong corporate, financial and market branding through effective advertising and promotion programme, media relation, investor relation activities and employee events is a critical factor.

2.1.2 External Communication

Any communication, on the other hand, going outside the business organization to the consumers, financiers, clients, suppliers, job-seekers, industry bodies and institutes, government agencies, media and general public is termed external communication. This is in various forms like public relations initiatives, corporate advertising in print, television or web, new product or service launch, trade show, job fairs, vendor or distributor meetings, press conferences, company website and corporate publications.

Externally, effective communication is crucial for achieving the perception of company and building respectful image and reputation about the company in the society. It serves to develop and maintain a coherent corporate identity, brings company values to life, shows value to customers and promotes the unique strengths, corporate governance, philosophy, social responsibility programmes and corporate citizenship while building an attractive employer brand. Not only does projecting an admirable positive image to the external public, build a sense of company trust, integrity, approachability and credibility. This also helps the company immensely in times of crisis by moulding a favourable public opinion and aiding crisis management.

By designing and implanting sensitive programmes using the cutting-edge tools, mechanisms and procedures, the company can carve a unique position in the minds of people, differentiating it from other peers and competitors. It can affect employee perception and its objectives facilitate to embrace the mission goals through vision, thus, influencing employee productivity and profitability. Above all, the long-term goodwill and solid reputation will help the organization to flourish and grow like never before!

As competition grows and reputation becomes more imperative, any company is serious about its image which it should always have for effective corporate communication. Therefore, both internal and external communication forms significant corporate functions, serving as a crucial liaison for the organization with its extended audiences. External communication is broadly classified into seven categories as presented in Chart 2.1.

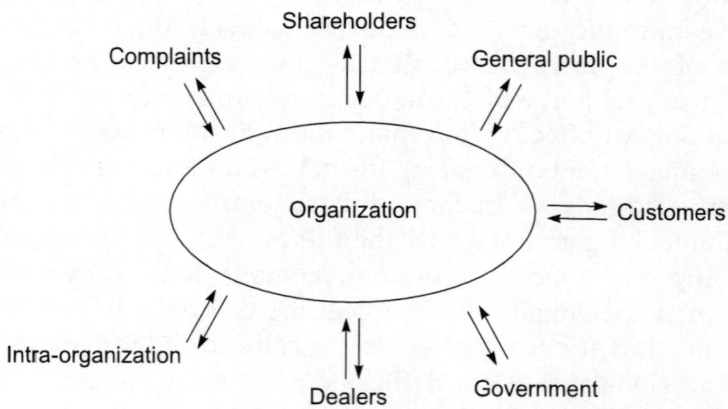

Chart 2.1 Outside Network of Communication

2.2 INTERFACE OF BUSINESS COMMUNICATION AND MANAGEMENT

A thrust need of business is to bring in together various components such as manpower, money, machine, materials, etc., and putting them on work systematically and coordinating their activities effectively to achieve production efficiency and profit. The latter can be achieved by rendering products or services to the society. It means business is concerned with two aspects, namely, production, and exchange or supply of goods and services with monetary profit. The activities of production and exchange respectively are called industry and commerce.

Industry utilizes the activities of human beings and other inputs engaged in production, extraction, processing, exploration, construction and fabrication of products and bring them into a useful form for final consumption or further production; and create a form of utility to those goods or services. Unless these goods and services are made available to those who need them, it may not fulfill the service of satisfying human wants. Goods produced by the industries should be made available to the consumers at right place, right time, right quantity and right price in right manner by an activity called **commerce**. Commerce provides all activities to establish a link between the producers of goods and the consumers of these goods; and maintains a smooth and uninterrupted flow of goods between them in the society.

Trade refers to sale, transfer or exchange of goods and services with monetary profit. Trade is internal (wholesale and retail) in the country and external (export, import and entrepot) across the boundaries of the country. The activities that facilitate trade are called aids-to-trade, also called auxiliaries-to-trade which are grouped into:

- Banking
- Insurance
- Warehousing
- Transportation
- Advertising

Of late, electronic commerce also called e-commerce is burgeoning as an 'aid-to-trade' and showing every sign of continuity to expand business. Arthur M. Weimar defined business as: "Business is that complex field of commerce and industry in which goods and services are created and distributed in the hope of profit within a framework of laws and regulations." According to Louis E. Boone and David K. Kurtz, "Business comprises all profit-seeking activities that produce goods and services necessary to an economic system. It is the economic pulse of a nation, striving to increase the people's standard of living. Profit is a primary mechanism for motivating these activities." In the words of Wright F.J., "Business organization is arranging or combining of resources to achieve an economic aim as either with the resources available to achieve the maximum profit or to achieve the given aim with the least possible expenditure of resources."

Rendering a specialized service of the specialized nature under the governance of professional bodies like Bar Council of India by lawyers, Medical Council of India by doctors, Institute of Chartered Accountants of India by auditors on professional knowledge, education and training is called **profession**. They charge a fee for rendering their professional services. A person who exercises the entrusted activity under the rules of employment or service is called employee and the person who provides this activity is called employer. Working in a college, office, factory, etc., are a few examples of employment. Even professionally qualified persons like doctors, engineers, auditors, accountants, etc., also work as employees in various organizations. Employees receive remuneration from the employer in the form of salary. The concept of business, profession and employment though distinguished from each other, but both have employees and professionals working with the business enterprise. The employees and professionals occupy a central place around whom, by whom and for whom business is run.

It is understood that business is an integral part of a society and an interface between connotes three aspects of economy. These aspects are (a) economic activity, (b) economic unit, and (c) economic process possessing the specific characteristics of change, diversification, competition, risk and profit on one hand and the society on the other. Thus, business is an integration of various available economic resources under the creative process system of management. The management is not a matter of pressing a button, pulling a lever, issuing an order, scanning profit and loss statement, and promulgating rules and regulations. In other words, any business encompasses the scientific know-how and technical do-how, encountering the challenges in converting inputs into saleable products or services (a) complying with legal regulations and government requirements, (b) meeting the social responsibilities, and (c) achieving the defined objectives of business enterprise.

The 2001 Nobel Prize winners in Economic Sciences, George Akeri, Michael Spence and Joseph Stieglitz said that information and communication is of utmost importance to the society and well-functioning of economics through acceleration of a broad based growth and increasing awareness. A good example is India's 'Operation Flood' in milk production which is the third largest milk producing country in the world. The focal point of communication is tapping of rich reservoir of knowledge on which depend possible sustainable economic futures of all the people in a society.

2.3 FOUNDATION

Communication as a foundation and management tool is elaborately discussed in the following pages.

1. Effective communication is important for managers to perform their basic functions of planning, organizing, leading and controlling. The process of communication makes it possible for managers to carry out their task of responsibilities. Planning requires communicating information to the top management. Similarly, the business organization requires communicating with others about their job assignments, leading requires managers to communicate to the subordinates so that the goals can be achieved and controlled which need to initiate necessary steps for maintaining accepted quality standards.
2. Such significant and well considered institution of business's success depends upon the environment which notably refers to the economic, social, cultural, technological, political, legal, global and natural factors wherein effective communication plays a catalytic role. The effective governance of them is a challenging task to the management. It means that no business enterprise operates in vacuum but derives its existence from the environment in the society. In making sound decisions, the management, therefore, does need to study the environment critically and analytically; and implement the decisions taken thereon. It is here that communication has a greater role to play in effective and prudence of business management. Today, communication has become the foundation upon which depends effective functioning of management.

3. Practically, management spends more than six hours in a day as per Klemmer and Snyder, on managerial time devoting to the activity of communication. The managers rarely are alone at their desks thinking, planning, directing, leading or contemplating alternatives. They may be busy on face-to-face or telephone conversation or writing or dictating memos, letters or reports sent to them. Management spends much time on communication, speaks about communication and how important it is!
4. In ancient times, business was carried out as barter system and communication at that time could remain at a primitive stage. The trade continued to grow both in size and competition; and became more complex in the competitive world functionally and geographically, i.e., locally, nationally and globally. Further, the management of business organization is more concerned in dealing with all the stakeholders – employees, customers, consumers, clients, suppliers, institutions, owners and the society. To safeguard the interests of all and earns profit for survival and sustenance, the management performs at 360°, its defined functions meaningfully and purposefully for which the management should need to have a two-way effective communication with know-how and do-how practices. This integrates the dynamic interactive process of planning, organization, directing, staffing and controlling, unifying all these internally and externally in the business organization for attaining the objectives. Thus, an efficient management function resorts to an effective communication process.

2.4 MANAGEMENT TOOL

Communication is not only an instrument of transmission of messages but an in-born quality or a talent of both art and science calling for mastery of skills. Essentially, the effectiveness of all the management functions entirely depends only upon an effective communication function. Simply, this shows how everyone in an organization participates/involves him/her directly or indirectly in communication process. Therefore, management and communication are interlinked; the end-result of the former can be achieved through the latter's effectiveness. The importance of communication is described as: What bloodstream does ensure health of individual, communication does supply information to all the concerned in the organization making effective functioning of it. "Well informed individuals will be 'sounder' than the ill-informed individuals."(Morris S. Vittles)

The use of letter was the only method of sending message before telephone. It is an important method of communication even in the advancement of electronic media in the modern times. It maintains a personal touch, avoids changes, serves as a record, and also serves as a means of keeping other persons/parties informed by sending copies. Even after the advancement in transmission of modern technologies like fax, e-mail, internet, etc., which have high speed rate of transmission instantaneously the message of written words through writing letter has become essential in terms of conveying the intended meaning. The importance of contexts in which letter writing is important in the following enquiries to answer:

- Getting and giving quotation
- Contacting customers and persuading potential customers to buy
- Making and answering complaints
- Making trade and trade enquires
- Collecting dues
- Informing the stakeholders
- Maintaining relations with public at large

A sound business organization takes every opportunity to write letters to all concerned in order to create and maintain goodwill. It is here that one needs the writing of letters with knowledge in clear and concise style of writing. Sincere, confident, self-respecting and friendly are qualities, which need to reflect in the style of writing a letter. Communication activates decision but decision without communication is useless while poor communication makes the decision ineffective. Communication and decision are thus two common parameters to all the functions of effective management in business organization. Communication, therefore, is the soul of management and is pervasive in everyday life and exerts tremendous influence on the success of business endeavours. Simple and true communication touches the emotions of soft-spot of employees with the right diction and tone of language as it will go a long way in improving organization's performance. Hence, communication is regarded as the basic function of organization and its absence; the business organization would cease to exist. In other words, the functions, objectives, procedures, etc., are visibly associated with management through communication.

2.5 IS COMMUNICATION A MANAGERIAL ROLE?

The organizational effectiveness and efficiency largely depend upon the management system and its driving wheels. These are provided by the communication system. Therefore, effective communication is as important as the other resources and systems used by the business organization. Therefore, communication in a business organization is indispensable. In the society, the fabric of modern man urges to satisfy wants or business organization wants to accomplish its goals entirely depends upon an effective and meaningful communication. The implementation of policies and programmes of management by an individual or an institution is possible only through a successful effective communication.

How does the communication so pertinent in business leads to its success? The management of any institution can initiate appropriate measures by adopting a sound communication system and getting involvement of the entire concern in the organization so that the issues or problems can be solved without much difficulty. The manager imparts the objectives of organization and spends about three-fourths of his time in transmitting information pertaining to business policies, producers, rules, programs, strategies, etc., to the subordinates as well as workers facilitating them to increase their work efficiency. A large part of manager's on-the-job effectiveness comes from how effective he is in communicating with clarity, precision and consideration. Katz pointed out that as a person progresses in the organization hierarchy; the importance of communication skills tends to increase.

Though communication is more a facilitator than an actual function of human resource, marketing, production, finance, etc., there is a strong cause for managerial communication to be treated as a significant 'functional' area of management since it conducts all the functional areas, age groups, experience levels and across genders. communication, thus, acts as a tool of management in managerial performance of business. This is explained below.

1. **Organization:** Assembly of various inputs or services for accomplishment of the stated objectives of an unit through production is referred as **organization**. Being informed or informing others is the basic factor of organization through communication. A major amount of time is spent on communication by most people in any organization, be it business, factories, hospitals, corporate bodies, religious bodies, military services, educational institutions and alike. Communication, fundamentally, is an interaction process between the people which keeps alive and maintains the organizational structure. In the absence of this pervasive process of communication, no organization could ever exist. Through communication better relations, through better relations better understanding and through better understanding better progress of organization is possible to achieve better performance. In fact, communication aids in managerial planning to be performed effectively, managerial organization to be carried out effectively, managerial actuating to be followed effectively and managerial controlling to be applied effectively. In other words, howsoever good plans, procedures and organizational structure exist; the business carries no importance, no value and serves no useful purpose until its functional areas are actually put into working operations. This is neatly summed up in the Pareto Principle of the 80/20 rule. It means that typically 80 per cent of unfocussed effort generates only 20 per cent of results; the remaining 80 per cent of results are achieved with only 20 per cent of the effort. By effective organizational communication, it can achieve the greatest payoff possible with time management. The areas for which communication focuses within a business organization are to:

   - Establish and disseminate goals
   - Develop plans for accomplishing goals
   - Organize resources in an effective and efficient way
   - Select, develop and appraise members of organization
   - Lead, direct, motivate and create a climate in which people want to contribute
   - Carry out management functions with controlling approach
   - Develop a clear line of authority with corresponding responsibility
   - Mobilize required inputs of production by means of informing well all the concerned
   - Spread and develop market for the goods or services

2. **Coordination:** Employees in a large organization are more in number and are working on the basis of division of labour. For attaining the goal of organization, there is every need of coordination among such workers which is possible to obtain by sound and effective communication. The essentials of communication, in the words of Marry Curling Nile, is that: "Good communication is a prerequisite to coordination. It is necessary upward, downward and sideways through all the levels of authority and advice for the transmission, interpretation and adoption of policies, sharing of knowledge and information; and more subtle needs of good morale and mutual understanding."
3. **Decision-making:** Providing all the needed information enables the management of business organization to take sound decisions at right time and transmit them to those who are in need of them. Chester Barnard says that, "The first executive function is to develop and maintain a system of communication." Communication plays a vital in discharging the managerial roles say, interpersonal, informational and decision.
4. **Motivation:** The Indian management needs to supplement faith in scientific management with the theories of motivation to achieve business excellence through human excellence in the competitive era of globalization. For exploiting the expected results from the functions of planning, directing, controlling, motivation is an unspecified yet critical part of management function. It is a process of keeping everyone in an organization well informed by speaking. In most organizations, the performance is through usual means, how people are informed, how they are encouraged and the extent to which they participated. The hierarchy of five needs with self-actualization, esteem, social, safety and psychological in Indian business organization, as stated by Abraham Maslow, entirely depends upon how effective communication motivates involving both parties of influencer and influence.
5. **Smooth Working:** Communicating the right information to the right workers at the right time discloses the real situation prevailing in the organization. This helps workers to perform their duties without delay with utmost care to lead to smooth functioning. In this context, it is worth to quote Terry G.R. He said: "communication serves as the lubricant fostering the smooth operations of the management."
6. **Peaceful Atmosphere:** Lack of communication or no communication is the main reason for industrial unrest in any nation in the world and consequently creates a strained relationship between the management and the workers. Both the management and the workers understand each other properly in an improved way for the communicated information to ensure and enhance the industrial peace.
7. **Leadership:** In forwarding ideas, feelings, suggestions and decisions to the employees by the management and employees' sending responses, attitudes, perception and problems to the management through a two-way communication, the management assumes itself as a leader of organization's employees. See Exhibit 2.1 for role of leader in a business organization.

Exhibit 2.1 **Leader and Communication**

The whole setup of an organization and new heights in business revolves around a particular individual who is said to be a leader. He constantly interacts with different groups of people and people in authority like lawmakers, persons holding positions, high political office and thought leaders for reaping the ultimate results of benefit or success. He articulates to address every situation and every person that he meets in daily course of actions. He has a choice of words to dot the speech and is able to put across thoughts with mannerism, certainly grab the attention of audience. If the delivery seems to come from a loudspeaker, but not a live speaker, then the audience can be seen yawning or inching to the nearest exit.

8. **Job Satisfaction:** If the management of organization keeps on informing the employees in time, what to do and what not to do for striving the objectives of organization, they can put their performance in efficient way and improve the performance if it is not up to the standards. Employees are always desirous of knowing their target with the possible reasons thereof. All these are potential through purposeful communication by which employees can get job satisfaction.
9. **Image Building:** An enterprise is very much concerned with its public image, sustenance and survival, to a major extent, depends upon the good public relations that it maintains. The customers, potential customers, shareholders, suppliers, people of the society, state and central governments and alike constitute public. So as to build up such a good public image, broadcasting of information about an enterprise is a must by means of communication. If the management of organization carries out active communication, it can create a good image in the looks of public so that it can maintain good public relations. There is a saying that "building a city needs more communication than concrete."
10. **Crisis Management:** Failure of effective planning mechanism due to problematic situations in achieving the intended result is called **crisis**. Crisis is a time of danger, difficulty and anxiety which may be brought about by an accident or any unforeseen event say, fire in a factory, collapse of a business building causing harm to employees and customers, a shot-out by robbers who break in, etc. In such situations, every business, big or small, public or private runs the risk of crisis.

    The crisis situations in the field of management may be production, marketing, human resource development, finance, conflict resolution, interpersonal situations, group dealings, etc. Crisis management refers to managing the non-conducive environment situation in the functional activity of production, marketing, personnel, conflict resolution, interpersonal situation, group dealing, etc., and finding a solution without loss of time. A golden rule adoption in this context is that crisis situation should be averted or anticipated with effective message sent through an appropriate channel and media with all the persons involved or affected. Thus, communication would help to fight against the risk of crisis. Give a thought to the crisis. Imagining a fire in a college building, the following questions arise in such a crisis:

- What is the immediate communication required?
- Who are to be contacted, for what purpose?
- Who are to be notified?
- How are the inmates to be directed and instructed to move out of the danger?
- How should the panic be controlled?
- Who should talk to the parents who arrive?
- What should be answered to those who call by telephone?
- What is to be said to the reporters who might call or arrive, and by whom?

11. **Cooperation:** If the flow of communication is smooth and receptive with cooperation, an effective mutual understanding between the concerned ones can be developed in the congenial atmosphere. This is the utmost need to promote peace and production without any interruption at the workplace. Herbert G. Hicks said: "Communication is basic to an organization's existence from its birth through continuing life."
12. **Stakeholders:** Individuals or group of persons who have some interest or stake in the business and work for its success are called **stakeholders**. A continued and sustained business is the result of good response of all the stakeholders: (a) owners expect smooth and efficient business and good return on their equity, (b) employees expect career progress, job satisfaction, reasonable reward and incentives system, customers anticipate quality products and services in commensurate to the price paid and the community to look ahead to the conduct of welfare scheme for its social progress adopting a variety of methods, types, channels and strategies. Effective address of all the issues would resort to a sound communication.
13. **Competitors:** The operations of inventory, production, marketing and other related issues in the market would need the involvement of communication with business management in the market. Notwithstanding the competitive nature, different business managements may arrive at some understanding to respond to the customers. Often clash of interest may crop up between them which needs to be sorted out. Thus, the management of business organizations for different reasons may need to communicate with its competitors and other operators in the market.
14. **Government:** The involvement of government in business needs no emphasis. Every business, in some way or the other, comes within the ambit of the central or state or quasi government in nature; and comply or compliance of tax payment, pollution control, stock holding, etc., of various rules and regulations of the government. Inadequacy of reporting could result in problems like levy of penalties or prosecution. Every business organization, therefore, respects the law of land in conduct of its business. Communication between the government and the business organization, thus, is a point of recognition and respect.
15. **Consumer Forum:** All organizations deal with the varied consumers, consumer organizations, consumer courts and consumer lobbies; and host of others like supervising agencies, employment agencies, courts and judicial organs, international

bodies, financial institutions, etc. Communication with the entire consumer forum plays a crucial role in modern-day business organizations.

16. **Media and Press:** Every business organization at one time or other in one form or other, expose by communicating or interacting to media, press, television and other media for the purpose of advertising, announcement, clarification, image building and alike. The press relations and the media contact is, thus, an essential function dealt with caution and attention.
17. **Common Correspondence:** Irrespective of businesses whether they are big or small, old or new, local or national, public or private, proprietary or partnership, monopolistic or competitive, manufacturing or service; they have certain common concerns and approaches within given business environment and deal with people. Also is organized into functional areas, viz., marketing, human resource, financial, production and so on with a wide variety of business letters in both ways: business organization to various agencies including individuals and agencies; and individuals to business organization. See Exhibit 2.2 for common business correspondence.

Exhibit 2.2 **Business Correspondence**

Department	Matter for Correspondence
Purchase	Calling quotations, tenders and orders for products and services Inviting tenders for job and supplies Asking for samples and drawings Placing orders Status enquiries Technical and commercial bids
Sales	Preparation of sales letter with terms and conditions Circular of letter Preparation of market survey report Report from sales persons to sales executive Offer of discounts and concession Launch of new product or scheme Mailing company literature Letter of acknowledgement
Personnel	Calling candidates for written test Interview call letters Offer of appointment Confirmation in service Changes in emoluments Disciplinary matters Leave and travel sanctions Training programs

Administrative and secretarial	Change in management Change in business hours Opening and shifting branches and offices Invitations and public notices Correspondence with directors and shareholders Agenda and minutes of company meetings Correspondence with shareholders and debenture holders Correspondence with agents and transport companies Representation to trade unions, chambers of commerce
Other communications	Job applications Preparation of bio-data and curriculum vitae Export and import related correspondence Preparation of bill of exchange, promissory note, hundi, etc Correspondence with foreign institutions Advertisement copy of various types Questionnaire and opinion polls Legal correspondence Publicity literature Preparation of visual aids Social letters in business Appreciation letters on achievements Goodwill messages

To sum up, communication as a function of management integrates the other management functions of planning, organizing, staffing, directing and controlling with the aim of making every person in the organization aware of expression leading to good working relations through a two-way approach. This becomes a sound base for achieving the intended results. In other words, the functions of management become meaningful only in the presence of communication as it has limitless universal boundaries. Vision is for mission and communication is for goal achievement of individual or business concern. In brief, good communication is a dire need which has direct bearing on the peace and progress of an organization and economy of a nation.

2.6 COMMUNICATION APPROACH

The approach in the communication process is commonly grouped into three which are persuasive approach, problem-solving approach and operational approach. These are discussed below.

1. **Persuasive Approach:** Regulating and balancing the information flow, facts and feelings in an organization is the responsibility of management. Winning or influencing the mind of employees towards better understanding as well as better relations to achieve the operational objectives is the task of management. The communication of a well planned programme involving rules and procedures for healthy and good environmental conditions of an organization is of the utmost

necessity. So, an organization always has a healthy communication trend with a balanced flow of information tending persuasive.

2. **Problem Solving Approach:** Effective communication tends to effective role of a concern. It means effective work performance and efficient problem solving. As theory of problem-solving approach, this creates a good managerial climate for providing to pervade and spring forth with the feelings of confidence, mutual trust and openness of people. This trend brings a problem-solving approach in business communication.

3. **Operational Approach:** Relation of individuals or group of individuals provides a major element in forming an organization. Communication in such organization is 'organic' covering all relationships including all the concerned activities with a message flow, upward, downward and across the line. Communication is nothing else, but human relations. Look at exhibits 2.3, 2.4 and 2.5; how communication helps the management in identifying the response of employees.

Exhibit 2.3 Employer Employee Communication and Outcome

An effective two-way communication between the employer and the employees is vital for any organization to succeed. Communication is necessary to manage information, share knowledge, avoid mistakes, gauge progress, know limitations, learn from failures, solve problems, innovate and support one another.

When the employer and the employees are clear with regard to the goals, agree upon the course of action and move together in organization to achieve its goal, any gap in communication or miscommunication results in unexpected outcomes. Such communication fails in two conditions. One, when an employee does not receive correct and complete information due to hiding information or failing to communicate the needed message properly. Two, when the employer fails to extract honest feedback from employees because of opinion not sought or disregarded. Failure of employer communication results in employee disengagement, damaged trust between the employer and the employees, missed opportunities, delay in project and failed initiatives. But, how can one ensure effective employee communication? What is the right way to measure employee communication and improve it.

First, when information is common to the whole workforce, then circulate it with focus on different aspects and call for discussion to ensure that they perceive the information in an appropriate form. If disparities are found, the employees must be told about what they should look for in the communicated information. Next step is measuring the output of employees, the quality of their work, or how it made their work easier. Next comes measuring communication from the employee end. To do this, communication from the employees should be documented and verified whether they communicated complete and correct information. Any barriers in the communication process like someone in the hierarchy hiding information or suppressing the source must be identified and removed. The different aspects like compliments, complaints, challenges, requests, ideas and opinions should be measured separately.

In measuring the employee communication, the whole workforce is so essential. All the aspects of organization, right from its performance in the market to the employee benefits are inevitably covered. Communication of employees improves relations between the employer and the employees which, in turn, improves the productivity of an organization.

The changing role of management in business changes the changing role of producer, marketer and consumer. In the context of buyers' economy due to many producers of output or services came into being in the society, it has been recognized and realized that the production of output/services and marketing of them must satisfy the wants of consumers. Exhibit 2.4 illustrates how a steady shift and changing role of management in business sector changes the future role.

Exhibit 2.4 Changing Role of Management

Past	Present
Producer: Most important in the economy and produced what found possible to him.	Takes direction from the marketer and consumer; produces output the consumer wants, strives things for what they need and employs technology to achieve ends, innovation, service and relationship management are on the agenda.
Marketer: Distributed production efficiently and faced competition to manage it mostly by price-financial management.	Constantly helps and leads the consumer to determine what he wants. Investigates possible improvements, innovations and changes. Realizes the quest which is an unending action greatly propelled by consumer behaviours.
Consumer: Purchased what was made available and what he could afford within means and tailored his lifestyle accordingly. His behaviour was somewhat inhibited.	Tries to achieve a better standard of living for acquiring goods and services with increasing income to meet the growing needs. Realizes that needs can be ever-growing and yesterdays luxuries are today's necessities. Exercises options and dictates creation of goods/services. All these form uninhibited consumer behaviour.

Exhibit 2.5 Wooing Through Communication Package

Godfrey Philips India found that its cigarette brands were not reaching the rural outlets. Though, it was advertising on television, there were not enough television sets in the rural areas. The company came out with an indigenous idea. It put on road, five of its own vans fitted with television sets. A road show consisting of an entertainment programme interspersed with advertising messages was undertaken. They visited shops, village malls, weekly markets and alike. Van carried stocks of cigarettes and supplied them to the rural outlets. Video vans helped the company in creating awareness, encouraged sampling of brands and in monitoring the market. Another case is that of Hero Honda. It has gone in, for special video films on serving or maintenance is shown in the mobile workshop. Its campaign also included billboards, hoardings and radio commercials in local languages.

In motivating employees, building high morale among employees, providing satisfaction in work, contributing to development and growth, moulding employee attitudes, coordinating among and between all the concerned employees internally and externally. Towards this, the role of communication is considered a catalytic role in business organization. In a word, it bridges the meaning between people which implies that a person can safely cross the road. To sum up, no price should be too high and no effort too heavy for the management of business organization in driving towards improving the communication system; which is fundamental and vital to all the actions of management.

2.7 DOES BUSINESS NEED COMMUNICATION?

Business communication is different from personal communication because business has distinct characteristics as well as distinct set of goals. So, one has a fair idea and thought of business in sending business messages effectively to become successful. A business is an institution with efforts to conduct sound business. All these are possible in the presence of good communication. A discussion is made on the need and rationale of communication in business for survival and sustenance of its growth and development in serving the people in the society because of the following considerations.

1. **Sustainable Results:** A business operates with long-term objectives by bringing all the required resources and courses of innovative thoughts to produce and supply products and services uninterruptedly. The player in the business should act continually and regularly to serve all the stakeholders. In other words, it should not become fly-by-night operators making fast money and disappearing from the scene. Since the large business organizations are perennial in character, they should recognize the long-term sustainability of results. An effective communication is a catalytic agent in tailoring the environment to attain the defined results.
2. **Business Dynamics:** Satisfaction of human beings is fast changing in the changing socio-economic-cultural environment; business too has to change for its sustenance. A business needs to adopt and respond to the changes of human beings towards the products with generic services. A progressive business can recognize the inevitability of these changes and make every effort to anticipate the changes in business environment due to changing behaviour of consumers in the society for making remedial actions. Mass production and mass marketing are the

order of day; both of which are becoming highly complex, then the jobs become intellectually critical where the employees need to become intelligent with up-to-date skills. In this scenario, it is the brainpower, i.e., knowledge which is more in demand.

The degree of business changes and extent of proactiveness is determined by the warranted situations of environment. Television in the place of radio, PVC pipes in place of gauging pipes, computer in place of type-writer, fax and e-mail in the place of regular mail, incandescence lamps in place of kerosene lamps and alike are some dynamics of business. All these business dynamics would not find market without the presence of a purposeful communication system under a healthy policy.

3. **Relationship:** The business relationships are with customers, buyers, suppliers, debtors, financiers and others with whom it interacts on an ongoing basis. Sound and healthy relationship sustains the business which results in profit earning with mutual benefits. A purposeful business communication is needed to establish, nurture and sustain mutual benefits in the long run.
4. **Business Information:** A strategic decision is necessitated in the modern complex and competitive business which depends upon the information. The information can be stored and retrieved through processing, analysis and interpretation for making strategic decisions. The decision-making is made feasible due to computer and electronic devices; and possible on better communication mechanism across the world. Hence, there is every need of sound and appropriate communication in the business.
5. **Business Discipline:** Discipline is primary aspect in every business concern to practice in the present context. The function of communication makes employees know the rules and regulations of organization and appraise themselves to the work situations, safety regulations, amicable relations, etc., accordingly. Towards this, the management must use appropriate channel and media for effective internal communication.

2.8 GOVERNANCE AND COMMUNICATION

The corporate governance in globalization scenario has a wide business spectrum with the cardinal principles of adequacy (made information available to all stakeholders for their fair assessment), transparency (openness without hoodwink), consistency (no contradiction between what is said and what is achieved) and shunning down short-cuts and unethical practices. The corporate governance encompasses the range of formal and informal actions and interactions for goodness of the society at large. Fairness, honesty and transparency of business organization pertaining to its dealings with stakeholders are imminent in the prudent management of business. Descriptions and thereon prescriptions of the board and the sub-committees need to contain a narrative cohesiveness, support of unit's performance and prospects, and its understandable assessment. The good governance of all these aspects inevitably and indispensably hinge upon the sound and effective communication system. Follow-up aspects for good and effective communication in business sector are as:

- Effective communication is a matter of accident or change happening but would need a desirable draw up communication policy in ensuring clarity of business transactions and interaction with media and public.
- The response to frauds, damaging press reports and other such adverse developments can be rectified by the issue of rejoinders, meeting the press, interacting with public or contacting the opinion-makers and alike; all such would need to control the damage. This aspect, indeed, is an important facet of any effective communication and public relations strategy.
- Effective communication presupposes not only strengthening of information pertaining to the positive developments but also addressing and dealing appropriately with the negative happenings.
- In an internal environment and work culture with freedom to express views at various levels and in all directions, communication is an aid and assists the management of sound governance.

QUESTIONS

1. Explain the interface of communication in business management.
2. Discuss communication as an aid-to-business.
3. Explain the scope of communication in business.
4. Write a note on governance and communication.

3 CHAPTER

Classification of Business Communication

Effectiveness depends upon ability to reach others through the spoken or written word.

— **Author**

Learning Objectives

This chapter will enable you to

- know written, oral and pictorial types of communication and their scope;
- describe body movements as channels of communication;
- know the essence and need of oral communication;
- understand the approach to conduct meetings and conferences; and
- understand how to prepare for an interview.

INTRODUCTION

Words are a familiar tool or type of symbol conveying intended message and stand for their meaning. In other words, they are employed as a means of balancing not only a sentence but also an idea. Spoken words are influenced by quality and volume of voice, pitch, speed of delivery and timing pauses. A speaker's communicating message takes a clear understanding only on his facial expression, gestures, movement, manner, appearance, etc. To make written communication effective, the choice of words, composition of phrases and sentences are important. English is a link language. See Exhibit 3.1.

Exhibit 3.1 **English is a Link Language**

English language has lived for a long period of time in our country, and therefore, it cannot be treated as a foreign language. Rather, it becomes one of the Indian languages. In the globalization process even countries like Japan, West Germany and Switzerland have started recognizing the importance of English in the recent years. In India, the states such as Gujarat, Punjab and West Bengal have given importance to English right from the school level. English and regional languages co-exist. As link language, English acts as a cementing force to unite the entire mankind across the globe. In view of the status symbol, no country can afford to neglect English especially in the contemporary context. Teaching English in educational institutions is now gaining momentum.

Communication covers a wide range of areas and dynamic activities of business transactions in an organization to upkeep the pace of progress with the lifestyle and occupations of people. The inevitable changes in communication style due to the advancement of technology have influenced all the people in the areas of commerce, industry, education and innovation, governance, thinking and daily lives. In business, the activities of goal setting, planning and budgeting, monitoring and control; and the functions of management including human resource development entirely depended upon the practices of sound and effective communication.

3.1 CLASSIFICATION OF COMMUNICATION

In modern era of management development, communication is a 'key' in clarifying responsibility, accountability, transference, improving organization structure, improving education and training needs, spotting talents for promotion, motivating and raising morale of employees, their counseling and warning, increasing productivity and ultimately earning profits. The methods of communication are broadly grouped into verbal and non-verbal. Detailed classification of verbal communication and non-verbal communication are presented in Chart 3.1.

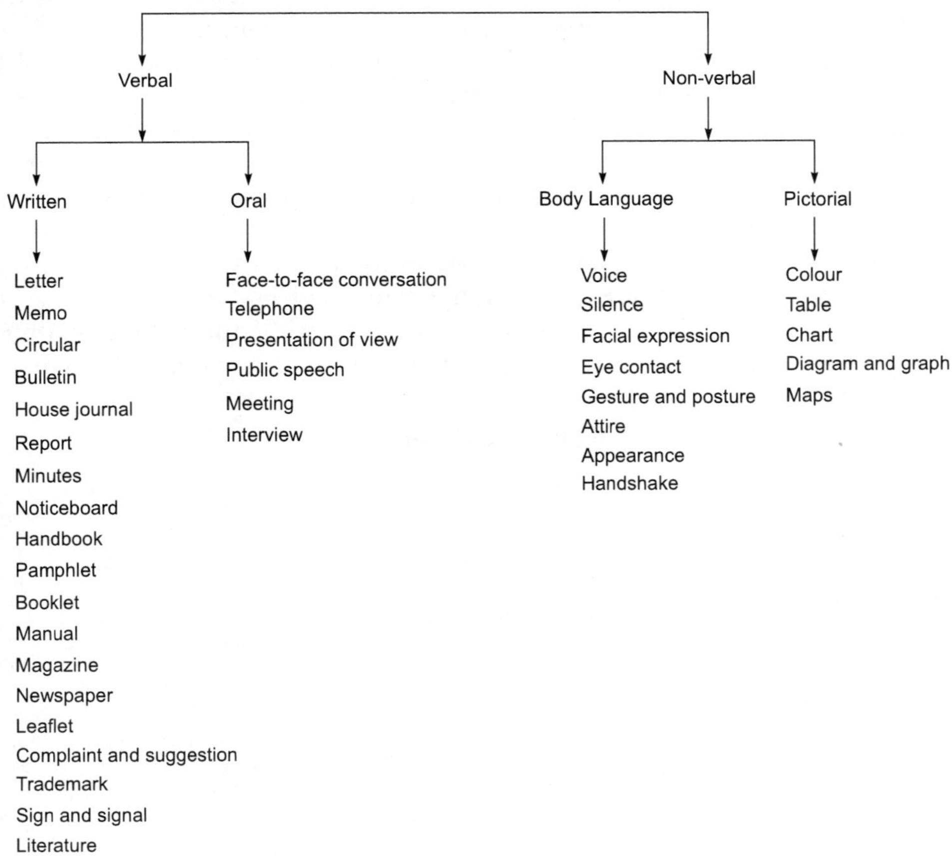

Chart 3.1 Classification of Communication

3.2 VERBAL COMMUNICATION

Communication through words is called **verbal communication** which classifies into written communication and oral communication.

3.2.1 Written Communication

Communication recorded in white and black is called **written communication**. It covers all kinds of subject matters like letters, resolutions, suits, affidavits, complaints, pleadings, financial statements, appointments, cost sheets, memos, notices, circulars, reports, bulletins, brochures, etc. Written communication is a powerful method of sending messages if properly and correctly worded. History is replete with instances where a piece of writing was involved in events of great significance say, love, war, peace, unions, songs, etc. The power of writing is beautifully described in the saying, 'the pen is mightier than the sword.' Jules Reynard opined that "writing is the best way of talking without being interrupted."

Well-structured written communication frames the message skillfully to the readers' receptiveness accomplishing the transfer of knowledge. Writing skills and word power of communicator comes into play energetically in making written communication forceful and purposeful. Scholarly writings and innovative experiences of knowledgeable persons' wisdom has institutionalized in the form of documentation as a record for the future society. In business world, Memorandum of Association (MoA), Articles of Association (AoA), Prospectus, Action Proposals, Arbitrations, Manuals, Appointments, Policy Statements, Reports, Memos, Notices, Minutes, etc., are examples of written communication. Each has a well accepted format and layout in disciplined communication by custom or convention.

Written message is said to have quality of readability for comprehending easily and quickly. Every written communication is to understand the level of the reader, ability, educational background, experience, etc. Readable quality of the subject matter is important in written communication for clarity and understanding of the subject matter.

3.2.2 Features of Written Communication

The features of written communication are as follows:

- Message presented in written structure
- Reaches people with no geographical barriers
- Forceful and purposeful thought is exhibited
- Wisdom record in documentation

Merits

Written communication has several merits such as:

- Aids in understanding clearly the given message
- Retains the message in document form for further references

- Helps in permanent record with permanent value
- Helps the concerned with many details in depth
- Ensures accuracy, consistency and quickness
- Avoids alternation
- Reaches large number of persons at a time
- Amenable to planning at a higher level
- Depends less on memory since facts are mobilized beforehand
- More reliable
- Most suitable for long distance communication
- Provides no scope for rumours and inaccurate and partial information
- Maintains secrecy and confidentiality of matter as much as possible
- Saves time and money
- Possible to make clarification and correction of errors if any

Demerits

The demerits of written communication are that it:

- Is impossible to have immediate participation and there is no scope for personal interaction
- Does not provide scope for immediate persuasion as well as motivation
- Varies through interpretations depending upon the audiences' interests and behaviour
- Has no immediate evaluation of audience reaction
- Lacks closeness and warmth
- Maintains no secrecy
- Cannot be withdrawn easily once the message is transmitted
- Costs more and consumes more time in preparation of draft
- Prepares messages through bureaucratic way and does things officially and strictly as per the letter than spirit.

3.2.3 Essentials of Written Communication

The management of business has to choose one or two suitable for the purpose among the media of letter, memo, circular, bulletin, house journal, report, minutes, notices, handbook, brochures, booklets, manual, magazines, newspapers, posters, etc. Care should be taken to ensure selection of an appropriate medium under the circumstance so that it acts as facilitator but not as a hindrance. Written communication helps in solving many management problems in business and industry, it proves to be indispensable at times in certain conditions and situation as well. The written communication has popularly been used as media to get information and other things in achieving the goal of an organization. A communication is said to be effective and good, if it has certain essential requisites.

Effective written communication calls for the attention of specific requisite skills, command over language, applying word power and spelling, following correct grammar, right phrases and quotations, right channels – courier, telex, fax, e-mail, etc., Focused attention on handwriting, printing and photocopying is to be considered to transmit a clear message. The effects of these essential requisites of written communication are presented in Table 3.1.

Table 3.1 Essential Requisites of Written Communication

Essential Requisite	Result
Clarity of Thought	Message must be effective and clear with logical and straightforward thought
Concrete Facts	Message must involve concrete facts but not abstract or generalized information
Command of Knowledge	Message with confidence, knowledge command and full information on the thought
Correctness	Message without flaws and exaggeration
Short sentences	Message in simple and short sentences
Pre-test	Avoid ambiguity, misunderstanding and misinterpretation of message by pre-testing
Coherence	State facts and figures plainly and intelligently
Completeness	Transmit comprehensive coverage of ideas
Accuracy	Communicate message correctly and accurately
Sequence	Arrangement of messages in sequence aids the reader to pick main facts easily and quickly

3.2.4 Types of Written Communication

A brief account of important types of written communication is presented below.

1. **Letter:** A letter contains one's own ideas about an issue in black and white, and is sent by post. A popularly used form of communication for different situations with perfection and quality is letter writing. The essence of good letter writing is to present ideas in a clear manner and convey the message in such a way as understandable by the recipient. The scope of letter is broadly divided into: introductory letter, business letter, application letter, letter of marriage, thanking and congratulating letter, condolence and obituary letter, advice and recommendation letter.
2. **Memo:** Memorandum, abbreviated as 'memo' is widely used in communicating a brief written note about a particular issue to all the concerned people in the business organization. Memo is one-way communication and also a good communication tool so far concerning internal communication in all forms of

business organizations particularly from top to bottom irrespective of whether it is small or big, private or public. Its basic advantage is a record of evidence and proof for future reference. Oxford English Dictionary defines memo as: "An informal epistolary communication without signature on address or subscription, usually written on paper with a printed heading, bearing the word 'Memorandum' and the name and address of the sender."

Form of memo may have the organization's name printed on the top; spaces provided for date, sender's name and department, and the receiver's name and department. Top executives of a business organization may have personal memo pads with their name printed on the top, for use within the department. A memo may or may not be signed.

3. **Circular:** A document with detailed information (instructions or orders) on a specific matter is called **circular.** It is meant for the purpose of informing the employees about the changes brought out in the organization. It has a number and a date for purpose of reference, and is signed by the authorized signatory of the issuing office. The institutions like government departments, universities, councils, corporations, firms, etc., may issue circulars. The occasions for issue of circular are:

   - Change in policy matters
   - Sale of goods and services
   - Dissolution or discontinuance of business
   - Change in the constitution of business
   - Granting or withdrawal of 'per pro' (proxy) authority

   The manager of business, for example, announces the starting of a new business which means carrying out the opening function; with which he contacts prospective customers who are already in the market elsewhere. His persuasive and straight-forward letter with an offer for an attractive trial order followed by a satisfactory result naturally entices customers and veers them away from other shops. Another example is that the management announces opening of a new branch or moving to a more spacious and grand building in a posh locality in order to expand its business and inform all its customers as well as clients. The circular will play a greater role and acts not only as an advertisement but withholding the existing customers and clients also. In a way, a circular speaks appreciably about the abilities and qualities of a business organization.

4. **Bulletin:** A bulletin is an official report and published news of topical interest. A well brought out and carefully edited bulletin provides an excellent means of communication with the employees of an organization. Trading establishments, industrial houses, public, private and government agencies, educational and social institutions often publish bulletins. Bulletin is a newspaper in every sense; and can be published probably weekly or fortnightly or monthly. The issue of bulletin aims to keeps focus, informing the employees on:

- Policies, practices, procedures, regulations, management objectives, plans, problems, success and failures
- Understanding of work and the product to be made
- Concerning themselves with news and their activities to feel homely in an organization
- Achieving the job objectives of an organization

5. **House Journal:** Often communicating about the firm's image as message among its own employees or members is referred to as **House Journal**. The youth news of Young Men Christian Association (YMCA) is an example. The communication in all directions through informal media provides an opportunity to employees to express themselves by contributing articles, notes and other writings. Further, it contains news, personal and social items, matters relating to promotion, retirement, honours, awards, etc. The operation of journal is carried out by some large sized business organization and distributed cost-free to all the staff in organization.

   To produce a really good house journal with quality, it should be manned by a person of high caliber who enjoys full confidence of the management. An advisory body with rank-and-file employees as members is always desirable to improve the contents of journal and its effective circulation. Clarity, brevity and honesty in presentation of information in a circular are the watch words. The house journal aims to:

   - Serve as an effective medium of communication. The top management advantageously makes use while writing information in the journal in an informal manner addressing to the staff of organization. This would mould the opinion and attitude of staff.
   - Foster and develop cooperativeness, team spirit and create a mutual relationship, confidence and trust in employees.
   - Act as a wonderful medium to disseminate information as quickly as possible amongst the employees.
   - Instill enthusiasm in employees so as to contribute their best by way of efficient performance say, quality control, cutting down scrap and waste, good house-keeping, safety and alike.
   - Act as a feedback channel to the queries and opinions of employees.
   - Act as an information media for messages of public relations say, informing local community, families, school, local press, civic authorities including welfare schemes which aims at their benefit in the organization.

6. **Contents of House Journal:** As rule of an organization, the contents of house journal are connected with the management and employees by way of business and social association. Commonly found messages in a house journal are listed below.

   - Visits and programmes of top management
   - Activities of different offices and branches
   - Personnel news such as promotion, transfer, retirement, etc.

- ➢ Information about commissions and committees and their deliberations
- ➢ Appointments of new officers
- ➢ News of VIPs visits and their messages
- ➢ Research and development results
- ➢ Articles of general nature, technical and social interest
- ➢ Training programmes to the employees and others
- ➢ Achievements of organization or individual employees
- ➢ Photos on jobs executed, products manufactured, etc.
- ➢ News of social activities like Union Club, Rotary Club, Youth Club, etc.
- ➢ Humour and jokes
- ➢ Information on festivals and participation in them

7. **Report:** A document prepared by an individual or a committee on the entrusted task of a given problem/situation of business for taking decision rectifying the situation is termed **report**. It requires collection or compilation of pertinent data to the issue on which investigation is to be undertaken, presentation of data for discussion, and drawing logical conclusions and offering suggestions. Report is of varying length from two pages to a book; the latter is divided into chapters/ units. Detailed discussion is made in chapter on "Business Report Writing."
8. **Minutes:** A written record of decisions taken at the meeting of a business organization is called **minutes**. Business organizations have their own conventions to record the meeting discussions and resolving resolutions. Minutes may be written by hand or typed and pasted in a minute book, or typed and filed in a minute file. Minutes are a legal document. Details on conduct of minutes and record of proceedings are discussed in the later part of this chapter under "notice to meeting."
9. **Notice Board:** The most commonly used method of communication in working organizations, among visual media of communication inboard is called **notice board,** also known as bulletin board. A decision pertaining to an issue is made on notice board. A simple, clear message that is brief and easily understood help the recipients to make meaning out of it.

   Notice board is a visual medium of communication used as the most economical carrier of one-way communication flow. For carrying facts-oriented information, even today, it is widely accepted as a visual medium of communication of considerable value and importance in an organization. Medium of notice board is so conducive in discounting rumours. Many business organizations adopt the notice board medium in sending messages to its employees and others within the business premise. A good design – bold type and standard pattern of notice board should be located at all strategic points or areas throughout the plant and business premises, and positioned in such a manner that is readily accessible to all the concerned employees. The task of displaying and keeping notices up-to-date is done by the Personnel Department in the business organization. Only visual notices as well as notices seeking prior approval and sanction for display by the management are put up on the notice boards.

10. **Content and Coverage of Notice:** Classification of notices and display of them on the notice boards is on the matters of urgent, official, statutory, trade union, safety practices, plant news and photographs, canteen, sports, personnel notices and recreation. The contents of notices displayed on the notice board include the following:

    - The statutory provision extracts from Indian Factories Act and Rules, Payment of Wages Act and Rules, Minimum Wage Act, Maternity Benefits Act, Electricity Rules, Working Condition Rules, etc., both in English and in vernacular versions.
    - Circulars and notices issued by the management for administrative purposes.
    - Range of materials say, safety posters, special meetings, 'for sale' or 'wanted' or 'lost' notices, selected clippings of cartoons, information service institutions like clubs, athletic and sports clubs, cooperative societies, cafeteria, children schools, etc.
    - Other relevant information from outside the organization with specific permission of the management.

11. **Purpose of Notice Board:** Intelligently, carefully and efficiently maintained notice board with notices serve many useful purposes. These are:

    - Stop rumours and their circulation. It means they can aid in removing any suspicion or misconception or misunderstanding. Otherwise, this misinformation or wrong information may affect the operational activities of the plant.
    - Minimize complaints and grievances due to its effective presence. Even getting the slightest information about displeasure amongst the employees getting ready to raise their heads, the management can take immediate action clarifying the position and posting the right and correct information on the notice board to the employees.
    - Boost up production by means of displays implies reduction in production costs and wastage.
    - Work as informative, educative and persuasive media.
    - Act as morale building of workers inculcating feelings of pride in their jobs.
    - Convey timely notices to employees' activities – recreation, athletic contests, etc.
    - Act as good media for employees' personal services, for example, lost and found, etc.
    - Serve as useful media for certain posting as per statutory provisions.

12. **Tips for Effective Notice Board:** To render notices as an effective medium of communication, the following tips must be followed. They are:

    - Notice boards be properly designed, well positioned, prominently displayed and notices properly displayed on them

- For special notices of the plant, specific space must be set aside on the boards
- Statutory notices, be kept separate from communication notices
- Employees benefits notices be displayed on a separate board
- Use different colour or type of designs for knowing differences between different kinds of announcements say employment, personnel, etc.
- Dates of posting and removal be exhibited on each notice; take care of posting and removing notices
- Employees' interests must be specially displayed on the notice board
- Displayed material should be brief and readable and sorted out intelligently

13. **Handbook:** Handbook is a usual form of written communication media and provides important information pertaining to policies, rules, procedures, working practices, etc., of business. The companies or business organizations are using handbooks to promote their image and impression in accordance with provisions of the board.
14. **Pamphlet:** Pamphlet has a fewer pages of sheet and serves as a very useful mode of written medium of communication. It covers a wide variety of issues like interior decoration, embroidery, cooking, sports, health, personal and family topics, etc. A person who writes pamphlets is called pamphleteer.
15. **Booklet:** Booklet is a small thin book containing the profile of concern or product, and provides an overall picture of the visitors, prospective customers, investors, executives, trainees, newly-recruited employees and other audiences to the organization. Its main motto is to tell the interested persons about the concern's evolution and background information effectively. It also covers messages of national security, educational benefits, awards, rewards, success, and expansion and development of business.
16. **Manual:** A document or small book containing all the information pertaining to the organization structure and responsibilities of each position, job, description, salaries, prevailing relationships among the members including organization procedures and methods is called **manual.** Through the manual, one can have knowledge about the particulars of organization or information easily.

    Manual is handy for use, kept as reference, a concise treatise and an abridgement containing practices, conventions, instructions and policies of business organization. It is an authoritative guide to the office of organization issued showing its performance. It contains history of organization, growth and development, objectives, positions, employees' functions, duties and responsibilities, accounting and auditing, welfare and working facilities.
17. **Magazine:** Magazine also called periodical is regular, say weekly, fortnightly, monthly, quarterly, half-yearly and yearly publication containing information on opinions, findings of studies, articles, etc. It is the most important medium of internal communication; the most important communicating tool and a vast scope for product advertisement medium too. One magazine with all languages is not suitable in a country like India where there are several languages.

Hence, we have both regional and national magazines. Examples include farm magazines are meant for rural people, consumer magazines are most useful for advertising product information and business magazines contain information on new products, their features, quality, durability, price, etc. Why magazines are so popular is explained by the Magazine Publishers Association of Marketing Division, America: "Magazine is a visual spectrum, believable, covers wide range of comparable values, selective reaching in, with most receptive ideas, flexible in covering the full range of prospects besides being authoritative."

18. **Newspaper:** A paper containing daily news and opinion of current events in the society is called newspaper. The word, news stands for North, East, West and South sides. It is an effective external mass communication medium. Some publications are on the basis of business; such as Financial Express, Economics Times, etc. A special feature of newspaper is attachment of a special section as a part of the main edition. Sunday special covering classifieds has, Monday Times Education, Tuesday Young World and Wednesday Opportunities with The Hindu are some examples of special section edition.
19. **Leaflet:** A leaflet is a small printed document meant for external communication to inform people outside the company about the product or service, its uses, features and durability. It is one-way communication. "A small sized leaf of paper or a sheet folded into two or more leaves, but not stitched and containing printed matter, chiefly for gratuitous distribution." (Oxford English Dictionary)
20. **Complaints and Suggestions:** Complaints and suggestions are one of the written communication instruments containing complaints and suggestions of employees in writing. A complaint and suggestions box is installed at a prominent place within the organization for employees to put in their written complaints on the working condition, facilities and general matters too with suggestions. In practice, the complaint and suggestion method is not effective. See Exhibit 3.2.

Exhibit 3.2 **Be Cool**

Emotions can and do play with words. A wrong word uttered or a letter drafted and dispatched in a fit of rage can cause unavoidable and unintended damage. Let the anger subside. Remember the Chinese proverb. "Never answer a letter when you are angry."

21. **Trademark:** Adoption of identifiable mark, say a word, name, symbol, number or device or any combination thereof, by a manufacturer as identification of his goods or services in the market and distinguishes them from those manufactured by the competitors is called **Trade Mark**. It identifies the origin of product or service, showing who is manufacturing or supplying it or who is selling it. Trademark gives legal protection under the Law as it is being governed by the Trademark Act in marketing of goods or services. Consumers can identify the product or service with the help of trademark of goods or services on their purchase. If the business organization applies trademark for its entire business instead of any individual product, it is called Trade Name.

22. **Sign and Signal:** A sign is visual fixed mark used to mean something. Servicing to warn, direct, or command as per agreement is known as signal. The traffic signs and signals must instantly convey information to the drivers about what lies ahead on the road. Show of a green light or waving a green flag is a signal to go ahead. Sound signals such as (a) siren used to warn about enemy in air-raids and in factories to warn of fire or accident, (b) whistles used by police and army to call members to assemble and convey instructions, (c) bells and buzzers used to indicate the starting and ending of work periods, and also used by special vehicles like the fire engine to warn the road users to give way and (d) bell associated with pleasant sound in worship areas indicating faith in prayer. Look at some examples of sign language given below.

    - A teacher put her/his finger on her/his lips in a nursery class (sign to keep silent)
    - A player raises two of his fingers in a V sign after the game (sign of victory)
    - Elders and priests convey blessings by placing their hands on the head of persons bowing before them (sign of blessing)
    - Youngsters and disciples touch the feet of elders and teachers (sign of reverence)
    - A hearing impaired person uses hand movements (sign language)

Further, a general sign in the case of road and traffic (red colour) or subject specific signs in the case of profession (in Mathematics, signs specific to arithmetic, algebra and geometry as also in Science, Engineering and Medicine) are in practice in the modern society. Awareness and understanding of signs and signals makes communication more meaningful as they may be overt or covert, explicit or in a code of language. Some examples of sign communication are presented in Exhibit 3.3.

Exhibit 3.3 Examples of Signs

20 mph	→	Speed limit of 20 kilometers per hour
][	→	Narrow bridge
+	→	Addition
/ or ÷	→	Division
Σ	→	Summation
=	→	Equal to
∞	→	Infinite
>	→	Less than
<	→	More than

3.2.5 Writing Skills

Today's business world demands professionalism in writing skills. Research suggests a vast number of employees are sabotaging their career by ignoring their writing skills. An employee regularly comes across at the workplace via written reports, presentations, proposals, executive summaries, memos, e-mails, instant messaging and all other forms of written communication. Here, it is appropriate to remember that education is an asset; skills are profit, and indifference and laziness a loss. It takes just a quick glance, may be three seconds, for someone to evaluate you, when you send out a written communication. In this short time, the other person forms an opinion about you based upon your writing skills.

In the rapid pace of technology innovation, writing skills are the life-blood of business in the corporate sector. Every employee is under the pressure of increasing to deliver better working results in terms of economic gains faster than the competition. A professional written communication gives a meaningful message and establishes a connection leaving a powerful impression in the receivers' mind. It is the appearance of the words with simple and correct wording of sentences. Content is well-organized and neatly formatted to assure the readers that the author presents quality message with professionalism. Sloppy thinking is entwined with sloppy writing. The key is to write concisely and clearly with clarity of thoughts. Here are some tips to be followed for all forms of written communication in business organization. These are as follows:

- State the objective in the title, subtitle or first sentence and allow the reader to quickly decide if he wants to go ahead with reading the document or not. For longer or more complex documents, consider stating the objective in the first paragraph.
- Knowing audience is important. Ask yourself – who will read this? What do they need to know and expect from you? Do some research on audience and pitch the points and suit the language.
- Stay on topic. Do not allow unrelated research to throw reader off-track. Focus on the subject.
- Start with the most important information first. Remember, the reader does not have ample time to go through pages of information to find what is relevant to him.
- Insert illustrations and graphics to keep the reader on track. It helps to reinforce the discipline of using modular structure; and leads to clear and simplified writing.
- Use formatting approach to organize the documents. It will allow the reader to find the information that he needs quickly and easily; and skip what he does not need.
- Emphasize major points. A word of caution, overuse of emphasis may result on the impact getting diminished and the text looking chaotic.
- Use simple sentences to communicate key points.
- Focus on spell-check and attention to details. An error-free report or proposal speaks volumes. It reflects author's professional attitude.
- E-mail etiquette. Be conscious about responding to the emails within 24 hours. People expect a response just like a phone call. Use email as a formal communication tool.
- Draft a good email. Summarize the messages but be concise. Avoid using adjectives, articles and adverbs.

3.3 ORAL COMMUNICATION

Oral communication (in meeting or conference or counseling or negotiation) goes on with one person speaking/talking and the other(s) listening and responding. Noteworthy skills to be followed pertaining to oral communication is as follows:

- Understand and use an appropriate language
- Speak clearly and pleasantly
- Organize and sequence thoughts effectively
- Use better vocabulary and word power
- Command over illustrations and phrases
- Use proper accent and pronunciation
- Reach voice modulation
- Follow listening skills
- Adhere to time specification
- Enforce effective telephone talk
- Self-control and self-confidence

Oral communication, also called verbal communication, has had a long journey that started with the early man. It occurs between individuals and organizations with the help of words and sounds. Further, it takes place in many ways – casual and serious, formal and informal, structured and unstructured. Oral communication encompasses conversation, monologue, dialogue, talk, speech and chat between persons. Some of these are pre-mediated and some are not. Formal speeches are pre-planned and well-structured while informal are unstructured and often loosely worded. Oral communication has developed across different regions, cultures, countries and continents with so many languages in the world. The specific feature of oral communication is used when sending the message is urgent.

Every individual and organization is empowered to express feelings or desires and makes copious use of oral communication in transactions and interactions. Talking and speaking is the commonly used approach of communication within the family and social groups. Oral communication has been used extensively and gainfully in the business activities of organizations internally as well as externally. In it, instant questioning and answering is possible between the parties or groups, i.e., the sender and the receiver till they get the best possible understanding, in which tone of voice, facial expression and mannerism weigh much. It is a successful tool for efficient and smooth communication with an immediate feedback.

Features

The essential features of oral communication are:

- Spoken words
- Structured and unstructured form
- Two-way process with speed

Merits

The form and structure of oral communication has certain merits. Oral communication:

- provides a quick and better understanding,
- is an effective media for exchange of information,
- works effectively among various hierarchical levels of management,
- expresses message more easily and completely,
- provides immediate feedback,
- saves time and cost,
- is free to change comments, and
- works very well in small groups.

Demerits

Oral communication is not free from limitations. The demerits of oral communication are as follows:

- It is liable to misunderstanding
- It causes distortion of messages due to distance factor
- It is not suitable where permanent and uniformity of communication is needed
- It cannot be easily transmitted if the message is lengthy
- It may create problems if the receiver acts as per his willingness in implementation
- It is a difficult media when the message is required to be transmitted a large number
- It is often dependent on memory
- It is, normally, not recorded or documented
- It is not effective when the target group is spread out geographically.

3.3.1 Principles of Oral Communication

An important skill in oral communication is the capacity to communicate; for which the speaker must make the message clear and easily understandable. Management of any business organization is not possible to get through without communication. Communication, therefore, in modern days of busy world is a 'valuable asset' particularly for teachers, lawyers, auditors, politicians, administrators, consultants, business executives, parents and children. Speech is for others to understand. Ineffective, faulty and vague speech leads a conversation to a state of confusion and misunderstanding. In making oral communication effective, no standard rules prevail but it calls for certain principles to be followed. Irrespective of circumstances, there are certain essential ingredients of good oral communication which are described below.

1. **Brevity:** Text of message to be delivered is as brief as possible resorting to being neither too short nor too long. It is because of time which is not only from the point of speaker but also from the audience point of view. Lengthy messages confuse and may lead to misunderstanding. Conversation in short sentences gives the

listener time and opportunity to follow what the speaker endeavours to put across. Therefore, use precise, simple and familiar words for effective communication.

2. **Clarity:** Besides brevity, clarity of message in simple words, short sentences and common words with a matter of style wherein man speaks is the foremost among the principles of oral communication.
3. **Precise Words:** Speaking exactly using the right words at the right place. The precise words are often called concrete words to convey real and correct meaning. Avoid use of vague words. No two words give exactly the same meaning. Hence, it is difficult to replace one word with another. Full knowledge of synonyms and antonyms is necessary to ensure precision of the message.
4. **Cliché:** Often the use of word with no meaning is known as **cliché**. An effective communication avoids clichés as they are stale in oral communication. The speaker may often use phrases that irritate the listeners, spoiling serious mood of conversation. Examples are 'yes', 'quite fine', 'I mean', 'ok', etc.
5. **Sequence:** Logic supplements precision of the matter to be used in oral presentation. Consistency, continuity and logic of the subject matter are of concern.
6. **Avoid jargon:** It is a language or terminology relating to Business, Commerce, Law, Defense, Sports, Military, etc. Use such words with which people are well-versed in the subject and can understand properly. Avoid the words of jargon which cause confusion in the minds of listeners.

3.3.2 Forms of Oral Communication

Today various organizations such as business, management, governance of country, judiciary, national and international institutes, etc., are achieving their goals for which they came into operation. In doing so, face-to-face conversation has become handy and efficient practice in a two-way communication process system. Face-to-face conversation, telephone, tele-conference, e-mail, speech, public speaking, lectures, broadcasting, participation, interviews, meeting, etc., are different forms of oral communication. These are explained below.

1. **Face-to-Face Conversation:** Conversation between two persons is known as **face-to-face** conversation or tete-a-tete, also called **dialogue**. It means an exchange of ideas and opinions between two persons or groups or countries on a particular issue, reaching a friendly and amicable agreement or settlement or solution. It is also a means between characters in a novel or play or film. Dialogue is a 'win-lose' spirit. A friendly, empathic and inclusive environment can set stage for a fair consideration to gain something from conversation.

   (i) **Skills needed:** Dialogue as business communication skill needs interpersonal skills tuning to build rapport and finally reach a closure with satisfaction. Persons who are good at dialogue can create an atmosphere of friendliness by being inclusive and having empathy. Empathy is a sense of understanding of how the person feels by showing respect to each other's point of view. If a 'win win' atmosphere is created, the conversation becomes more fruitful and leads to a comfortable closure.

Skills development is required for controlling and carrying out successful dialogue. A conversation with skills is an art of dialogue contributing to clear and pleasant talks. It makes other(s) listen patiently through eye contact, vary the voice to avoid a monotone, be brief and to the point.

(ii) Self-control: Developing self-control takes time and patience. In business dialogue condition, control of one's desire to talk particularly in controlling the impulse to interrupt another person whose statement he does not agree with. Hence, a great deal of self-control is needed to remain cool and composed in case of one's views. Holding one's tongue is difficult, but if you have the ability to maintain peace and keep silent you reach the right moment to speak.

(iii) Listening: Broad mind of tolerance of speaking styles, thorough knowledge of topic in conversation and genuine desire to reach a satisfactory conclusion will assist in exercising listening skills. Imposing one's own frame of reference on everything is nothing but frustrating the other person, and leaves the other person's purpose worthless. Finally, it does not lead to conversation through good dialogue. A good listener focuses on the speaker's line of interest and tries to understand the intention of his framework. It wins goodwill of the other party.

(iv) Understanding Non-verbal Behaviour: Ability of sensing the feelings behind the words with aid of body language comes with practice. Use both eyes and ears in seeing as well as listening respectively. Please put cautious attention as others watch your body language. If both the parties clarify their points of view, certainly a dialogue can go on peacefully and usefully with an intended goal.

Questioning is powerful tool in dialogue. So, cultivate carefully the way and style of asking questions with clarity to make people comfortable. Assertiveness without aggression achieves win-win results in most business situations. Stating wishes directly and honestly considering others' needs into account is assertive while talking all the time and hurting others is aggressive. It involves careful and attentive listening. If there is any unsettled issue, it may be scheduled for another dialogue. By summarization of conclusions, dialogue comes to an end on a pleasant note benefitting the relationships.

(v) Dialogue on Telephone: Telephone conversation is lively and effective. How much message is conveyed in face-to-face conversation? Only 7 per cent, 38 per cent and 55 per cent is conveyed by the words, tone of voice and body language respectively.

Clear articulation and correct pronunciation are more essential in dialogue conversation. English is spoken all over the world and in varying accents; hence pronounce correctly with accuracy, clarity and obviousness. Speed of speaking can affect clarity in dialogue conversation to some extent. Talking very fast, say more than 150 words per minute affect clarity and also gives impression of speaker being in a hurry. Similarly, high pitched voices are unpleasant and appear uncultured while the extremely low pitch seems to be sound in a mechanical way. In view of this, find the dialogue speech, right speed, pitch and volume making it simple, clear and easy to follow.

Tone is expressiveness of voice and carries 38 per cent of conveying the message through communication. Words are used to describe tone of voice such as cheerful/sad, respectful/impertinent, interest/bored, energetic/tired and sincere/false; the person who hears the tone voice is affected. Therefore, learn how to use the voice effectively.

(iv) Telephone Etiquette: Initial contact with some people is through telephone is etiquette. The way the telephone is answered makes first impression about the person and the company. So, telephone etiquette is essential for everyone to send messages. The guidelines for making a positive impact by telephone etiquette are given below.

(vii) Make Call: Prepare all questions to be asked and comments to be made on the basis of information before making a call. Greet as soon as the call is answered and introduce yourself and ask for the person to whom you want to speak. Concentrate and pay attention only to the person you have called. Avoid unfamiliar words and long sentences but use simple language. Ask questions for clarification if conversation or used words is not clear or not heard attentively. The main points should be repeated at the end to check the understanding of conversation of both parties. At the end, politely thank the person for giving his time.

(viii) Take Call: On the first or second ring, answer the call promptly and identify yourself by a phrase like 'Nirvi here' or 'Nirvi speaking'. When the caller is not identified, ask 'May I know who's calling or who is speaking?'. Make positive welcoming impression with the tone of your voice when you speak. Keep cool and be patient with a difficult caller.

Owing to the presence of voice, tone, expression and movements of body being attached to the words, face-to-face conversation offers better communication.

2. **Telephone:** Voice is the only prerequisite for telephone talk without physical presence of the speaker or listener. Clarity of speech and skilful use of voice is the most essential. Confusion may prevail while using similar sounding words such as pale and bale or no and know, etc.

3. **Presentation:** Face-to-face communication is more likely to synchronize with each other and uncovers access between the speaker and the listener; facilitates cooperation and deals in expansion. Touch of humour enriches the presentation; but the tone of it is business like as the purpose of presentation is to provide information. To enhance the quality of presentation, use visual aids if required. The presenter is expected to answer questions at the end and has responsibility to ensure a clear understanding on all aspects of the topic among the audience.

Thus, face-to-face presentation and body language – nodding, smiling, making gestures, eye contact and verbalizations affirm the other person with a message, for what it stands as 'politeness ritual.'

4. **Public Speech:** Public speech is a face-to-face setting with the distance between the speaker and the audience gathering. Ensuring the purpose of public speech depends on the speaker's skill in using gestures and microphone. Applause rather than questions from the audience is followed in public speech and feedback is very little as the speaker can hardly see facial expressions.
5. **Meeting:** In a democratic setup, meeting is a common method which is used as medium of communication. Meeting is carried in family, democratic institutions and corporate management (in statutory, annual general body, extraordinary general, board of directors, shareholders, debenture holders, creditors, etc.) facilitating transaction of business in an orderly, deliberate, planned and democratic manner for the purpose. A meeting may be a public meeting or a private meeting.

   Organized assembly of a group of people's communication with togetherness for deliberating on the topics and issues pertaining to the business interests is called **meeting**. The word, meeting denotes an arrangement to come face-to-face with advance plan for a purpose. It is a gathering, assembling or coming together of two or more persons for the purpose of transacting some objective of business. "Meeting is an assembly of number of people for entertainment, discussion or the like" (Oxford Dictionary). A meeting is, thus, referred to as involvement of all the concerned persons on fixed agenda with a person (usually leader) in the chair to guide the communication and maintain proper order for arriving at a consensus. The size of meeting depends upon the nature and kind of meeting. Oral communication is backed up by note-taking and writing the minutes.
6. **Interview:** Interview is a meeting at which one person or an expert of the committee called **interviewer** asks questions on the subject matter with another person or applicant called **interviewee**. Assessing of the latter's performance is the main purpose of interview. The features of interview are structured and question and answer type of communication.

   In oral communication, the guiding principle is 'talk less, say more'. 'Speaking is like sowing seed and listening is like reaping fruit.'

The word-of-mouth works better in communicating the intended message to the concerned people in the society as they feel friendly because (a) it is highly credible which impress the receiver the feel friendly and (b) it is certainly economical and has a multiple effect which favour the sender. Similar approaches have been used even by the big organizations like Air India, Readers Digest, Taj Hotels. Examples illustrating the power of word-of-mouth are presented in Table 3.2.

Table 3.2 Power of Word-of-Mouth

Message	Concerned
'Do tell us if you are not satisfied and do tell others if you are satisfied.'	Notice in the restaurant
'All returns within a week are replaced without questions.'	Notice in supermarket
'We welcome you. Please let us know who recommended us to you. We would like to mail a gift.'	Walk-in customer
'Please record names and address of your friends who may like to use our services. You will be doing a good turn by recommending our good services and we will express our gratitude by sending a gift to you.'	Customer feedback
'Please fill in these pictures on post-cards with the addresses of your relatives and friends. We will mail it to them at our cost.'	Airlines and hotels

The terms meeting, conference and committee are almost synonymous which means coming together of a group of persons for the purpose of discussion to arrive at a common decision. Meeting and conferences are an integral part of modern day business life. Sound business management needs an exchange of views which is being facilitated by the conduct of meetings and conferences. Thus, interactive communication, i.e., face-to-face contact is the lubricant of the business engine helping the messages to reach out to the target audience effectively.

3.3.3 Learning to Speak

A speech is given on the occasions of anniversary or an inauguration with a purpose usually to encourage, appreciate, congratulate or entertain followed by applause from the audience. Its content is light. On other hand, presentation is heavy and delivered to a small, knowledgeable audience at a seminar, conference, or a business meeting with purpose to inform, explain, persuade or present a point of view. It is followed by questions from the audience. In any profession, being able to speak well is an asset. Cultivate and develop speaking skills with some knowledge of formal aspects of public speaking with practice. This needs preparation at four junctures:

- Environment for talk to be delivered
- Text of presentation
- Care of physical appearance and body language
- Visual aids

1. **Environment:** Environment forms the venue wherein the speakers present their messages to the audience. The speaker is familiar with physical environment. If it is on home ground, check the room a few minutes before the talk begins. Get familiar with the room, arrangement say lighting, ventilation, visual aid equipment, etc., and speaker position say platform, mike, podium, etc. if the venue

is outside the room. For any speaker, the most important is the target audience which requires careful analysis of the message delivered in terms of form and style, occasion, content and tone of speech suiting the interests of audience with their economic and education status.

2. **Text:** Next most important thing in speech is preparing the text suiting the required message. Speech must be logical and have a smooth flow from one point to the next. Write down the whole speech including the address, opening sentences if the speaker is a beginner. Average speed is 150 words per minute, but varies according to the audience capacity to understand and familiarity of ideas presented. A 2-minute speech does require one page typed in one-and-half line spacing in 12-point font size. Formality in official speaking is distinguished from social or personal style of speaking. Avoid bad words and repetitive phrases such as you know, you see. An interesting element of speech is that it adds light, enjoyable and relevant humour to the topic in course of speech that makes the audience more attentive and prevents disrespecting any listener.
3. **Presentation:** Any presentation needs to follow the beginning, middle and end with introductory remarks, main speech and closing remarks respectively. The opening remarks fulfill the purpose of building rapport, focus attention and arouse interest of audience. Text presentation depends upon the occasion and objective of speech. For instance, the motto of a commemorative speech at an inauguration or annual function is to encourage and felicitate; then mention the highlights of achievements, elaborate the value of effort and express faith in the ability of participants to do even better. End-up speech with supportive encouragement and close with good conclusion expressing confidence in further achievement. It must not be abrupt but graceful and smooth highlighting the main issue in the minds of audience. See Exhibit 3.4 for learning to speak.

Exhibit 3.4 Learning to Speak

Speaking well is a fine art which can be cultivated. It needs conscious efforts on the part of the speaker. Nobody is a born speaker. Good speaking is not effortless, although it looks so. As one moves up from the classroom to the boardroom, the fine art of speaking well is mastered. To quote Emerson, "All the great speakers were bad speakers first."

4. Visual Aids: In communication, a stronger impact than spoken words is visual material as most persons retain much more of what they see than what they hear. Visuals can be added in three ways: (i) Flip charts which need a stand to arrange an overhead projector and a slide projector being portable. High visuals can be obtained for a reasonable price if the use of computer graphics is within the reach of people. (ii) Speech – visuals need to be prepared as an integral part of any conversation to enhance a point with illustration; a chart or graph being referred to as a person talks. (iii) Cram-visual should not be crammed. One (OVD) overhead projector transparency should have only one simple graph/chart or five to six short lines of text. Creating mental pictures in the minds of listeners with words, pictures and graphic description can certainly enliven a talk.

3.4 INTERACTIVE COMMUNICATION

Through meetings and conferences, any person associated with a business organization can arrive at a decision through his innovative thoughts and ideas.

3.4.1 Conference

A meeting of large group of persons (ranging 10 to 500 or more) assembled for the purpose of discussing a theme of common problem or issue is referred to as **conference**. It is divided into sub-themes with small groups for the purpose of discussion. The participants may be from different parts or places of the country or world.

Members participants pool together and share their knowledge and experience in the conference in a direct face-to-face interactive communication approach. Due to advent of technology, the teleconference and videoconference which came into being have facilitative interactive communication between the participants without necessitating physical presence of all the concerned at the venue. Conclusions arrived during the discussions in the conference are included in the report of conference and the conference report is given to the participants, concerned organizations and authorities. Though a conference does not have any authority but may make suggestions since the participants are persons of rich experience as well as expertise on the field theme. Thus, conference is an enriching intellectual exercise.

Conference is, normally, a meeting of longer duration and larger participation depending upon the subject. It may be Annual Conference, Bi-annual Conference, Zonal or Regional Conference of one day or two days and so on. Business organizations conduct regular conferences inviting experts on the issues of business relevance. The form of conference would depend on the objectives of it. The form of conference would depend on the objectives of it. For instance, the conference:

- reviews the operations; simply it covers presentation of reports and their evaluation
- reconciles clashing views and interests between management and workers; it focuses on 'free and open' interchange
- conducts departmental works; it thrusts on the need for discussion of departmental heads
- solves problems arising in a work area or passes on information or instructions; the reference is to collect facts to solve issues.

3.4.2 Appraisal of Conference

A conference is normally scheduled annually and bi-annually. Preparation and attention in conference is, by and large, the same to those of meeting. Sometimes, conference may have the features of a function and in such case, it will have a chief guest, introduction of the speaker or the dignitary, invocation, lighting of the lamp, keynote address, presentation of bouquets, distribution of brochures and other details. A good presentation at the conference includes the following measures. They are:

1. **Preparation of Text:** Preparation of text is an important aspect. Even a person who has natural skills in speaking needs preparation to deliver a good speech. See Exhibit 3.5 on how long it takes to prepare a speech.

Exhibit 3.5 **How long it takes to prepare a reply**

If I am to speak for ten minutes, I need a week for preparation; if fifteen minutes, three days; if half an hour, two days; and if an hour, I am ready now.
The message is clear. The shorter the presentation, longer is the time taken for organizing it. One should carefully decide what is to be included and what is to be left out. The speech should be carefully prepared keeping the essentials of the topic/issue and leaving out those which are not directly relevant to the message. On the other hand, when one is making a longer speech with more time at his or her disposal, preparation need not be that much elaborate. To be brief yet effective in accomplishing the focus of presentation calls for careful choice of words and ideas.

2. **Text Presentation:** Delivery of speech to knowledgeable audience at a conference, a seminar or a business meeting with purpose to inform, explain, persuade or present a view on a topic followed by questions from the audience is called presentation. Ability to speak well is an asset in any profession. The presentation involves oral communication with the support of audio-visual aids (if required) on the specific topic/issue or concept to the audience in a participative approach. It has been a popular means of communicating various business concepts and ideas, features of products and services, analytical studies, status reports and alike through demonstration being explained by means of visual aids. For instance:
   - In selecting the contender, a particular assignment is given to him for presentation; and the evaluation is made on the basis of contents and skills being presented. The presenter should be well versed and synchronize verbal delivery with the visual message suiting the target audience and complete within the time allotted. In other words, the person making presentation should encourage response from the audience and sustain it. A good presentation requires a careful cultivation of subject knowledge, confidence, communicative ability and interpretation of skills.
   - Audio-visual aids include slides or transparencies, handouts, screen projector, pointer, etc., that form part of presentation. The multimedia (a personal computer or a laptop) is the latest aid in making good presentation as it facilitates storage and retrieval of written text and very colourful appeal, clarity of pictures and charts, readability of words and figures. In view of its appeal, communication of messages through multimedia presentation has become popular in business and training. The communicator finds it easier to put across the message forcefully with purpose since the visual messages and the material prepared beforehand act as aide-memoir.

- Address the dignitaries and gathering suitably. Begin the presentation with introductory remarks and focus by highlighting the core aspects of the topic/ issue which are important to the audience, and close with a clear message. The closing of presentation should not be abrupt but graceful and smooth, touching the main issues. A quotation or a parable or question can mark the conclusion like this: 'We need competition in business, but cooperation on the road'. Finally, thank the organizers, and the audience for their attention.

3. **Appearance and Personality:** Physical appearance, presence and personality impact presentation. Even before beginning to speak, the audience notice body language. Body language includes personality (comfortable posture, good standing), lively rapport with the audience, facial expression and gesture, accompaniment of speech enhancing the meaning, making short pauses at suitable times for ensuring attention and hold the microphone six to nine inches away from the mouth to ensure speech volume.

   The following points summarize a good presentation at meetings and seminars. They are as follows:

   - Preparation for a presentation
   - Know your audience and tailor the contents of your presentation to suit them
   - Update the facts and figures
   - Practise till you get confident
   - Anticipate probable questions to be asked and be ready to respond
   - Make the presentation participative and involve the audience
   - Be at the venue in advance and familiarize yourself with the focus of programme
   - Sport a smile avoiding being grim
   - Conclude with a recap of all the main points

   Oral communication is the most common method of communication in use ever since man learnt the use of language. Spoken communication, telephone talks, interviews and discussions are all the forms of active and direct communication orally. Effective oral communication skills are imperative for becoming an effective speaker; good speaker more often than not, carries the day. The essentials of a good speaker are:

   - Right posture in a befitting manner
   - Speaking artistically
   - Preparing ideas and thoughts, and expressing logically
   - Knowing your audience
   - Pausing and punching the ideas for the listeners to understand
   - Structuring ideas and thoughts suiting time
   - Modulating voice, body language and quotes to reach out to the audience
   - Speaking without hurting
   - Speaking worth to the listeners' time and not speaking unnecessarily
   - Speaking responsibly with authority and respect

Properly conducted meetings are the most valuable means of communication in a business organization. They provide participation and give members a sense of belonging and importance. Therefore, meeting is a way of managerial life to an organization. A meeting is necessary to promote:

- Understanding and accepting an organization's policies as well as procedures
- Understanding employees' needs and desires
- Collecting and exchanging ideas and suggestions
- Intelligent cooperation and coordination
- Saving time and saving repetition as well as paper work
- Arriving at a consensus on issues
- Understanding and solving a problem/situation
- Informing and explaining issues pertaining to organization
- Getting feedback for decision-frame
- Learning and training to remain up-to-date

3.4.3 Meetings

Meetings are interactive forums in the corporate sector to facilitate face-to-face discussions at the level of (i) employer-employees meeting and conference, (ii) employee-employee meeting and conference and (iii) employee-customer meeting and conference. Meeting relates to fewer persons; even two persons, and takes place any number of times during a day, week, or month. Thus, gathering of meeting is very limited but held more often, pre-planned and impromptu whereas gathering of conference is large but held normally once in a year and structured in advance. A distinction between meeting and conference in the corporate sector, as commonly followed, in practice is that the former refers to an assembly of persons particularly for an activity and workshop; and the latter refers to a meeting of any organization, association, etc., for consultation, deliberation and alike on the specific issues.

Meetings and conferences are organized and conducted effectively in order to have an effective and significant role in business communication in terms of exchange of information, elaboration, clarification and articulation of concepts and ideas as innovative thoughts, deliberation on specific issues, removal of misconceptions, finalization of plans and strategies, review of performance, enlistment of support and a host of such other needs of communication. These aspects are dealt in depth at length and achieve much more than any written communication. Meeting and conferences are thus becoming an indispensable tool as a useful medium of interaction between the people of different business organizations.

3.4.4 Notice of Meeting

Notice of meeting typed or printed on the letterhead of an organization include (a) Name of the body/group to meet, (b) Day, date and time of the meeting, (c) Place of the meeting (with address and specific room/hall) and (d) Agenda of the meeting. For example:

Notice of Meeting

To

All Members

Notice is hereby given that the Annual General Meeting of Members of the Indian Managers Association will be held on July 18, 2017 at 4.00 p.m. at the Taj Mahal Hotel, Mumbai 400042 to transact the following business.

1. To receive and adopt the Income and Expenditure account, the Balance Sheet, the Report of the Auditors and the Report of the Committees for the year ending March 31, 2016.
2. To declare the results of the election of the President, Vice-President, Hon. Secretary, Hon. Treasurer and Four Ordinary Members of the Executive Committee for the years 2012-15 in accordance with Rule 35 (iii) of the Rules and Regulations of the Association.
3. To appoint Auditors for the year 2015-16 and fix their remuneration.
4. To consider any other matter that may be brought forward; for which a written notice of at least seven days has been given.

Mumbai — By Order of the Executive Committee

Date: May 16, 2017 — (C R Rao)

Hon' Secretary

Agenda: The list of items to be discussed at the meeting of an organization is called **agenda**. It is determined on the type of meeting and is sent along with the notice of the meeting. It may be sent later if it takes time to be prepared. The items of agenda are: (a) the agenda begins with the item "minutes" also called (in detail) as "approval of minutes of previous meeting", (b) after this, the business items are set out, (c) any other business (if not mentioned in the agenda, then the Chairman himself raises a matter which is not included in the agenda) and (d) next meeting (usual practice to fix the date of next meeting before the close of the current meeting).

The Chairman has to take great care in putting order of items in the agenda as some item/items are likely to be controversies over any of the item(s). Usually, the urgent and non-controversial items are put first. Order of agenda items cannot be changed during the course of meeting except by the consent of members. See Exhibit 3.6 for specimen agenda.

Exhibit 3.6 Specimen Agenda

1. To confirm the minutes of the last meeting held on March 15, 2016 (enclosed)
2. To approve the revised budget for the year 2012-13 and budget estimates for the year 2014-15
3. To consider and approve the recruitment done by the Selection Committee
4. To review the working results of the concern
5. Any other matter permitted by the Chair
6. Next meeting

3.4.5 Conduct of Meeting

A meeting of any kind is conducted by the convener. A convener is one, who calls and arranges for the meeting. The chairperson usually follows the rules and regulations say, 'Rule Book' for conduct of the meeting and maintain the correct procedure. In case of voting and ties, controversies and wrangles, the chairperson gives a ruling and casts his voting.

Meetings may be highly formal or very informal. The formal meeting follows the procedures or rules laid down in the Memorandum of Association and Articles of Association, and are convened by the Chairman and the Secretary. The Chairman leads and guides the discussion and the Secretary notes down the minutes of discussions. Examples of such meetings are Annual General Meeting, Board Meeting, Executive Committee Meeting and alike. The informal meetings do not follow such strict rules or procedures; and may be held without the Chairman or Secretary in the Chair. No record is to be maintained concerning the proceedings of the meeting. Examples of such meetings are Group Discussion, Advisory Committee Meeting, Consultative Committee Meeting, etc. Really, there are three stages in any meeting said to be healthy practice. These are (i) before, (ii) during and (iii) after meeting.

Before the Meeting

Effectiveness of the meeting depends upon adoption of certain rules as follows:

- Develop a valid purpose or reason for calling the meeting to solve a problem and to secure positive attitudes
- Consider carefully whether the purpose could better be achieved by some other means say, by telephone calls
- When the meeting is to be held, make sure that all the concerned people must attend
- Carefully decide what subjects are to be taken up for discussion and in what order

During the Meeting

To conduct the meeting effectively, the following issues should be adhered to:

- Start the meeting on time
- Introduce the participants to the purpose of meeting and the agenda cutting all irrelevant discussions
- The Chairman should use good humour, gentle persuasion and have a sense of timing
- Provide opportunity to each participant and maintain time schedule
- Summarize the conclusions in a fair way
- Finish the meeting on time. If inevitable, extend the meeting for half an hour or so
- Thank the participants for their contribution to the achievements

After the Meeting

While implementing the decisions taken at the meeting, the following points should be kept in mind for creation of a healthy atmosphere in working of a business organization.

- Follow-up the most essential. It is as essential as the meeting itself.
- Actions taken on the resolutions arrived in the meeting has to be informed in writing to all those present in the meeting.
- To evaluate the actions carried out, if necessary, an Evaluation Committee Meeting should be called for.

3.4.6 Minutes of Meeting

Record of the decisions passed at the meeting is called **minutes**. It is an official record of the deliberations and conclusions carried out at the meeting in a systematic manner and finally signed by the Chairman. Drafting minutes into resolution for implementing them is a matter of skill and judgment. Minutes are a legal document and can be produced, if necessary, in a court of law as evidence.

Minutes include only the resolutions without details of the discussion transacted at the meeting. It is a short summary of discussion at the meeting with the statement of reasons followed with the name of the proposed and the seconded. An essential part of minutes includes:

- The name of the body and nature of meeting
- The day, date, time and place of meeting
- The name of Chairman of the meeting
- The names of persons 'in attendance' including the invited officials like Auditor, Solicitor, Management Consultant, Cost Accountant, Legal Advisor, etc. who are not members of the meeting
- Write absence against those who are not present
- The Secretary should finalize the minutes of meeting in consultations with the Chairman
- Each item should have a separate minute under a separate number
- The controversial discussions, abusive language, irrelevant points, defamatory matters, etc., should be carefully avoided
- The minutes should not reveal the secret matters pertaining to the organization

3.4.7 Record of Minutes

The business after conducting the meeting with agenda invariably records the minutes in a book called **Minutes Book**. The record of minutes is as:

- First item of the minutes is always the reading and confirming of the minutes of the previous meeting, e.g., the secretary reads out the minutes of the last meeting held on March 15, 2016. They were signed as a record of the meeting. Pass condolence resolution, if any, before the confirmation of the minutes. A condolence meeting is in three parts; first part states that the Chairman refers the demises and a resolution was passed, the second part outlines the person's achievements, nature and ability, etc., and the third part mentions the meeting stood in silence for two minutes. The secretary is authorized to convey the condolences of meeting to the bereaved family.

- Ending the minutes with a vote of thanks to the Chairman and there is no other business, and the meeting ended with a vote of thanks to the Chair.
- Every item on the agenda must have a corresponding item in the minutes.

3.4.8 Format of Recording Minutes

The format of recording the minutes of business meeting is illustrated as:

MINUTES OF THE MEETING OF THE BOARD OF DIRECTORS OF ABC COMPANY LIMITED

Minutes of the 18th Meeting of the Board of Directors of ABC Company held at the Registered Office of the Company at Valley Chambers, New Delhi on Monday, August 24, 2017 at 10.00 A.M.

Present:

1. Mr. Ram (in the Chair)
2. Dr. Gopi
3. Mr. Kavarkar
4. Mrs. Hema
5. Mr. K. Samy
6. Mr. R. Buchhan

In attendance:

Mr. M. Dhoon (Auditor)

Various items included in the agenda are discussed and resolutions passed as is given below.

1.
2.
3.

The Board decides to hold its next meeting ....

Sd/Ram

Exhibit 3.7 Meeting at What Cost

The American Management Consultants, Booz, Allen and Hamilton have conducted a study in the recent past and reported in the press disclosing that 299 managers at an average salary of $50000 a year have spent half of their time in meetings. A large proportion of this time was wasted on useless discussions, political maneuvering and personal conflicts. Based on their study, the consultants advised the organizations not to call a meeting that costs $10,000 for a decision worth of $1,000.

3.4.9 Types of Meeting

1. On the basis of formality, the meetings can be classified into three. These are:

Very Formal Meetings: The meetings of Parliament, State assemblies, company shareholders meeting, management-union negotiations, university senate, university council and university executive council are referred to as very formal meetings.

Formal Meetings: The meetings of the management councils, general body of voluntary organizations, briefing session, advisory body and management meeting are known as formal meetings.

Informal Meetings: The meetings of group discussion, ad hoc meeting and brainstorming session are referred to as informal meetings.

2. On the basis of purpose, the meetings can be classified into five. These are presented below.

Decision-making Meeting: A meeting of committee, board and such other specially appointed bodies hold with the powers to take decisions on behalf of organization is known as decision-making meeting.

Briefing Meeting: Reading a note on the concerned information to an issue and answering questions or requests with clarification is called briefing meeting. No discussion occurs at the briefing meeting.

Consultative Meeting: A body of experts holding a meeting to discuss and advise the concerned employees or people is called consultative meeting. But such body does not have powers to make any decision or action. Consultations between the different departments or sections are an example.

Negotiating Meeting: A meeting to settle the differences between the two parties of competing interest on its brief is known as negotiating meeting. Seller and buyer or employer and employee or two separate organizations desire to collaborate; the representatives of these parties discuss and arrive at an agreement. Meeting of exit interview and grievances have the element of negotiation.

Group Meeting: A meeting of group of persons with stimulation for understanding and exploring the possibilities and solving the problem is known as group meeting, also called group discussion meeting. It is used as a tool for selecting candidates by observing the behaviour and abilities of the individuals taking part in the meeting.

Merits

The merits of meeting are:

1. Enormous amount of information and knowledge with complexity makes it difficult for one person to handle the task. This can be made easy through discussion enabling to get benefit from the expertise of specialists.
2. Group activity and discussion provide the social and emotional support to the participants.

3. Tend to democratic approach in discussion of various ideas and problems.
4. Easy access to information due to openness and being in touch with members.

Demerits

Galbraith J.K. once said: "Meetings are indispensable when you don't want to do anything." The demerits of meeting are:

1. Meetings of formal and informal nature may turn out to be time consuming and expensive.
2. Meeting may end without any useful conclusion if much disagreement exists among the members.
3. If meetings do not provide useful outcomes to the members, they may not be taken seriously.
4. There is a great deal of useless talk if the chairperson has no skill in conducting a meeting. It causes others to feel frustrated for no opportunity to express their views.

3.4.10 Committee Meeting and Its Types

In modern business organization, the entire administrative task cannot be performed by a single person alone. Rather more persons are required to perform the same administrative task collectively. This shapes into a committee. A meeting of a small group of persons upon whom is entrusted a special task by authority to scrutinise the issue and submit a report with conclusions to the authority is called committee meeting. It often meets and maintains the minutes of each meeting. Hicks defined committee meeting as: "A committee is a group of people who plan to discuss or make a decision for a particular subject." The committee meetings are of several types.

1. **Executive Committee:** A committee consisting of line officers for taking decisions or review of recommendations made by other committee and implementing them is called executive committee. This committee is permanent in nature. The Board of Directors of a company is the best example for the executive committee. The executive committee holds a meeting and passes orders giving instructions for implementation.
2. **Sub-committee:** A smaller committee constituted by the larger committee from among its members for the purpose of completing an aspect or a part of larger committee's task is referred to as sub-committee.
3. **Ad hoc Committee:** A committee formed on the spot with a small group or during the meeting from among members present as well as others who are knowledgeable about solving a problem is called ad hoc committee.
4. **Standing Committee:** A committee forming a part of the organization with members by their position, title and office held is known as standing committee. The committee is permanent in nature with recurring task assigned and its members may be of one or two years' duration and may change by rotation. It

often meets to examine the nature of recurring problem and has high powers to implement its decisions.

5. **Special Committee:** Appointment of a committee for handling a special task is referred to as special committee. Its members are selected carefully taking into account their special knowledge and experience in the field of the entrusted task.
6. **Fact-finding Committee:** A committee formed for the purpose of collecting information on a particular subject and submitting a report on it with recommendations to the management is a fact-finding committee.
7. **Advisory Committee:** The committee that examines the problems that are referred to it is called advisory committee, also called problem solving committee. This committee calls for information or opinion of all those concerned or connected to the issue of problem and analyses it from different angles and gives advice considering both pros and cons of the proposed solutions.

Merits

The merits of committee are:

- Decisions are more acceptable since they are impersonal and democratic
- Examines the matter from different angles and puts together more information, knowledge and experience than a single person does
- Spreads responsibility to the members and relieves the manager's sole responsibility
- Hasty decision is avoided
- Decision is the best one, as saying goes like: "two heads are better than one."
- Members express their views, ideas and feelings freely which minimizes the clash of interests among them
- All the members of the committee have authority and responsibility

Demerits

A humorous and sharp remark on committee: "A committee is a group that keeps minutes and loses hours." "If you want to kill an idea, get the committee working on it." The demerits of committee are:

- Takes more time in arriving at final decision as each member expresses his own ideas, feelings
- The manager, sometimes, may appoint a committee as a delaying tactic when he is faced with a troublesome situation
- The decisions, sometimes, may be taken on compromise rather than consolidation of opinions
- More expensive as it takes more time to attend the meeting, secretarial help, stationery, refreshments and all expenses of committee for taking decision
- Fails sometimes to arrive at any useful conclusion
- No secrecy is maintained about decision arrived
- Responsibility cannot be thrust on any one member if the decision leads in unfavourable results

3.4.11 Measures for Productive Meetings

An alert participant finds that a meeting is an opportunity for continuing education in business management. An attentive and active participant should possess the following for productiveness of the meeting. These are:

- Work on the agenda and get information
- Read thoroughly the papers distributed, if any
- Keep an open mind for correcting any mistake in thinking or information gathering
- Have a sporting spirit for any idea or suggestion which is defeated
- Show appreciation towards those who make a good point
- Never personalize a difference of opinion
- Keep comments as short and precise as possible
- Be a good listener
- Be courteous in terms of the meeting manners, say as good as social manners

It is known that within any organization's operations, meeting plays an important role in passing information to employees, explaining new development or policies and gaining input from others. In fact, meeting is a powerful communication tool in employees' involvement in the workplace. Have you ever come out of meeting thinking to yourself that this meeting was waste of time? Non-productive meetings are not only a loss of valuable time; but they actually demoralize the employees who are otherwise self-motivated and highly productive.

When the need of having a meeting is essential, a few objectives need to be understood well in advance: Can you make the meeting productive and effective for solving organization's problem and decision-making? What is the purpose and specific outcome of the meeting? Is the meeting appropriate? Will you communicate information? Any meeting held just for the sake of being held is ineffective in positively boosting staff morale. Consider the following checklist when necessary to hold a meeting.

- Check the meeting room in advance to be sure it is ready.
- Arrange a semicircle or open U seating with space between members of group creating conducive atmosphere in problem-solving and decision-making.
- Provide every member of meeting with note pads, pencil along with agenda copies.
- Start meeting promptly at the scheduled time even if there are latecomers. This shows that the time of those who arrived on time is valuable.
- Limit introductory announcement to not more than five minutes. Clarify the objectives and outcomes. Remind attendees of previous meeting; allow up to three minutes for a review.
- Remove distractions from the room.
- Ascertain to write a running account for the activities. Good ideas are often forgotten because of lack of proper record-keeping.

- Keep the meeting focused on the agenda. Politely interrupt any meeting and ask the person recording the points to summarize within sixty seconds due to limited time.
- Get everyone to participate. Brainstorming exercises can be the best method for problem solving if everyone keeps an open mind, feels welcome to contribute and can express ideas without criticism. Compliment all who participate.
- Spend five minutes for summarizing the main points discussed and decision made in a positive and upbeat way.
- Schedule the next meeting. Adjourn the meeting on time.

3.4.12 Telephone Talk

An important facet in an interactive communication and integral part of responding to customer enquiries is through telephone talk. Banking, contact services, marketing and making sales calls on telephone are becoming popular particularly in metros. In modern business or other organizations including the political organizations, everyone makes use of telephone. Since telephone talk does not have the advantage of physical presence, clarity of speech (in similar sounding words like 'pale' and 'bale') and skilful use of voice are important. Many organizations, therefore, decided to train their employees on telephone manners either in calling or receiving; and bring out literature on it for the benefit of their staff. Some aspects to be kept in mind pertaining to telephone talk are given below.

- Lift the receiver before the 2nd or 3rd ring
- Announce your name/organization and greet the caller
- Respond politely and courteously
- Make sure that the calls are returned promptly
- End the conversation with a "thank you" or a "good day"
- Replace the receiver gently in its place
- If the person called is not available, make a note of caller's name, telephone number and message and communicate to the person concerned at the earliest
- Keep personal talk on the official line to the minimum
- Make your talk cost-effective
- Speak slowly but think quickly

3.4.13 Farewell

A farewell is a bit of emotional speech but short. The content is a summary of the achievements, contribution, and best and notable qualities of the person who is retiring from the service. This is being emanated from the speaker's own personal experiences with him. The speech can be made by narrating a specific incident to illustrate the person's qualities.

The farewell speech hinges, to a great extent, on the relation between the speaker and the person who is being given a farewell. The tone should be appropriate to the occasion avoiding too much emotion or too much humour. If the occasion is a send off to a person going to a higher position or on a special assignment, the tone is congratulatory. The speech ends with good wishes for health, success, happiness and further achievement. For example see Exhibit 3.8.

Exhibit 3.8 **Congratulatory Tone**

(a) A man of wide interests and capabilities, Dr. Raizada is hardly going to sit idle after he has retired. I have noticed that he has already planned to work on a number of interesting projects which he has assigned to himself. I wish him excellent health and all success and happiness in whatever he chooses to do.

(b) We shall miss Mr. Pool very much. But, we also rejoice in his good fortune and his abilities which have brought him this opportunity to serve in an important and responsible position. We wish him every success and all happiness in his new assignment.

3.4.14 Condolence Meeting

A condolence meeting is a solemn occasion. Speeches on such occasions are brief and in a serious tone. Humour of any kind or reference to any humorous incident is out of place. There is no elaborate address even if there are many persons on the dais. The speech opens with a brief address like: "Friends, it is a sad occasion for us today when we have to mourn the loss of ….. who was with us for so many years!"

The cause and circumstances of death are mentioned after the opening sentence. A brief life sketch of the person, a reference to the person's contribution to the organization and to the society is mentioned. The speech ends with an expression of a sense of grief and loss. It is customary to send a condolence speech with the words, "May his/her soul rest in peace."

3.4.15 Comparison between Written and Oral Communication

Objective of both the oral and the written communication is to convey the intended message to the target audience. In some instances, oral communication might be more useful while in others written communication is necessary because of its own relative merits and demerits. As one cannot depend upon a particular medium of communication; and both are complementary to each other. Because of this feature, both media are used. Oral communication is more useful where the subject matter is complex and a final decision requires deliberations from the persons concerned. Where the messages are required to be kept for future reference, written communication is the only possible way. Differences between oral and written communication are presented in Table 3.3.

Table 3.3 Comparison between Written and Oral Communication

Written Communication	Oral Communication
(1) Speed: Takes more time to draft, dispatch, receive, read and understand message	Takes less time to speak, hear, listen and understand the message
(2) Record: Serves as documentary record and can be used for future reference. It has a legal evidence	Authenticity may be questioned as it saves no legal document record. Messages can be edited and distorted
(3) Precision: More precise and accurate message	Not always possible due to choice of words and no time. But, receiver can get clarification on the spot and body language enriches the meaning of words as well
(4) Expense: Need of stationery, preparation and transmission costs	Need of channel costs

3.4.16 Meta-Communication

Verbal communication refers to the exchange of messages through the use of written or spoken symbols while non-verbal communication refers to anything that transcends written or spoken symbols. If separated, the verbal part of a message conveys information whereas the non-verbal part indicates how the verbal message should be interpreted and thus becomes meta-communication. Accompaniment of an additional idea to the every expressed idea is known as **meta-communication**. Wherever, verbal and non-verbal messages contradict each other, the latter is more likely considered. In fact, Donald D. White and David A. Bandar have suggested that the total impact of a message is the function which is as: Total impact = 1.00 (verbal 0.07 + vocal 0.38 + facial 0.55).

3.4.17 Need of Communication Skills

A key element in skill management of competition is communication. The communication skills which are relevant across all methods are insight into human behaviour, removal of emotional blocks and effective use of personality. There are three types classified as skills in oral communication, skills in written communication and skills in non-verbal communication. These types of skills are presented in Table 3.4.

Table 3.4 Skills in Communication

Oral	Written	Non-verbal
Understand and use appropriate language	Command over language	Power of observation
Organize and sequence thoughts effectively	Word power and spelling	Awareness about the body movements and other expression

Contd.

Vocabulary and word power	Correct grammar	Interpret properly the non-verbal messages
Command over examples, illustrations and phrases	Structure properly the written messages	Supplement with oral communication
Proper accent and pronunciation	Correct use of phrases	Self observation and practice
Proper use of sound system and other aids	Simplicity, brevity and clarity	
Voice modulation and reach	Attention in handwriting, typing, printing and photocopying	–
Listening skills	–	–
Adherence to time specification, effective telephone talks	–	–

3.4.18 Types of Interviews

In an oral or face-to-face communication, eminent person(s) called interviewer ask questions to the other person called interviewee with a specific purpose; this is known as **interview**. Interview is used in an organization to get feedback on specific situations and to find out information for decision-making besides selection for employment. Interview is classified into six types as given below.

1. **Promotion Interview:** Conduct of interview to an employee elevating him to higher position is called promotion interview. It is informal and serves as induction into a new team with new responsibilities. Suppose, there is competition for promotion in the organization, this interview helps in selection process and serves as an opportunity for a discussion of career opportunities of each candidate.
2. **Assessment Interview:** A face-to-face confidential talk between the supervisor and the employee on several issues periodically is called assessment interview. In this, more discussion is made on the career development of employee, areas which need improvement and to be strengthened, training and job enrichment.
3. **Exit Interview:** Conducting an interview for an employee who has resigned is called exit interview.
4. **Leaving Interview:** An organization can conduct this interview to know:
    - Precise reasons for leaving the organization whether ill-feeling or misunderstanding, etc., with which a decision can be taken to maintain good relations with the employees
    - Feedback on employee's attitude and opinion about policies of organization
    - Updated entry of details and information in the personal record file
    - The payment of final pay cheque and its handing over

- ➢ Accrued benefits like sick leave, earned leave, if not paid in the past
- ➢ The payment of benefits of Provident Fund, Group Insurance, etc.
- ➢ Whether books like manuals, tools, equipment, etc., were returned

5. **Problem Interview:** Conduct of interview with a problem employee whose performance is unsatisfactory in spite of warning is called problem interview. To know the reasons like domestic problem or ill-health, lack of training or dissatisfaction with the job, failure to adjust to the environment, etc., for the poor performance of employee in face-to-face interaction and to suggest a solution rather than warnings and notices is the motto of this interview. If behaviour is unsatisfactory, the interview can be used for giving a clear understanding of what is expected and what will be the consequences of unacceptable conduct. The interviewer needs counseling, persuasion and negotiating skills for such interviews.
6. **Stress Interview:** Reaction to the external environment and inner thoughts and feelings is referred to as stress. An interview that puts the candidate in a difficult situation in order to test his/her reaction to stress is known as stress interview. It is used for knowing a person's capabilities to what extent he/she can face the difficult situation without getting upset. A stress interview tests qualities such as courage, cool temper, tact, self-command, etc., which are needed when confronted by employees or people in big or small groups.

   Rapid fire questions on the topics, questions asked by different members of the panel together, cross questioning and arguing, disputing the candidate's statements, ridiculing the answers, subjecting him to silence and inattention are some methods used to throw the candidate out of balance. At the end, the candidate is informed that it was a stress interview.
7. **Selection Interview:** The process of assessing the suitability/potential of the candidate for a specific job is known as selection interview. The main motto is to assess the candidate's credentials and capabilities along with skills to assign a job. Thus, it becomes a basis for decision of both the employer and the candidate. A panel of experts usually conduct selection interview to draw out the candidate's personality – subject knowledge, skills of presenting right answers to questions, behaviour, gentleness, etc., for the job. Interviewers spend more time on good candidates; gather enough information about the candidate's suitability to join the organization. Many organizations recruit promising candidates by holding interview at campus in professional colleges and institutions.
8. **Campus Interview:** Campus interview is a complex situation to a student to face during the final year of the course, where the sense of excitement and enthusiasm is optimum. A candidate, who is able to handle this situation in a systematic and planned manner, emerges successful in such interviews. To emerge successful on a campus interview one must know: the SWOT analysis indulging to identify the strengths, weaknesses, opportunities and threats. The next step is to prepare a resume in simple and straightforward language, one's academic and professional skills in a polished manner. The last step is to prepare and be well versed and thorough in a few subjects related to the discipline of study, areas of specialization

or areas of interest in short must be worked upon sharply and deeply by the candidate.

During the interview process, the student's presence of mind, analyzing skills and aptitude will be tested. In recent times, corporate engaging campus recruitment also tests the emotional quotient in addition to intelligence quotient. Thus, a student must prove to be intelligent and updated in diversified fields possessing stress situation to be placed in reputed concerns. It is widely instructed that the candidate must remain calm, emotionally balanced and utilize effective verbal and non-verbal communication.

Gestures or body language or non-verbal communication is the area to be improved and concentrated as most of the interviewers assess the real personality of the candidate through his or her body language; how one enters the interview lobby, the gaiety, the manner of sitting, the keenness in listening and answering questions, all these exhibit the personality of the candidate. Presentation (attire and appearance, shaking hands with confidence and maintaining polite conduct), punctuality and preparation are 3 P's of professionalism.

Campus interview is conducted at two or three stages. The first stage may be a technical round to test the technical skills and aptitudes, usually in the form of a written test. The second stage may be a group discussion round to test the language skills, the presence of mind and the ability to work in a group to solve a given problem and arrive at a solution. The third stage may be a personal interview round to test the background and general information of the candidate. Essentials for succeeding in an interview can be seen in Exhibit 3.9.

Exhibit 3.9 Essentials to Succeed in an Interview

Campus interviews are part of recruitment drive by many software companies to find talent for their current operations and projected future needs.

Young graduates from different streams and branches are available at one spot and the companies get prior knowledge of each student's performance in their courses, behaviour and attitude from the college faculty. This makes the recruiter's task easy at the first step. But, they do have the need to assess the candidates from the perspective of job role, ability to work in teams and blend with the organization's culture.

The candidate's knowledge in the branch of his study will be tested. He must be able to answer each question – be it in core subjects, project work or attitude in a manner that will prove him to be brighter than the rest of the class. People with desire to learn more, work in teams and attitude to excel, etc., are what the companies look for. On the interview day, the candidate needs to carry all his records on his project work and any internship he might have done.

9. **Walk-in-Interview:** The candidate should arrive at the place of interview at least 10 to 20 minutes before the time given. A candidate's moment while entering the door till he comes out of the door is under full observation. Generally, the procedure of interview consists of four parts, namely, entry, answering questions, asking questions and leaving; each one of these is performed with utmost attention.

3.4.19 Process of Interview

Interview is the process or activity during which a potential candidate is evaluated as employee by the selection board. The process of interview for selection involves presenting oneself, answering questions, asking questions and leaving interview room. These are highlighted below.

1. **Presenting Oneself:** Entering an interview room means the candidate must become familiar with room, its size and appearance and adjust accordingly. Way of opening and closing the door, walking, greeting and taking the chair will show whether the candidate is well-mannered and graceful, and composed and confident or nervous. Though entry takes only a minute, it makes first impression and impact. A better impression aids in a natural and pleasant expression. While the candidate presents oneself before interviewer – use formal and executive clothing, carry a pen in folder or a file, carry only relevant testimonials, a copy of resume, and a recent photograph. Do not present any certificate unless asked for.
2. **Answering Questions:** Answering questions takes a major part of interview time. The interviewer finds out the qualities and suitability of the candidate for the job through his/her comfort factor. A nervous and uncomfortable candidate does not show his/her best qualities. Avoid humorous or ironical answers, avoid repeating an answer or phrase or word and avoid answering in a raised voice. If the answer or opinion is rejected by the interviewer, do not hesitate to say 'sorry.'

   Ask questions from the subject, education and experience, special abilities, personal hobbies, family background and circumstances to any problem faced and handled in the past. In other words, the questions are meant to test the candidate's knowledge, personal qualities, character, attitude to work and life, career goals, motivation, etc. Some questions are common and almost indispensable in such interviews. So, the student may prepare well in advance for effective and convincing answers. Some repeated questions are as:

   - 'Tell me about yourself!',
   - 'What is your strength?'
   - 'Why should we appoint you?'
   - 'What do you know about the company?'
   - 'Do you have any reference?'
3. **Asking Questions for Information:** Once responding to the questions in interview is over, the candidate is clear about the job position, its related aspects and the company. If not invited, he may seek permission to ask for information by saying, "may I ask a few questions?" Or "may I ask for some information?" The candidate's questions pertain to working conditions, prospects of career growth, working relationships, etc.
4. **Leaving:** The interviewer generally indicates when the interview is over by saying something like, "Thank you; we'll get in touch with you later," etc. While moving out, step back first, then turn and walk away.

Success is the sum of small efforts, repeat day-in and day-out. Hence, work hard, work systematically and work with commitment. The candidate should keep in mind the following:

- Thank the interviewers
- Collect and pack all papers and files quickly and neatly
- Get up gracefully, without dragging the chair
- Wish them good day
- Do not offer to shake hand. But if any one offers to shake hand, be quick to take it.
- Put the chair back in its place
- Walk away with good bearing
- Shut the door carefully and noiselessly

Tips in brief, what to do at the interview are given below. The candidate should be conscious of the interview and attentive to:

- Answer to the point
- Answer in a clear voice without fumbling for words
- Maintain eye contact with the person
- Pause while answering, if he needs to ask some questions
- Elaborate on the point asked and continue with your answer
- Be thorough about the subject and be honest. Never take credit for work done in the project by others. You may be caught if you lie.
- Dress up formally.
- Remember that you will not get many opportunities in campus recruitment. So, you must present yourself as a confident and enthusiastic person ready to plunge into the world of work.
- Asks questions in a mild manner, if you have any doubts regarding the job or company. But, remember never ask silly questions.

In selecting a candidate to the position, proper procedure is to be followed. The view of the Executive Director, Human Resources, Procter & Gamble is given in Exhibit 3.10.

Exhibit 3.10 Recruitment

- The candidate fills-in a company provided Application Form.
- The company conducts a simple problem-solving test.
- If the candidate's application has progressed beyond the first two stages, he is interviewed anywhere between one to three times by the manager of Procter & Gamble.
- The decision to hire/not hire is to be communicated to the candidate post-interview.

3.4.20 Candidate Preparation

At the interview, it is not only information and knowledge of the candidate assessed but also the whole personality – mental, psychological and physical. How a candidate faces an interview physically, mentally and psychologically is discussed below.

1. **Physical Preparation:** The candidate should be dressed up neatly with properly combed hair, personal hygiene, well-laundered and well-fitting clothes, clean and well-cut nails, neat footwear and a suitable paper-file. He should exhibit posture by impressive walk and self-confidence. He should possess good conduct. The candidate may need some physical preparation as well. The following points may be helpful:
   - Greet in an acceptable form
   - Do not shake hands unless offered by an interviewer
   - Do not sit until asked to sit down or if you are not asked to sit, ask politely for permission to sit
   - Pull out the chair without dragging it and sit comfortably in a good posture
   - Put your file on the lap; in case you have a briefcase, put it down on the floor near the chair
   - Keep hands comfortable when you are not using them
   - Maintain comfortable posture throughout the interview
   - Remember to thank the interviewers and wish them 'good day'.
2. **Mental Preparation:** The candidate must review and revise subjects studied in his/her course of graduation having up-to-date knowledge including current events and interests mentioned in the resume. Read newspapers or listen to news, and discuss current issues which become useful tips. Opinions or views on current issues may be asked; for which discuss issues intelligently and support opinions with well considered reasons. The candidate must find out as much information as possible about the company wherein he/she seeks employment. Last but not the least is that the candidate must know about biographical questions.
3. **Psychological Preparation:** Questions in interview may embarrass the candidate, for which he/she should be prepared. Then, preparation of psychological issues becomes a part of personality and character development. Answering questions honestly is the best policy. Admit inability to answer a question than to pretend and guess. Being able to admit lack of information on the topic is a strong point. No one is expected to know everything and anything. Dishonesty as well as inability create a bad impression.

   Compensation package is a topic to be discussed at the interview. One's qualifications and good self-assessment give a candidate confidence to negotiate the compensation package. The candidate must know and get information on the nature of duties, future prospects, other benefits and any other desired information before leaving. This information is necessary for taking decision, especially if there are other job offers.

3.4.21 Competencies of Candidate

A set of competencies, which assumed, will determine the future success of the candidate. This includes:

- ➢ Passion for winning
- ➢ Ability to lead
- ➢ Strong analytical skills
- ➢ Ability to think innovatively
- ➢ Ability to identify and work constructively towards opportunities
- ➢ Ability to work collaboratively with others
- ➢ Drive for continuous self-improvement

Service organizations, sometimes, give greater weightage to the attitudes rather than academic qualifications and experience. Good service hires people with a helpful attitude and those who are service-oriented. See Exhibit 3.11.

Exhibit 3.11 **Hiring Attitude**

South West Airlines of the United States of America is a consistent topper in customers-service polls and has been rated as the safest Airline for over twenty years. It has also the distinction of being one of the ten best companies in America.

The recruitment process in South West Airlines is understandably rigorous. There would be at least half a dozen interviews. But, these are not psychological tests. Here is what the company looks for.

- ➢ "What we are looking for first and foremost is a sense of humour."
- ➢ "Then we are looking for people who have excelled to satisfy themselves and work well in a congenial environment."
- ➢ "We don't care much about education and experience because we can train people to do whatever they have to do."
- ➢ "We hire attitudes."

People who can listen, who care, who smile, who say 'Thank you' and who are warm are the people the Airlines hires for accounting jobs, as reservation agents and flight attendants.

An old proverb says: "opportunity knocks your door only once." Generally, people can never look for opportunities with their busy nature with problems, and in the process of solving those they lose time, interest and enthusiasm in life. Successful people understand that many of the problems are self-made; see in them an opportunity. Troubles arise in three ways which are (i) by us for us, (ii) by others to us, and (iii) by us to others. See Exhibit 3.12.

Exhibit 3.12 **Opportunities in Problem**

By Us for Us: A student who could not reply to a question due to tension in an interview in spite of knowing the answer, should blame no one but himself for not practicing public speaking and developing communication skills during his college days. A person becomes obese because he cannot control his food habits, which makes him lazy and thereby losing interest in things. Ultimately, this becomes an insurmountable problem for him. Such type of problems include fear, tension, insecurity, laziness, lack of communication, etc. All these are not problems but weaknesses which, in turn, metamorphose into problems. A crisis may be unavoidable but a weakness certainly can be defeated. If this simple fact is known, half the battle is won.

By Others to Us: Problem, sometimes, crops up when one wants to say 'no' but says 'yes'. A friend calls on a newly wed couple without a prior appointment, notices that the couple is about to go out for a movie, but still engages them in conversation. The husband is unable to ask him to leave or at least tell him about their program. It is called 'gentleman's syndrome'. A person is said to be suffering from this disorder, when he wants to be good to everybody, works for their appreciation and seeks other's approval for his deeds at the cost of his own happiness. Signing the surety bonds unwillingly, obeying other's demands reluctantly, etc., are some other examples.

By Us to Others: A person misplaces an important file at the office. He comes home irritated and scolds his son for not keeping the room neat. The sensitive son fails in the examination next day. Another example is that a person never sticks to his schedule and wastes others' time. This type includes lack of time management, anger, selfishness, etc., which cause trouble to others but in many cases boomerang to create personal loss to us.

Non-verbal communication is the earliest type of communication developed much before the oral communication language came into being. It is distinct from verbal communication and takes place extensively at various levels of family, individuals, institutions, society and organizations. Silence or action is a mode of communication and speaks louder than words. The media of non-verbal communication such as silence, gestures, handshake, attire, facial expression and body movement; all have meaning and hence communicate with others. Ray Bird Whistle observed that "the words spoken account for less than 35 per cent of the total meaning produced while the remaining 65 per cent is obtained by non-verbal cues." Non-verbal communication is divided into body language and pictorial communication.

3.5 IMPORTANCE OF NON-VERBAL COMMUNICATION

Consciously sparing facial expressions and created visual symbols can enrich the message presented in its true sense of meaning to the receiver. The feel of soft velvet and plush on the skin conveys the impression of luxury. Non-verbal communication occurs even in verbal communication and discloses truth which the communicator or writer is hiding behind the words. Albert Mehrabian observed in his study that "Only 7 per cent of a message effect is carried by words and listeners receive the other 93 per cent through non-verbal means." A saying also goes like: "non-verbal actions speak louder than words." The importance of non-verbal communication is highlighted below.

- Non-verbal communication presents large amount of complex data in a compact form at a glance.
- It provides instant response. Green and red colours tell the road users about the safety and danger of proceeding journey respectively.
- It is being responded by people immediately and powerfully. A film showing actual events is more effective than a narrated or written story.
- It is the best method of conveying even to illiterate people. A skull and cross-bones on the bottles and containers of poison warn people for immediate action. Similarly, a sign of burning cigarette in circle with red colour with 'x' mark indicate for action of 'no smoking'.
- It overcomes the barriers of language.

The power of observation is a major characteristic feature of the message received in the system of non-verbal communication. As such, the receiver should be in a position to clearly see the face, the gesture, the tone, the dress, the appearance and the voice of communicator. Non-verbal communication may be both intended and unintended which implies that the communicator conveys message through (a) posture, appearance, gestures, attire, and (b) other forms of body language respectively. In the latter, the receiver has to interpret the message properly in its true sense. For example, a sloppy picture may be interpreted as lack of seriousness although the speaker may be quite intent. Non-verbal communication, thus, thrives on (i) observation and (ii) interpretation while verbal communication thrives on (i) reading and (ii) listening.

Non-verbal communication is said to be effective when conscious efforts are made with regards to the body language – appearance, smile, behaviour, postures gestures and attire. Communication skills of non-verbal communication are the basic factors for reaching messages to the intended ones effectively. The skills of non-verbal communication are:

- Power of observation of all senses – vision, hear, smell, touch and taste
- Noticing power and awareness about body movements
- Interpretation of messages properly
- Supplementing with oral communication, if necessary
- Self-observation and practice

Non-verbal communication is grouped into (i) body language and (ii) visual (pictorial) presentation. The cognizant efforts are needed to express properly and understand the hidden meaning of message.

3.5.1 Body Language

Facial expressions, gestures and postures, attire, appearance, voice, sign and signals, timings, personal behaviour and other body movements are called body language. Body language was used obviously by the pre-literate man. In non-verbal communication, body language is an important mode and supports most parts of the words in a speech and gives meaning without using words. If the listeners are unaware and insensitive to the body language of others, they cannot understand the message as clearly and effectively as possible. The body does not lie and body language tells the truth. If you are sleepless, your eyes tend to shut; if you are tired, you tend to yawn, and so on are examples. Today, use of signs and signals perhaps evolved as the methods of communication for the hearing impaired. How the Bharatanatyam dancer conveys the meanings through her/his expressions using different parts of the body? The study of body motion is called **kinesics**. Love is the universal language used in non-verbal communication. Love and compassion of Mother Teresa and peace movement of Mahatma Gandhi all over the world are good examples. The speechless movie is another example of effective non-verbal communication. Thus, non-verbal communication is more effective than words in some instances. Until such time, no communication credibility gap signifies confidence or trust. How communication through the body language is effective is explained through Exhibit 3.13.

Exhibit 3.13 Body Language

According to research, an overwhelming impact of non-verbal communication is discerned. It is said that more than 85 per cent of the effect of a speaker on an audience is accounted for by the non-verbal part; of which 50 per cent of the effect is accounted for the body language, appearance, facial expression, postures and gestures, and remaining 35 per cent for visual factors like colour, sign and signal.

The important parts in body language in communicating the intended messages are discussed below.

1. **Voice:** Tones like harsh, soft and whisper; pitch of high and low; quality of controlled and uncontrolled; rapid and slow pace; and force of intensity are the distinctive features of voice. A high tone is louder and heard at a longer distance than a low tone. High pitched voice is often unpleasant and shows immaturity or emotional disturbance which, naturally, struck a person with fear. Speed of speaking is another aspect of voice. Rapid speech indicates excitement. When telling an interesting message, we increase the speed of speech while in explaining a difficult idea, we reduce the speed of speech. Clear pronunciation of rhythm and accent will have an effect on the listener.
2. **Stress and Sound:** Stress and sound on a particular word can change the meaning and implication of the sentence. Try saying a sentence like: "Did you attend the dinner last night?" This can be expressed in different ways putting stress on a different word each time and the difference in the meaning implied can be noted. Just one word and a look can convey what might take several meanings. For example, an explosively uttered word, 'what' could mean what are you saying. Do you really mean that? I just cannot believe what you are saying? Such non-verbal aspect of spoken words is known as **para language**.

3. **Silence:** The state of wordlessness is called silence. Facial expressions and posture may indicate the feeling behind the silence. People say that 'silence is half truth'. Saying goes that 'silence can crop up many a problems.' Silence may be deliberate or unintentional. The former conveys a powerful message while the latter results in awkward situation. In dealing with an irate customer, the officer would be well advised to observe silence and listen to the customer before reacting. "Silence is gold in many cultures and it is a force" (Warren Keagan).

   Silence shows several things in a face-to-face situation. Person deliberately becomes silent when he in anger or displeasure; and also keeps silent to express sympathy with someone who has suffered loss. Further, in skillful presentation, silence can be used effectively to replace words. For example, a pause before or after certain words makes the words stand out from the rest. Therefore, silence in many instances is an effective medium of communication. For instance:

   - A pause has power to make the listener more alert. A leader at the time of climbing up the stage or platform to address the public finds an environment of applause by the audience when he takes his position near the mike in a silent posture. In a way, silence is usually considered approval in a number of personal, business and social transactions as practice, custom, tradition or understanding.
   - Under the law of contract, legal doctrines speak on silence. The acceptance of an offer can neither be implied through silence nor by his failure to answer. Sometimes, silence is considered equivalent to speech; it is considered fraud in some cases and otherwise in other cases which depend upon the way of raising a question. See Exhibit 3.14 how silence is gold.

Exhibit 3.14 Silence is Gold

When a lady enters a cloth shop, the salesman shows her ordinary saris first, allows her to say 'no' for some time initially. He knows that no lady prefers to buy saris first shown no matter how gorgeous it may be. He pulls out some more saris to show and at a particular point notices the spark and approval in her by eyes. She is still uncertain. Then, he starts impressing her by saying it is the best one in quality, and, above it, suits her preferably. Playing on her ego and indecision, he thus wins. The principles involved here are: (a) a good idea does not succeed if the timing is not right and (b) it is important to be patient till the other person (customer) is helpless and seeks your advice.

   Therefore, silence is what keeps you from saying more than you need to; makes the other person want to say more than he means to.

4. **Facial Expression:** Face is said to be the most expressive part of the body. The thought of mind and the feelings of heart often find an expression on the face on account of facial features and eyes movement. A good relation exists between the facial and emotional feelings of the speaker. Expression through face without

words is known as facial expression. A cheerful face or appreciative smile conveys the attitude and reaction to success in communicator's endeavour. A yawn is interpreted as a symbol of sleeping. A single nod implies consent; many times it may mean dissent or refusal. Putting down the head shows reverence of a feeling of shyness whereas keeping it backward means indifference. The features of facial expression are as follows.

- Happiness shows most in the lower face and eye areas
- Sadness shows in the eyes
- Surprise shows in the eyes and lower face
- Anger shows in the lower face and eyebrows, forehead
- Disgust shows in the lower face
- Fear shows in the eyes

Thus, human face is capable of conveying wide range of expressions and emotions such as happiness, anger, surprise, boredom, fear, disgust, sadness, liking, disliking, love, jealousy, agreement, pain, pleasure, etc. When a subordinate approaches his superior to get his approval after the completion of the entrusted task assigned, the superior expresses his silent approval by a smile. So, smiling at a subordinate communicates meaning. The expression or movement to make forehead wrinkle and eyebrow moved down indicates disapproval or worry of deep thought. Range of responses from facial expression is listed in Table 3.5.

Table 3.5 Response from Facial Expression

Acceptance	Rejection
Like	Dislike
Friendship	Hostility
Interest	No interest
Anger	Love
Agreement	Disagreement
Surprise	Fear
Ease	Discomfort
Pleasure	Pain
Attention	Boredom

5. **Eye Contact:** Expression of message through eye positioning is called eye contact. In expression of love, affection, sincerity and alike, it becomes crucial. The words and expressions used in common parlance while reading the eyes are: twinkle in eyes, fortitude glance, eyes emitting fire, worried look, sad look, etc. Eye contact

serves as a signal of readiness to interact and its absence tends to reduce the chances of such interaction. Eye contact assumes a considerable significance in:

- Dealing with customers at the counter
- Facing interviews for recruitment and promotion
- Making presentations and sales talk

Eye contact comes in, for scrutiny in legal cross examinations, negotiations and such other business situations. Unblinking eye contact means that the person is lying and watching your reaction. If a person exhibits full eye contact for too long together with angry expression, it implies that it is shooting darts at someone. Thus, eye contact creates a behavioural change and also shows the need for oral communication.

Career Builder India conducted a survey on 400 employees, that most of them within five minutes of interview can figure out if the candidate is fit for the job or not. Majority of them consider failing to make eye contact as the biggest body language mistake made by the applicants. Further, stated that 56 per cent of employees come to know within the first five minutes of interview if a candidate is fit for a position. Facing the job interview is not just about how you answer the interviewer's questions, but it is also about what your body language says about you. Employees look for those non-verbal cues to indicate a candidate's level of professionalism and, if they have, they will be the right for the position.

6. **Gesture and Posture:** Movement of limbs, or hands or head or body as natural accompaniment of speech is called gesture. A person who does not make any movement while speaking is said to be stiff and mechanical. As gestures is closely related to personality, no two persons make exactly the same gestures; but easily recognize general meaning of it. TV news readers keep gestures and even head movements under strict control.

   Holding body in a certain position is known as posture. A polite and well-bred person is more attentive how he stands or sits in the presence of visitors and informal situations. Graceful posture is an asset.

   Nodding, shaking of head, smiling, patting the back, putting the hand over one's shoulder, clasping hands, shrugging, arm folders, eye signals, sitting positions, thumb and finger rub, thumbs up, touching, frowning, scowling, blinking, yawning, crossing and uncrossing of legs, etc., are among the types of physical actions and gestures. These are used to convey the meanings and messages and are interpreted by the receivers accordingly. Postures and gestures with actions are of much use in the context of organization. For instance:

   - A traffic constable is able to direct traffic on roads through gestures of hands and arms, without verbal communication.
   - People in a face-to-face position indicate they are in bargaining or stranger position. People standing or siting in the right of one another shows cooperative situation or friendship.

7. **Attire:** Dress conveys cultural background of people. Good taste is indicated by what one wears. Combination of appropriate colour and design for the occasion,

formality of occasion, the time of day, season, cultural background of people present and the convention of organization would provide guidance to dress up. Dress of people from different countries varies. Dress of army men differs from civilian, land army, air force and naval personnel according to their rank. Dress of religious heads, political leaders, lawyers, judges, doctors, nurses and sports persons differ from one another.

For example, an official addressing an important meeting, making an important announcement, receiving dignitaries or making an appearance at a high level conference, court of justice, etc., has to wear a formal dress. Organizations have dress codes to ensure the desired impression by its representatives. Any breach of this unwritten code is likely to dilute the effectiveness of the communication.

8. **Appearance:** People, in modern society, have the habit of judging others by their appearance. The factors that contribute to good appearance are personal hygiene and neatness, care of skin, nails, hair, tie, footwear, jewellery, careful selection and comfortable wearing. Untidiness in appearance indicates indifference.
9. **Handshake:** In the modern society, it is well accepted that people greet each other and introduce themselves to one another with a handshake. Handshakes are varied assuming description and interpretation. It may vary as:
   - A firm handshake – the right way of showing confidence and keenness
   - A clasp handshake (using both hands) – high degree of warmth or respect
   - A tight grip handshake – some kind of aggressiveness and dominance
10. **Smile:** Smile speaks the language of love, compassion, sincerity, courtesy, confidence and dependability. In communication, a smile is a potent form of facial expression. The significance of smiling is beautifully described in the saying: "You are never fully dressed unless you wear a smile." In making business transaction and interacting with team-mates or colleagues in every such transaction, smile can create a favourable impact and earn goodwill. Awry, artificial or platonic smile conveys messages quite contrary to those of natural and pleasant smiles.

3.5.2 Pictorial Communication

Pictorial communication, also called visual communication, is a means of not only appealing to the logical reasoning and conclusion but also to have an aesthetic value. Without diluting the main focus of message, thoughts or ideas can be expressed through pictorial or graphical presentation which is extremely a valuable part of written communication. This often substitutes or complements written statements and makes the communication focused with an attractive appeal.

Pictorial communication includes graphs, diagrams, charts, etc., that are developed to convey the intended messages. The communicating information inscribed in them can be seen at a glance and the relationship exhibited in them can be known easily. Organizations make use of pictures like blueprints, progress charts, maps and visual aids in training programmes. Such means of communication are increasingly used in training of employees, educating the students, researching of researchers and making people aware of products or services in the society. A picture can provide powerful visual images as suggested by the Chinese proverb. It says that "A picture is worth a thousand words." Many business organizations, in fact, have designed their advertisement copies in which only pictures are used and no words are spoken. To be effective, pictures should be combined with well-chosen words and actions in order to convey the complete message with accuracy. The governing rules of pictorial presentation are:

- The communicator has to keep in mind the 'value addition' of inserting pictorial mode of presentation – table, chart or pictures. To what extent the pictorial presentation is substituting or complementing the written text is to be taken into stock. Brochures, sales literature, booklets, advertisement, motivational communication and reports of business constitute a key area amenable for pictorial presentation.
- Select an appropriate pictorial mode for presenting forcefully or emphatically the messages to the target audience. The target audience is the general public and not highly literate and well-versed group; hence simpler tables, charts, graphs and diagrams are appropriate.
- Due attention is to be paid to present all the relevant details which make the messages clear and complete. A clear title and narration is to be given to each table or chart or graph mentioning source of the data at the bottom.
- Mention of (a) source of data and (b) details like quality, amount, period, etc., which indicate the authenticity of data and render clarity of data respectively.
- Appropriate scale is to be taken fulfilling the governing rule of 1:1.5 on horizontal and vertical lines respectively.

3.5.3 Utility of Pictorial Presentation

The pictorial presentation adds value to the text of message and makes the business reports including literature more effectively readable friendly. The utility of pictorial presentation:

- Breaks monotony
- Simplifies and amplies facts and figures
- Strengthens the memory and improves recall value
- Adds colour and variety to presentation
- Provides scope for creativity in communication
- Brings out relative and time values with greater clarity

Merits

In conveying the intended message, the pictorial presentation of data is more extremely useful. The merits of pictorial presentation media are that it:

- Understands quickly the interpreted message
- Enables to understand at a glance

- Helps to remember the message that may long last
- Facilitates comparison
- Gives a bird's eye view of the given subject matter
- Is dynamic and carries a greater force in demonstrating the message
- Is more revealing as well as appealing to the eyes
- Aids to save time as very little effort is required to understand, and draw meaningful inferences

Demerits

The limitations of pictorial presentation are that it:

- is used to show only limited subject matter at a time
- takes a lot of time as it needs technical expertise
- is a costly matter as it incurs both installation cost and revenue cost in most of cases
- is approximate and as such pinpoint accuracy is not possible in all circumstances

3.6 NEW DIMENSIONS TO VISUAL COMMUNICATION

The use of above-mentioned visual communication in business has been considerable creativity in business literature. The addition of colour and presentation of skills brings a new dimension to visual communication which further adds value to the written communication in business.

1. **Colour:** Colour is an important and powerful means of formal communication which has become so much a part of daily life of human beings. Pleasant and cooling colours in the work context have good influence on the concerned ones in business say, stakeholders including employees. In traffic signals, chemical industry and cosmetics industry, colour is mainly used for classification and identification. Red colour indicates 'stop', amber colour 'wait' and green 'go' in traffic signals. Red colour cylinder is used only for cooking. Attractive colour is used for soaps and shampoos of various types. In office, carbon copies of forms are made out on papers of different colours in order to distinguish copies meant for different Departments. The use of logo in modern-day business is a printed symbol representing the company or organization with mission of vision.

   There are several colours classified into warm and cool. Blue and green colours are cool colours as they associate with the sky, sea, trees, and grass; while red and orange are warm colours as they associate with passion, action, excitement and fire. A well-matched and softly blending colour is pleasant and smoothing with objective of its use. A sample of applicable colours to Indian local, ethnic and cultural connotations and symbolism beyond what it exhibited is presented in Exhibit 3.15.

Exhibit 3.15 Examples of Colours with Meanings

White	→	Symbol of purity, freedom, simplicity and peace
Grey	→	Symbol of supremacy
Green	→	Symbol of growth, prosperity, hope, freshness
Blue	→	Symbol of prosperity, well-being, manliness
Black	→	Symbol of strength, seriousness
Red	→	Symbol of excitement, passion, intensity
Yellow orange	→	Symbol of auspiciousness, robustness
Pink	→	Symbol of softness, tenderness, good health

2. **Symbols:** Representation of ideas or credo through signs is referred as symbol. It is used to convey a specific characteristic meaning and understanding of a situation. A logo is a printed symbol commonly used by every company or business organization. Its usage in right place enhances the effectiveness of communication in business. Given are some examples for symbols.

Lion	→	Symbol of strength or supremacy
Balance	→	Symbol of justice
Monroe	→	Symbol of sex
ISI mark	→	Symbol of quality
Rolls Royce	→	Symbol of status

3. **Map:** Representing a territory, map is used to convey the space relationship between the places and the geographical information of all kinds such as transport routes, seas, mountains, boundaries, railway lines, climatic conditions, distribution of population, crops, animal and vegetation including sociological factors like religion, literary, health and nutrition. Map can also be used in showing the surface of the moon, position of stars in the sky, solar system, planetary movements, etc.
4. **Cartogram:** Drawing a mark of fun of something is called cartogram. Cartogram represents quantitative information on the basis of region or geography by using symbols like shades, colours, dots, points, crop seeds, plus marks and alike with variables to be shown. Distribution of rainfall, population, density, etc., can clearly be shown comparing regionally or geographically in cartogram.
5. **Table:** An orderly arrangement of data through rows and columns is called **table**. Table is presented with an appropriate heading and number to serve ready-reference. Gainfully, tables are used for presenting: (a) time series data, (b) details of several products or services, (c) demand-supply gap position, (d) values, volume, prices, etc., (e) relationship and ratios, and (f) several relevant parameters. Relationship between any two or more can be obviously depicted in a table. For instance, as the price of a product increases, its quantity demand decreases; and vice versa. It means an inverse relationship exists between the price and the quantity demand of a product. Price, total revenue and marginal revenue relationship is so important to understand the revenue implications of

law of demand. Total sale receipts divided by the number of units sold gives an average revenue, i.e., $AR = TR/Q$. Total revenue is the price multiplied by quantity, i.e., $TR = P \times Q$. Marginal revenue is an additional revenue earned by selling an additional unit. The marginal revenue is, thus, calculated as:

$$MR = \frac{R_2 - R_1}{Q_2 - Q_1} = \frac{\Delta R}{\Delta Q}$$

Data given in Table 3.5 shows clearly the relationship between the average revenue, the marginal revenue and the total receipts.

Table 3.6 Relation between Revenue and Quantity

Average price (₹)	Quantity Demand (units)	Total Revenue (₹)	Marginal Revenue (₹)
10	100	1000	–
9	200	1800	8
8	300	2400	6
7	400	2800	4
6	500	3000	2
5	600	3000	0
4	700	2800	(–)2
3	800	2400	(–)4
2	900	1800	(–)6
1	1000	1000	(–)8

Data presented in Table 3.6 communicates

- The rate of fall in marginal revenue is more than average price
- As long as marginal revenue is positive, total revenue is rising
- At a point where marginal revenue is zero, total revenue is maximum
- Total revenue is decreasing where marginal revenue is negative

6. **Chart:** A device showing non-numerical information is called a chart. It portrays managerial position and relationship in the business organization. Terry defined chart as: "An organization chart is a diagrammatical form which shows the important aspects of an organization including major functions and their respective relationships, channels of supervision and relative authority of each employee who is in-charge of each respective function." In a chart, all the essential particulars are included. Accuracy, clarity and simplicity are the basic features of a good chart. The following are types of charts of an organization.

- Chart showing a vertical line of command flow from top level to the bottom is called a **vertical chart**. Most companies follow this chart.
- Chart showing the lines of command flowing horizontally is known as a **horizontal chart**. No company uses it.
- Chart showing the lines of command of the top executive at the centre and subordinates of this top executive in all directions outward from the centre is called a **circular chart,** also called a **concentric chart**. It shows the status of subordinates at different levels and each person's responsibility. It represents relationship among the existing employees in an organization at its best.
- Chart showing the entire organization and a particular division or section of organization is called a **master chart** and a **supplementary chart** respectively. The former gives a clear picture of organization with major sections or divisions of the organization while the latter shows the details of relationship, authority and duties within the specified area.

A distinction between the graph or diagram and the chart is that the former depicts quantitative relationship while the latter depicts non-numerical relationship. Organization structure, decision-making process, production process, information flow, etc., can best be depicted in a chart. Chart 3.2 shows the hierarchical position and prevailing reporting relationship in a business organization.

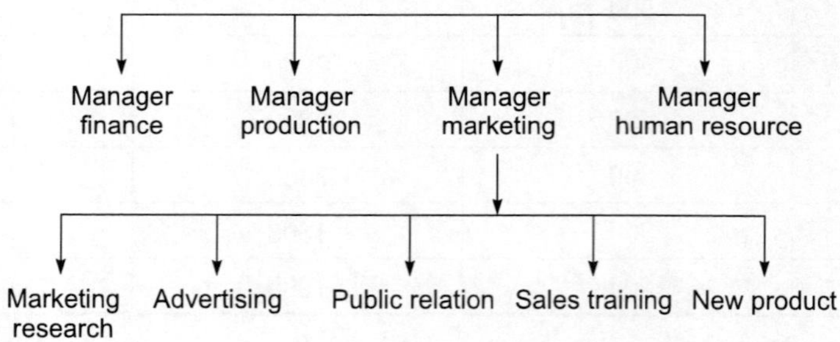

Chart 3.2 Hierarchical Position and Reporting System

7. **Graph and Diagram:** Graph is a symbolic representation of statistical, economic or mathematical data and communicates with accuracy. Graphs are used in all types of reports for conveying the intended message at a glance. For interpreting correctly and honestly, a graph needs the efforts of minds to think wisely and precisely. Drawing used to explain and present numerical data in an attractive, eye-catching and interesting way is known as diagram. Diagram is one-dimensional, two-dimensional, three-dimensional, cubical or cylindrical. Thus, diagram and graph are commonly used to present volumes, proportions, ratios and relationships. They can also be used to present historical or time series data.

   Graphs and diagrams are of different types, ranging from the simpler and ubiquitous to the complicated ones. While presenting data in the form of diagrams and graphs, due attention is paid with regard to: (i) caption or heading, (ii) description of legends, (iii) neatness and proportion, (iv) clarity of composition, (v) class intervals, and (vi) drawing scale. Some illustrations are expressed in the following diagrams and graphs given below.

Whatever, the graphic devices are used to present data, care and caution may be exercised while drawing accurate and precise analysis; otherwise the reader may infer unintended meanings. An expert who knows the merits and demerits of diagrams and graphs representing the given data, meets the important objectives of study.

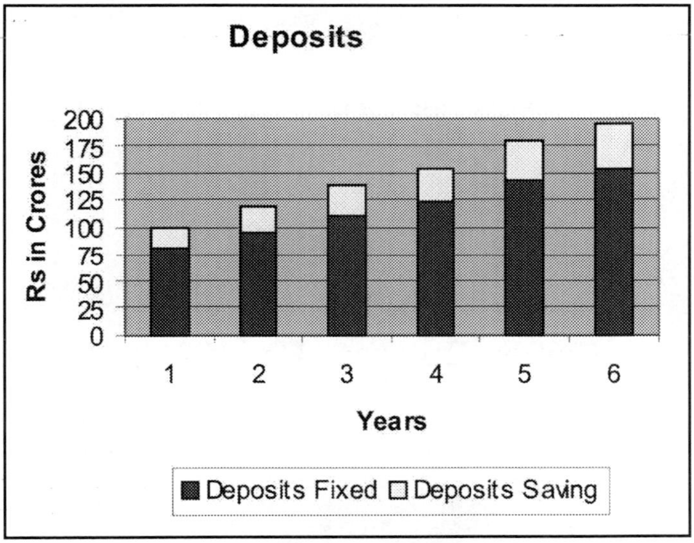

Figure 3.1 Subdivided Bar Diagram showing Deposits

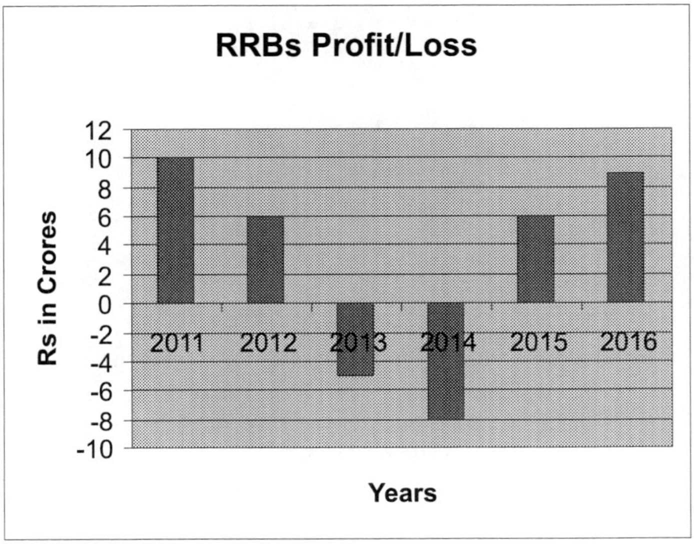

Figure 3.2 Bilateral Bar Diagram showing Profit and Loss of a Bank

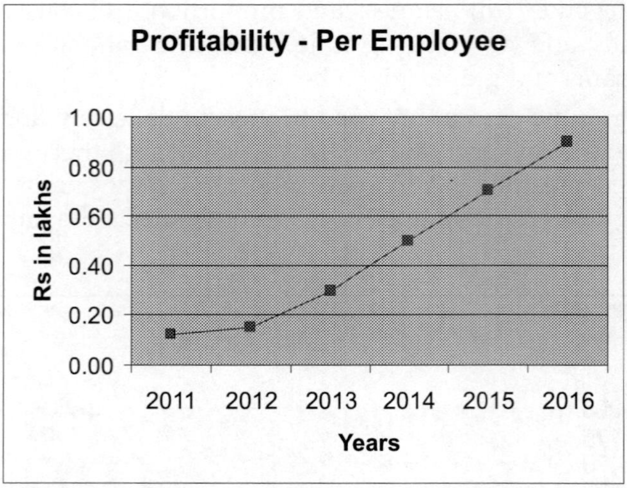

Figure 3.3 Graph showing Per Employee Profit

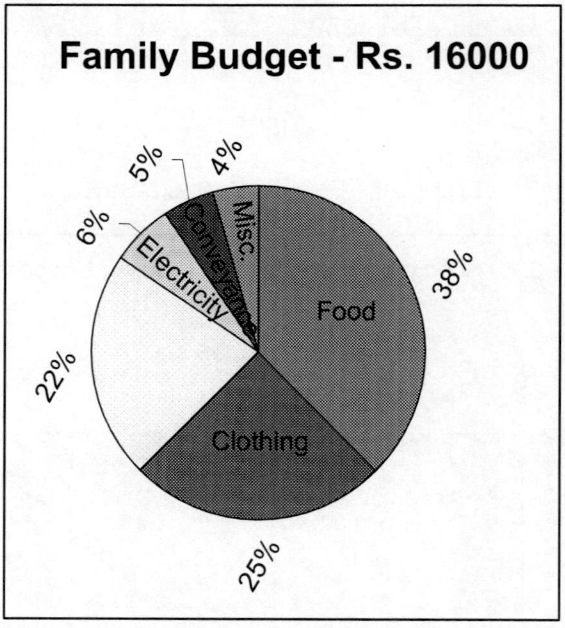

Figure 3.4 Pie Diagram showing Family Budget

QUESTIONS

1. What is written communication? What are the essentials of written communication?
2. State the features, merits and demerits of written communication.
3. What do you mean by oral communication? State the skills to be followed in it.

4. Write merits and demerits of oral communication.
5. What are the principles of oral communication?
6. What is dialogue? Explain it in business communication.
7. Briefly explain various types of written communication.
8. What is house journal? State its objectives and contents.
9. What is notice? Explain the importance of notice board and state the tips for an effective notice board.
10. What is conference? Explain the presentation at a conference.
11. Explain a model note on preparing text of presentation.
12. What is meeting? Why it is necessary?
13. What are minutes? Explain how to write minutes with an illustration.
14. Discuss the conduct and various types of meetings and their relevance.
15. Discuss merits and demerits of a meeting.
16. State merits and demerits of a committee meeting.
17. What are the interview types? Discuss.
18. Explain the candidate's preparation for an interview.
19. State the features, merits and demerits of oral communication.
20. What are the principles and forms of oral communication? Explain them.
21. Compare and contrast written and oral communication
22. Explain why non-verbal communication is important in communication.
23. Discuss briefly various forms of non-verbal communication with suitable examples.
24. Explain the following.
    (a) Memorandum
    (b) Circular
    (c) Manual
    (d) Bulletin
    (e) Face-to-face conversation
    (f) Trademark
    (g) Dialogue
    (h) Signs and signal language
    (i) Essentials of participative member
    (j) Agenda
    (k) Competencies of candidate
    (l) Opportunity in problem

4 CHAPTER

Channels of Communication

LEARNING OBJECTIVES

This chapter will enable you to

- know the areas of channels of communication; and
- understand the significance of grapevine.

INTRODUCTION

The way by which a message flows from the sender to the recipient is referred to as channel of channel. This channel is formal and informal communication flows to satisfy employees' needs of the organization.

4.1 CHANNELS OF COMMUNICATION

In an organization structure of business, the positions of employees must often interact as well as interface in exchange of facts, ideas, opinions, etc., for effective business through proper conduit is called channel. The messages move upward, downward, vertically, horizontally and reciprocally through the formal or informal channel of communication. The way a message flows through a channel from the sender to the recipient is referred to as **channel of communication**. The form or mode through which the message is placed is called **media**. Both channel and media are necessary; their combination together is known as means of communication in an organization.

Communication flows through the channel of network required to establish the soundness of an organization properly. The information flow is determined by its direction. Various types of communication channels are presented in Chart 4.1.

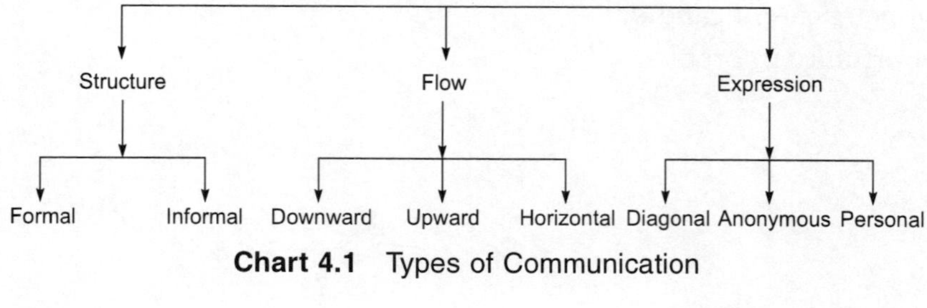

Chart 4.1 Types of Communication

On the basis of structure communication is broadly divided into formal communication and informal communication.

4.2 FORMAL COMMUNICATION

Flow of messages smoothly, orderly and timely in an organization through officially prescribed route with a fixed pattern is referred to as **formal communication**. Its main objective aims at the organization's managerial efficiency. The management of organization frames the governing rules and transmitting ways of communication where it is interdependence, interrelationship between individuals and groups, or within the groups. This frame on formal communication governing the system is meant towards:

- The increase of production and productivity with control measures
- The coordination of activities as well as resource allocation
- The regulation of environment and competing system
- The creation of conducive climate

Precisely, formal communication is applicable to the big business corporations, central and state government departments, multinational corporations, universities, etc. The network of formal communication is of four types in terms of directional flow of information. These are:

- Downward channel
- Upward channel
- Diagonal channel
- Horizontal channel

Features of Formal Communication

- Authority with responsibility and accountability
- Well-defined channel structure for transmission of information
- Vertical downward communication
- Delayed as it needs to pass through various levels in the organization
- Correct information with substantial evidence
- Rigid, inflexible and controlled
- A fixed and proper channel in organizational structure

Merits

- The organization to fix responsibility easily
- To make available information to the right person
- The boss and the subordinates to understand each others' attitudes and behaviour
- The authority to protect senior staff
- To allow anybody to by-pass the rule of proper channel
- To maintain morale and discipline among the employees

Demerits

- Is possible to filter the information
- Cannot be formalized, action-based information
- Increases the workload of line officers
- Entails delay in communicating as it passes through many persons before reaching the right person

On the basis of flow communication in business organization is grouped as shown in Chart 4.2.

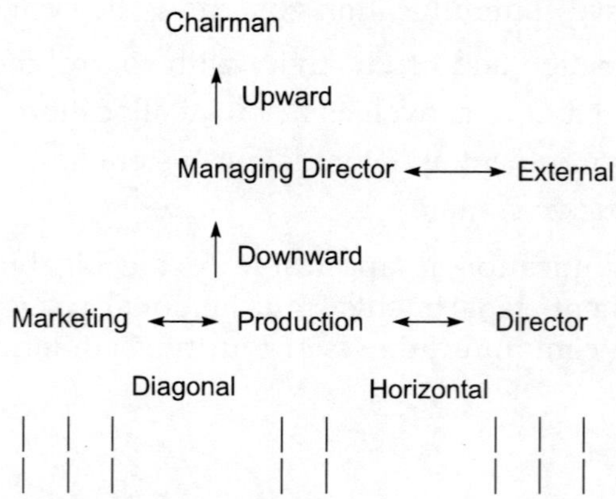

Chart 4.2 Flow of Communication in Organization

4.2.1 Downward Communication

Moving communication downward from the chief executive officer to the lower functionaries through middle management is called **downward communication,** also called **top-down communication**. Information involved for communicating in downward communication channel is both of direction and controlling nature, and includes all the official messages. It passes through written (orders, reports, rules, instructions, manuals, policy directives, etc.) in the form of folders, manuals, periodical reports, bulletins, posters, letters, memos, etc.) or oral in the form of interviews, public address system, conferences, meetings, mechanical devices like telephone, face-to-face conversation, etc. Here, a scalar chain is followed. Business goals, business priorities, motivational letters, work related instructions, newsletters, manager's desk letters, etc., are the major issues that follow in downward communication.

The purpose for which downward communication is required: (a) to get things done, (b) to prepare for changes, (c) to discourage misinformation, and (d) to let the people feel the price of being well informed. The motives in using downward communication are as:

- Instructs about a specific task
- Designs a product

- Supplies feedback to employees about their performance
- Motivates and develops high morale among the employees
- Informs about organizing policies, orders, decisions, goals, etc.
- Creates a sense of belonging to the organization

An effective downward communication makes employees know about their task of work – how to do, when to do, where do to, etc. This obviously creates positive trend in the minds of employees in achieving organization's objectives and thereby making them feel a sense of identification in organization. One should keep in mind that the instructions are simple and carefully explained as most of the persons at lower levels of hierarchy may not have sufficient education and knowledge. While moving information downward, there may occur a loss of information due to misinterpretation, lack of understanding, neglect, delay and distortion particularly in organizations with a long channel.

In a rapidly changing environment in order to ensure the information moves fast without loss, a direct approach in the form of cluster channel is preferred. This provides an opportunity to seek clarification and avoids loss of information. Computer networks in the organizations makes flow of information easy free of delay and distortion. Chart 5.3 shows downward communication channel.

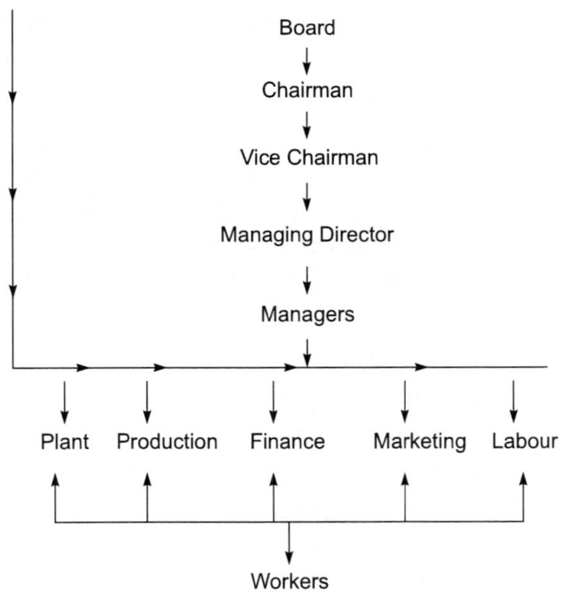

Chart 4.3 Downward Communication Channel

Downward communication is the first type of directional flow of communication carried officially. The media used in downward communication are orders, memos, instructions, manuals, explanations, house journal, office orders and notices, circulars, brochures, bulletins, handbooks, posters, telephone, etc. A combination of written and oral (face-to-face) media is always preferred to operate rapidly with maximum validity.

4.2.2 Upward Communication

Vertical communication is both downward and upward. Upward channel permits to know the rational and emotional reactions of the message passed downward. It implies a two-way communication effect.

Communication moving from the bottom to the top levels is called **upward communication**. It moves from the employees to the supervisors, supervisors to managers, managers to executives, regional managers to general managers; and also from the branches to the regional offices, regional offices to zonal offices, zonal offices to head office. Employees' suggestions, market reports, performance reports, feedback on new products and requests for facilities are the issues that come up in upward communication. This communication is non-directive; and primarily of reporting nature, i.e., feedback. The management knows the acceptance or rejection of rational and emotional reactions of the message passed down and also the achievement of subordinates' work progress. The management of organization encourages a free-flow of upward communication because it is important for the following reasons:

- Provides useful information so as to make decisions
- Serves growth and development of democratic leadership
- Motivates and encourages team spirit
- Promotes loyalty, honesty and participative attitude for effective functioning
- Conveys feelings of subordinates about the job and company
- Facilitates an effective inbuilt feedback mechanism

The information available in upward communication is of two types, namely: (a) personal information about the performance, views, ideas which is vital for employees relations and morale, and (b) technical feedback which is key aspect for smooth working of organization. In Chart 4.4 is shown upward Communication channel. Most business organizations have this upward channel to encourage and ensure upward movement of communication for the following information.

- Periodical review meetings with individuals and groups
- Reporting system existing in the organization
- Matters related to making ideas move forward
- Matters concerning the organizational personnel
- Matters concerning grievances and complaints
- Open-door policy providing every employee access to authority
- Comments and reactions
- Matters concerning moral surveys
- Matters concerning suggestions
- Matters concerning round table discussions
- Matters concerning performance appraisal and accomplishment of employees
- Matters concerning rumours of which employees are aware
- Exit interviews with employees who are leaving the organization

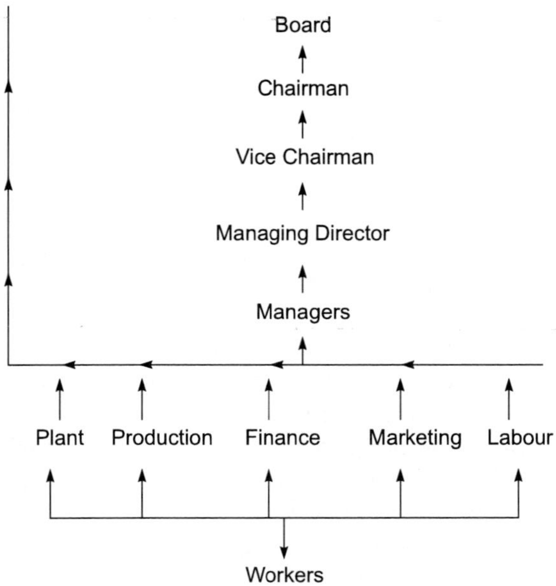

Chart 4.4 Upward Communication Channel

Merits

- Addressing the subordinates' grievances at the earliest
- Providing information for decisions-making
- Developing democracy and leadership in the workplace
- Promoting a sense of loyalty and respect in the employees
- Acting as a device for having ideas of employees and their suggestions
- Providing an opportunity to employees to feel free to convey opinions to the management

Demerits

- Ignores the subordinate's information by superiors
- Distorts information
- Creates problem when the top executives are unwilling to listen to grievances and readdressing them
- Consumes a lot of time

Subordinates, in fact, have to get initiative in responding to the information received. Communication is not simply downward but involves both transmission and reception. In practice, there are several circumstances in which subordinates are reluctant to communicate upward. The reasons for this are:

- Lack of confidence in superiors
- Lack of common sharing

- Lack of ability
- Fear of critic
- Lack of self-confidence
- Distrust due to superior's bossism
- Non-listening attitude of superiors
- Physical distance

4.2.3 Horizontal Communication

Passing on information between peers, i.e., persons of equal status in an organization is called **horizontal communication**. It was developed by French management pioneer, Henry Fayol in 1916. He styled this communication as a 'bridge' of organizational communication between one superior and the other making possible direct exchange of information. This communication is also called lateral communication, cross-wise communication, inter-scalar communication and sideways communication. The sender and the receiver of message may be in the same department or different department with the motto of coordinating their activities.

Features

- It takes place within or outside an organization between the peers
- It exchanges messages openly, freely and frankly
- It is based on common understanding
- It coordinates the function (downward flow is authoritative flow of messages and upward communication provides feedback on operational performance)
- It is both formal and informal (speed, quick decisions and readiness to accept)
- It is applicable in big business organizations including transnational corporations

The focus of horizontal communication is on:

- Exchange of information about the activities, process and progress
- Discussion of plans and problems, review, conflict issues
- Coordinating issues
- Finding solutions to the problem through brainstorming
- Friendly give and take advice
- Social support among peers

Merits

- To coordinate the activities of different departments/ persons
- To avoid duplication and thus reduce waste of time, money, material and labour
- To faster, accurate and speedily sending the messages than vertical communication

Demerits

- Gives possible scope for arising difference in opinions among the executives which, in turn, has adverse impact on productivity and efficiency of organization
- Does not give due importance to the message
- Does not have any control over the receiver of message

4.2.4 Diagonal Communication

A communication between two or more persons who are neither in the same section nor on the same hierarchical level of organization in different sections is called **diagonal communication**. It is a short-circuiting channel and direct passing of information which saves considerable amount of time, money and efforts. The need for diagonal communication does arise because (a) the other system of communication fails to convey the information effectively, and (b) the person or persons of a group are neither under the direct control and supervision nor subject to the authority of the functional heads of supervisors in hierarchy.

In conglomeration where communication between the parent company and its subsidiaries, the diagonal communication channel can be adopted. This communication channel can be effectively used in the multinational and multi-market business organizations which have multiple line operations in a wider geographical area or number of countries. Another area where this channel can effectively be used is that between plants spreading across a wide geographical area within each product group and among various product groups. It is only media in a heterogeneous group of business organizations. Flow of information from the salesman to the finance manger is an example. It is a top-to-bottom as well as bottom-to-top exercise. Performance budgeting of an organization is a typical example to a two-way process of communication.

On the basis of expression, communication is classified into written communication and oral communication.

4.3 ANONYMOUS COMMUNICATION

Anonymous or pseudonymous letter which is under false name(s) plays a role in communication. The name of author does not disclose its identity to everyone except to whom the letter is addressed. For many crimes often clues came out as anonymous sources. The effective working of departments such as customs, excise, police, anti-corruption, etc., to a greater extent, depends upon the receipt of anonymous calls or letters giving valuable information. Further instances are that we often see letters to the editors in a newspaper like 'A harassed in-laws', 'A cricket lover', etc. These letters are unsigned or unnamed.

4.4 PERSONAL COMMUNICATION

The communication that takes place between any two individuals be it in a family, group, community or even an organization in an individual capacity informally. Since privacy prevails in personal communication; it takes the form of personal letters, personal telephone calls, conversations, one-to-one meetings or e-mail messages. It is purely private in nature and nothing is official. It is private and confidential conversation between two individuals, hence it is termed tête-à-tête.

4.5 THREE-PHASE COMMUNICATION

Communication at the scalar level is another approach consisting of inter-scalar, intro-scalar and extra-organizational.

1. The two-way communication is also referred to as inter-scalar communication. Information flows between different levels of authority – upward communication and downward communication.
2. If information travels between two departmental managers or any two or more persons having equal relationship, it is termed intra-scalar communication. This communication increases understanding, accentuates group unity, speeds up action, aids morale and provides supplementary information. This communication tends to weaken the organization if it is over-emphasized to serve the interests of a particular management level rather than the general interest.
3. Flow of information between outside the company and the employees within the company is termed extra-organizational communication.

4.6 CONSENSUS

Communication through an understanding and agreement of unanimous opinion is called **consensus**. Different group of people and different categories of employees in an organization are sure to have different interests; each group naturally wants decisions benefiting its members. It is natural that each group has resentment on other when a decision or policy is implemented. For instance, a decision taken to be implemented certainly affects the working and service conditions of employees. Here, both the management and the employees make use of channel provided by the committees. On the part of management, there must be willingness, understanding and patience to prepare the material for discussion so as to suit the understanding of the employees' responsibilities. On the part of the employees' representatives, there must be courage, knowledge and understanding to discuss matters usefully. Both sides must be skilled in the art of persuasion. Thus, consensus on all important matters and major changes creates a sense of participation to help develop motivation and high morale. Thus, a consensus needs to be arrived at by organizing meetings with a full discussion for a peaceful negotiation and understanding. The organization as a unit has to function with all the groups pooling their efforts towards the goal on consensus which is so essential.

4.7 INFORMAL COMMUNICATION

Information passing not in accordance with any existing formalities and regulations of an organization is called **informal communication**. It is also called grapevine, because it denotes informal means of circulating information or gossip. Management of organizations can use this channel for effective and speedy communication of messages. In view of this, certain messages are not suitable to circulate by formal means. Koontz and Donnell said, "the most effective communication results when the managers utilize informal organization to supplement the communication channels of the formal organization." Most of this communication is oral which supplements formal communication. Informal communication is simple, glance, gesture, smile or mere silence. It helps in gathering information and preserving in a cordial and friendly atmosphere in the organization of industry and commerce.

Merits

- Spreads quickly
- Is transmitted without any difficulty
- Helps both the sender and the receiver to exchange information freely
- Promotes sound cooperation among the employees
- Passes any amount of information

Demerits

- It is not in order
- It carries inaccurate information very often and hence no use
- It may create a lot of confusion or misunderstanding among employees
- It is difficult to fix responsibility

4.8 GRAPEVINE

The word, grapevine originated during the Civil War period in America where telephones were strung loosely from tree-to-tree in vine like fashion. Unclear and confused messages, that often come forward is known as **grapevine**. The message is spread by gossip and rumours. It is a kind of informal communication which prevails in the organizations and travels through informal networks. It often travels faster than formal messages and also gets, sometimes, more powerful and becomes more receptive than the formal communication. Grapevine as an effective communication tool is often put to the beneficial use by the prudent business management in announcement of information of new products or bonus to workers, etc., which come into widespread circulation quickly as well as satisfactorily.

Grapevine co-exists with the formal structure. It is fact that informal channel cannot be predicted and designed. As such, it cannot be deliberately planned and structured along with the formal organization. It is because of the fact that grapevine is more a product of situation than it is of person. The management in order to know a possible reaction to a proposed plan or decision, may plant a bit of information in grapevine. An organization should use it in a constructive way for making sound decision as it moves so fast. Davis has stated that under a given situation and motivation, anyone tends to become active on grapevine. Grapevine is of four types. These are as:

- Single strand (individual communicates with other individuals through intervening persons)
- Gossip (individual communicates non-selectively)
- Probability (individual communicates randomly with other individuals)
- Cluster (individual communicates with only those individuals whom he trusts)

Of the four informal networks, the cluster is the most popular. The operation of grapevine as a cluster chain is illustrated in Chart 4.5.

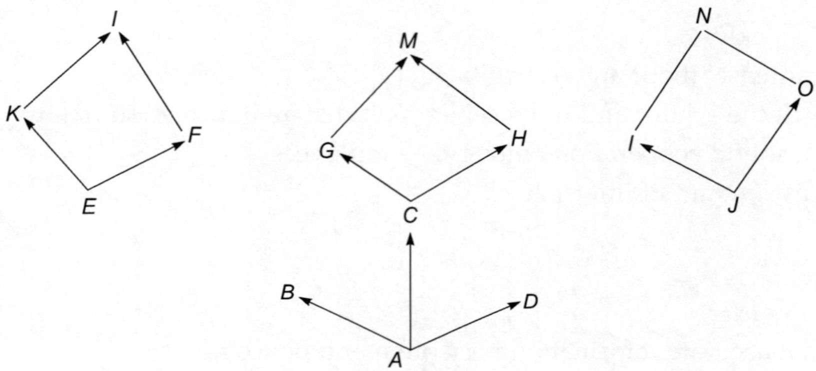

Chart 4.5 Cluster Chain

In Chart 4.5, A tells something to three of his well-known persons who, in turn, tell something to two of their (three persons) known persons. The two persons tell something to only one of their known persons. The receiving persons are gradually reduced in number. The reason is when the information becomes stale and those who know it do not retransmit. Remember, only a few persons are active in the grapevine system of communication. The active communicators are known as liaison agents. The characteristic features of grapevine are:

- Grapevine often works with amazing speed in transmission
- It has no definite pattern
- It does fill gaps left by ineffective formal communication
- It is generally related to the working place
- It is random diffusion, i.e., passed in unorganized fashion
- It is usually downward or sideway
- It works effectively and rapidly irrespective of consequences

As one of the benefits, grapevine is an effective tool for developing corporate identity, building team-work and motivating employees. It supplements formal communication channels to make the total communication system as effective as possible. A deep psychological need of employees to talk about their jobs and their company is being reflected in a lively grapevine as life interest.

Keith Davis in his paper "Care and Cultivation of the Corporate Grapevine" stated: "Without grapevine, the company would literally be sick." Grapevine information is accurate about 75 per cent and the remaining 25 per cent is inaccurate which forms rumour. It is dangerous because of its potential to fish out in troubled waters. See Exhibit 4.1 which explains how major portion of grapevine may be true but inaccurate part may make the whole grapevine meaningless.

Exhibit 4.1 Examples Showing how Grapevine becomes Meaningless

1. On one grapevine, a story about a clerk marrying the General Manager's daughter was true with regard to his getting married, the date, the location and other details. The one wrong detail in this 90 per cent accurate story was that the woman was not the General Manager's daughter but only happened to have the same last name. This one wrong point made the whole communication wrong in general meaning even though it was 90 per cent accurate in details.
2. On Pulse Polio Day, i.e., December 22, 2008 in the state of Tamil Nadu rumour triggered like this: A TV channel said that after administering polio drops to two four-month old boys, they died. This spread across the state like fire and led the parents thronging many hospitals in panic, sporadic incidents of stone-throwing and road blockades across the state. Then doctors checked the children on whom polio drops were administered and found that one child died around 10 a.m. not due to polio drops at the D.G. Pudur Primary Health Centre but due to hydrocephalus (abnormal accumulation of cerebrospinal fluid in the brain) who underwent a surgery at a private hospital in Coimbatore two months ago. Doctors asserted this on examining 188 children on whom polio drops were administered at that health centre. Irate public broke chairs and tables, tore up patient registers and even damaged few equipment at the Government hospital in Salem. Doctors fled the scene and heavy police was rushed to the hospital to bring the situation under control. At some places, even doctors used the public address system to convince that the polio drops were safe. This shows how speedily the rumour spread creating ambiguity and anxiety among the parents.

It is understood from these examples that even though the grapevine tends to carry the truth, it rarely carries the whole truth. However, rumour serves the purpose of:

- Structuring and reducing anxiety
- Making sense of limited information
- Signaling sender's status or power that he is the only person possessing the information

Can the management eliminate rumours? The answer is no! Instead; the management must live with them and try to minimize the adverse consequences limiting their range and impact. Some tips for effective management of rumours are:

- Get the root of rumour and examine it with facts
- Announce schedules for making important decisions
- Explain decisions to those who appear inconsistent
- Identify the rumour-mongers and discipline them
- Take the assistance of labour union to fight rumours

The differences between formal and informal communication channels are given in Table 4.1.

Table 4.1 Comparison on between Formal and Informal Communication Channels

Formal Communication	Informal Communication
Emerges out of formal organizational relationship	Emerges out of social interactions among people
Channels of communication are prescribed	Channels of communication depend upon individuals' relationships
More rigid as need no deviations to follow	Quite flexible because nothing is prescribed
Speed of message travel is slow due to formalization	Message travels faster
Chances of message distortion are low	Messages are often distorted
Treated as authentic	Not authentic even if the message is correct

QUESTIONS

1. Draw a sketch of business organization's channels of communication and explain them in brief.
2. What is formal communication? State its features, merits and demerits.
3. What is grapevine? State its features. Illustrate how a major portion of grapevine is true, but less portion untrue may make the whole grapevine meaningless.
4. What is downward communication? State its purposes. Draw an illustrative of downward communication channel.
5. Explain the upward channel communication with a suitable sketch and state its merits and demerits.
6. What is lateral communication? Mention its merits and demerits.
7. Distinguish between formal and informal communication channels.
8. Explain the following:
   (a) Diagonal communication
   (b) Cluster chain
   (c) Inter- and extra-communication
   (d) Three-phase communication

5 CHAPTER

Corporate and Mass Communication

"Reading makes a full man, conference a ready man and writing an exact man."

— **Bacon**

Learning Objectives

This chapter will enable you to

- know the relevance and significance of letters in business;
- know presentation and punctuation of business letter;
- describe the layout of business letter; and
- know the effects of media modes on business.

INTRODUCTION

By very nature, mass communication addresses through its channel—public speaking, newspapers, magazines and journals, radio, television, dotcoms, etc. Each of these calls for distinct skills.

5.1 CORPORATE COMMUNICATION

Generation of communication in a business organization and making it reach its target population say financiers, suppliers and all stakeholders is termed **corporate communication**. It covers a corporate identify, image building, media relations, advertising and intended message to the all the concerned ones. To develop effective communication in the corporation sector whose arena of business operations are beyond the boundaries of a country, one certainly needs to develop practical thinking and writing skills. Writing facilitates one's own ability to recognize instances of faulty thinking like inconsistency and unproductive message to communicate. Knowing the relevance of communication in the corporate sector, the American Universities introduced paper on the subject of 'Corporate Communication and Indian Companies', for instance, Hindustan Lever, had the Department of Corporate Communication.

Thinking is an artistic skill that must be learnt. Creative thinking is not a talent but is a skill which can be obtained through learning. It empowers people to add strength to their educational abilities for improving teamwork, productivity and appropriate business profits. Core thinking skills are the specific cognitive operations on sound basis in innovation and theoretical literature in terms of:

1. Comparing
2. Classifying
3. Induction
4. Deduction
5. Error analysis
6. Constructing support
7. Analyzing perspectives
8. Invention/investigation
9. Decision making
10. Problem solving

In the process of thinking with these aspects, one can improve healthy practical skills in problem-solving. Here, one should remember that mind is like a knife when it is sharpened; but it is more effective in solving the problem.

A business organization needs to make special efforts to take care of its relations with the public internally and externally. To maintain the good relations, it has got its visibility and maintains high profile in the competitive world with the other competing organizations. Many organizations can perform the task of maintaining good relations with public through their public relations department. Sam Black has defined public relations as: "The establishment of two-way communication to resolve conflicts of interest by seeking common ground of mutual interest based on truth, knowledge and full information."

For the aspect of marketing, a manufacturer has to communicate to his sales and delivery staff, servicing of experts, wholesale and retail agents, importers, exports and overseas agents, retailers of line chain-store owners, departmental stores and down to the smallest road-side stall-keepers. Success or failure of products distribution is being influenced by the way the producers make packaging and arrange printers, transport contractors, advertising agents and media owners. Opinion of leaders, consumers and government officials are more concerned too. Yet marketing is not only the activity of a manufacturing organization. Apart from marketing activity, the business organization is also concerned with the finances, people (that need education plus skills) for recruitment and cooperation of various public services including non-commercial and non-profit organization to maintain good relations. Thus, public relations can be described as: "The inward and outward seeing eye."

All the activities of public relations depend upon two elements of action and expression; begin with good acts and express with good communication. Implicitly, the public relations are an art and technique of promoting various activities. These activities can be carried out by the corporations, organizations, government and individuals.

The objectives of public relations are focused on building and maintaining awareness, achieving acceptance, winning trust, cooperation and recognition, cultivating understanding. The goodwill of public relations depends upon its conduct and relations with others along with its products and services. The best way to appreciate public relations of varied type of organizations is to list them. For instance, the public relations for a cosmetics manufacturer are:

1. Beauty parlours
2. Whole sales
3. Retailers
4. Staff
5. Trade unions
6. Community around the factory
7. Laboratories and testing organizations
8. Food and drugs administration
9. Consumer guidance society
10. Doctors
11. Department of chemistry in colleges
12. Government department/local authorities

5.1.1 Business Letter

In corporate communication, both internal and external communication is in the form of business letter.

Modern business letters are becoming sophisticated like modern business machines. Successful business letter-writing is an art, and the writer is a man of devotion to business. Build arguments brick by brick to reinforce truth with truth. In a way, dresses the business letter and addresses in making a real impressive letter to mesmerize the receiver what the sender wants. Wren and Martin viewed letter as: "The art of letter writing is not merely an ornamental accomplishment, but something that every educated person must acquire for practical reasons." John B. Opdycke beautifully described the business letter:

I am the letter
I am the bearer of the tidings of great joy
I am the cavalier of culture
I am the courier of commerce
I am the ambassador of production
I am the winged mercury of industry
I am the plenipotentiary of finance
I am the alpha and omega of big business
I am the bearer of tidings of grave import
I am the letter

Views of some authors on business letter are:

Cicero says "A letter does not blush."

Charles E. Elliot states that letter is: "Carrier of News and Knowledge,
Instrument of Trade and Industry
Promotion of Mutual Acquaintance,
Peace of goodwill among Men and Nations"

James J. Howell expresses that "the letters are the Soul of trade".

5.1.2 ABCD of Letter

Rikhab Chand Jain and Subhkaran Dugar said on writing letter: "As one writes, so one reads. So one is careful enough to note the salient features of communication masterpiece or good writing. In this process, one can have insight of how the writer has written letter so well. On experienced lessons, adopt the same in an appropriate situation while he has opportunity to write." What is needed is the ability in expressing clear ideas, simple language and precise terms. So, in writing business letters, follow the ABCD of letter. Acronym of ABCD stands as: A for Accuracy, B for Brevity, C for Clarity and D for Dignity. The writer keeps this spirit in mind and should develop an efficient business letter without faults. Keep away the overused and shopworn phrases to aim at the ABCD letter and its crispness.

Organizations of business, bank, hotel, hospital, college, department of government, etc., dealing with people curiously and obviously follow written correspondence for enquiries, offers, quotations, announcements, invitations, price lists, due notices, new arrivals, clearances and disposals, recoveries and reminders, orders and host of other activities of everyday relevance. Business is corresponded through writing to customers, branches, auditors, suppliers, bankers, media persons, employees, shareholders and others with whom it has a business relationship. Written communication has wide reach covering various business aspects – production, finance, marketing and human resource development and geographical area. The merits of written communication outweigh its demerits; hence it is imperative for any business whose operations are widely spread out.

5.1.3 Essentials of Good Business Letter

Writer to be said good has to look at certain standards from the angle point of language, content, context, length, structure, layout, taste, tone, impact and purpose in addition to accuracy, brevity, clarity and dignity (ABCD) of letter. A quality of letter is good in many counts while undesirable features put a letter into a poor light. But for this, conscious efforts, concerted action and correspondence prudence is the call of the day to improve consciously a good letter with impressiveness and appearance. The efforts in writing a good letter are:

- Creating goodwill and favourable impressions
- Attracting and creating interest
- Wooing customers
- Reaching prospects
- Building relationships

A letter addressed to the target, must also address the business prospects, viz., target sales, effective salesperson, strengthening connection and providing details to the existing customers, maintaining relationship, dispelling misinformation, making announcements, sharing relevant information, keeping in touch with people who matter and creating goodwill. The essentials to make a business letter are given below:

1. **Plan:** Plan before writing anything about the purpose and the expectation of the receiver and the sender, i.e., receiver's response makes sure of inclusion of all the relevant information in a logical order and in good structure. The contents of letter differ from case to case, situation to situation, time to time, and also in its contents intending to transmit favourable, neutral, unfavourable or persuasive nature. Therefore, planning renders writing an effective letter. The writer must bring all the relevant and connected points together, and arrange them logically and systematically; expressing proper arrangement of thoughts in writing. Answer one question in one sentence.
2. **Purpose:** Aim of writing a letter is to serve the underlying motto for which it is intended. Creating an impact calls for establishing an appropriate wavelength – skill, knowledge, status and comprehensiveness of the addressee with coherence in use of words, phrases and clauses clearly.
3. **Brevity:** An important attribute of a good letter is brevity. The time essence is crucial as the addressee may not have unlimited time at his disposal to spare adequate time towards reading, re-reading and drawing a message in its entirety. Whatever be its merits, a long letter is often kept aside for later reading. Without scarifying completeness and comprehensiveness, a letter should stand to convey what it is meant for. See Exhibit 5.1 for brevity of letter with meaningful message.

Exhibit 5.1 Brevity is Best

The style of writing varies from person to person. Classic example for people who can communicate effectively even with minimum words is that of a letter from the great French writer, Victor Hugo and the reply to it from his publisher. It is as:
Hugo's letter was just "?"
He wanted to know how his newly published novel was faring in the market.
The publisher's reply was just "!"
Understandably, it would be virtually impossible for anyone to communicate so effectively and yet be so brief. To be brief and yet convey effectively is indeed a fine art of effective communication.

4. **Language:** Words and ideas are raw material. The writer communicates messages through the vehicle of language (see Exhibit 5.2 selecting the right word). Grammatical errors and spelling mistakes create a poor impression in the minds of readers, so draft the letter carefully. With care choose the right words and avoid repetition to make a writing and possession of what is called good style. The artist considers, selects and blends tints to get strength and delicacy in a finished picture. So also, the writer is with words. See Exhibit 5.2 and 5.3 on using words.

Exhibit 5.2 **How to Select the Right Word**

A farmer couple in a British countryside farmhouse was discussing the food to be served to the expected guests next morning. The farmer told his wife, "Prepare omelette for breakfast and bacon for dinner." As soon as he said this, the pig which was in the corner started jumping around shrieking. The hen, on noticing this, asks the pig, "What is wrong?" The pig laments, "Didn't you hear, they are planning to have you for tomorrow's dinner. The hen says, "So what?" They are having omelette for breakfast, which means I have to sacrifice my eggs and yet I am not that perturbed." In response, the pig makes an agonizing remark, "My sacrifice is a lot more than yours. Yours is participation, but mine is involvement."

Exhibit 5.3 **How to Play with Words**

Words have a meaning, both in absolute and relative sense. It is often possible to convey a powerful message by grouping together the thought and words. For example,
Lies, Damn Lies, Statistics
By this line, one gets a hint about statistics that is the superlative degree of lies.

5. **Appeal:** A business letter should be elegant which means taste, beauty, decenc and empathy and appealing to the reader's sensibilities. It ensures an appeal c aesthetics. Mistakes and corrections, striking, overwriting, improper ink flow unintended gaps, etc., are deficiencies of a good business letter appeal. The appea of letter should be thoughtfulness to visualize the reaction of the reader. In othe words, the business letter should attach the feelings and interests of readers.
6. **Style:** The way of presenting things or impression and manner of writing lette with proper use of words in proper places refers to style. The style of writin should create a conscious impact and bring to bear a reader's stamp on the lette An individual identifies his style of writing a letter if he is reading regularl letters emanating from a particular source. The simple, informal, thoughtful an focused style of writing scores high in building up a rapport with the reade Good writing style of letter implies the proper use of idioms and expressions and encompasses politeness or courtesy. The writer should not hesitate even t apologize for occurrence of omissions or errors.
7. **Positive Approach:** The ultimate aim of a business letter is to create a positive an friendly atmosphere motivating the readers to act or respond. Towards this, th writer with his proper imaginative frame of mind can write really a good lette presenting thoughts into words synchronizing in the context. It is viewed that positive approach in writing a letter generates and creates goodwill for the writer This approach does not mean that one has to say 'yes' for everything or anything Since the business has deliberations, say rules, norms and compliances, one canno say 'yes' if it is commercially imprudent. Good letter writing has the followin essentials:

- Variety in writing as it adds spice to writing
- Creativity and clarity
- Ethical and moral standards
- A distinctive style of writing
- Accurate message without misrepresentation and out of context passages
- As short and straightforward as possible retaining the essence of message

A bad letter, on the other hand, with undesirable features can mar the spirit and beauty of the entire letter; and can cause avoidable damage to the reputation of business. Following are the deficiencies of a business letter:

- Poor use of words and expressions
- Lack of clarity
- Incorrect spelling and grammatical errors
- Too short or too lengthy
- Flow of too many ideas in a letter
- Factually incorrect
- Failure to convey the main purpose
- Too many jargons and technical words
- Lack of aesthetic sense
- Use of unfamiliar language
- Absence of personal touch
- Absence of relevant information
- Lack of courtesy
- Written out of context
- Use of poor quality paper, cover, etc.

5.1.4 Punctuation of Business Letter

Punctuation is essential for composition of an idea into a message to be said effective and repose confidence to react. In oral, voice rise and fall, its pauses and stresses make up the punctuation of spoken word. Similarly, in writing business letters, one needs full stops, semicolons, dashes, commas with apostrophes, colons and question marks. A letter requires proper punctuation than a report. The general rules of punctuation are explained below.

1. **Full Stop:** The full stop (.) is the basic mark of punctuation and shows the end of a complete sentence. It is also used in abbreviated form of a word like Co., Pvt., and Ltd. The use of full stop is not practised after the common abbreviations like Mr. or Mrs. Still, the standard books use it. Full stop is not required at the end of each phrase in a list of items in an agenda and also in the words coined by using initials like UNESCO, SAARC, WHO, etc.
2. **Comma:** An absolute element is a word or a group of words which has no grammatical bearing on the rest of the sentence. It must be set off by a comma.

The punctuation mark comma (,) is used to show a shorter pause. Use of comma as in:

- ➢ Between three or more items in a series, say 'intended to visit Delhi, Chennai and Mumbai'.
- ➢ After a salutation as in Sir, and after the complimentary close as in 'Yours faithfully'.
- ➢ To separate the elements of a date as in 'Friday, July 16, 2016' (no comma is required if the month and year are given as July 2016.
- ➢ To separate the elements of an address except the city and the PIN code as in, '1-1-267, Vivekananda Nagar, Anantapur - 515 004'.
- ➢ Adverb or adverbial phrase as in, 'Despite rise in price, many people bought goods'.
- ➢ To mark off in large numbers, beginning with the unit as in, 1,20,00,00,000.
- ➢ Parenthetical need as in, 'please note that', 'for the purpose of records'. Examples are: However, Therefore, Hence, Thus, Besides, etc.
- ➢ Punctuating for clarity as in - 'Outside, the rain was falling in torrents'.

3. **Semicolon:** Semicolon (;) is used after a sentence is completed grammatically, but the sentence continues the same idea since it is not a complete break. It conveys a sense of therefore or hence or so on. An example is that, 'a person has not made a phone call to his messages; but fear he is dissatisfied with his goods'.
4. **Colon:** Colon (:) is used to introduce a list or series or an explanation. The use of colon in a good letter: (i) after the phrases (as follows: the following: given below (:) and (ii) for separating title and subtitle of a book, e.g. (Reforms of Commercial Banks: A Case Study).
5. **Question Mark:** Question mark (?) is used as the terminal punctuation mark in an interrogative sentence. A direct question ends with a question mark while an indirect question does not have a question mark at the end. How many copies of the circular will be needed? I want to know how many copies of the circular will be needed as examples for the above two questions respectively. Some other examples are: Have you seen a devotional cinema last night? How many copies of this book you are required? Is this your pen? If a question is to be rhetorical, i.e., no answer expected, the question mark may be replaced by exclamation mark as in, was ever a man so tortured!
6. **Apostrophe:** The function of apostrophe (') is used in (a) possessive, and (b) contractive approach. In case of possessive apostrophe, it is used:
   - ➢ For singular nouns as in – company's product
   - ➢ For plural nouns which do not end with 's' as in - children's park, men's tailor, women's hostel
   - ➢ For plural nouns that end with 's' as in – companies' representative, workers' requirements. Adjectives as in – his, its, and pronouns as in hers, yours, theirs do not have any apostrophe. In complimentary close of letter, no apostrophe as in 'yours faithfully'

- ➢ In phrases as in – a month's holiday, half an hour's interval, sixty days' credit, a week's day course program
- ➢ In possessive compounds as in – father-in-law's house

In case of contractive apostrophe, it is used only in oral communication and not in formal business writing like letters, reports and minutes. It is used to indicate that letters have been dropped as in - it's (it is), can't (cannot), we'll (we shall/ will) don't (do not), etc.

7. **Hyphen:** A short stroke (-) is used to join two parts of a word or phrase. The commonly compounded words as in - layout, inputs, outlay, nowadays, etc. and business titles like Vice President, Vice Chairman, Vice Chancellor, Deputy Governor, Deputy Secretary, etc., are not hyphenated. The compound adjective is hyphenated as in cases such as attitude-orientated, sales-oriented, etc. Some examples are: Co-exit, Co-operation, Co-education, Co-terminus, Anti-government and Ex-employer. Hyphen is used to avoid a perplexing combination of letters as in re-evaluate (reevaluate).
8. **Parentheses:** Parentheses ( ) are used to express the matter in between them. Received with thanks a sum of 1000 (Rupees one thousand only).
9. **Brackets:** Brackets [ ] denote the enclosed matter as is not part of the original text and is used to mark off the words, sentences and phrases explaining a certain context. For example, Ramu [picking up the telephone directory] does not know his telephone number.
10. **Exclamation Mark:** Exclamation mark (!) shows a strong feeling like surprise, admiration, enthusiasm. It is not in official writing except in sales letters. Some examples are: Stop! Look! Listen! Oh! What a wonder! Alas! Hurry!
11. **Dash:** Dash (—) is used to denote the change of thought or break in continuity of the sentence. Well-wishers, friends and relatives – all left them.
12. **Marks:** Quotation marks ("...") are used to (a) indicate the exact words of the writer or speaker and (b) a word or phrase which is not in common use but has become known among a group of people. Usually, a full stop and also a question mark become part of the quoted sentence. If quotation occurs within a quotation, then use single quotation marks for quotation within the quotation. Some examples are: Who I asked, "Is your boss"? Gunnar Myrdal says "Borrowing of credit a universal phenomenon."
13. **Ellipses:** Ellipses (...) are used to signify the omission of letters or words in sentences. Generally, ellipse consists of three dots with intervening space. "The Reserve Bank of India ... renders services to the public." "... thus ended a great era which..."
14. **Double Commas:** Double comma („) is used to indicate "ditto" or the same. For example:

    May 15, 2017
    " 16, "

15. **Caret:** Caret (^) is used in printing or typing to show where to insert the word or words, phrase, figure, etc., was missed originally.
16. **Prefix:** It is placed in front of a word to add or change its meaning or function. Examples are: de (decode), dis (dishonest), im (impossible), in (inability).
17. **Suffix:** A small part added to the end of a word or stem which changes the meaning and often grammatical function. Examples are: -ness (correctness), -able (predictable), -ly (greatly) and -full (purposeful).
18. **Synonyms:** It means the words that have same meaning or merely the same meaning. For instance, balance and remainder.
19. **Antonyms:** Antonyms mean the words that have opposite meanings. They are formed by adding prefixes like un, dis, im, non, etc. For instance, un (unimportant), un (unpleasant), mis (misplead), dis (disagree), im (impossible) and non (non-semester).
20. **Capitals:** A capital letter is used at:
    - The beginning of a sentence
    - The titles of public officials such as President, Governor, Prime Minister, Chief Minister
    - The official positions and designations in an organization such as General Manager, Chief Accountant, Chairman, etc.
    - The proper nouns – Names of (i) persons, countries, cities, states, rivers; (ii) months and days; (iii) institutions, (iv) festivals/holy days, (v) trains, (vi) ships, (vii) companies
    - The courtesy titles such as Mr., Mrs., Miss, Dr. whether in full or in abbreviated form
    - The first person singular pronoun, I
    - The salutation words such as Dear Sir, Madam
    - The complimentary close only the first word capital, as in 'Yours truly', 'Truly yours'
    - The name of bodies' acronyms NABARD, RBI, IDBI, ICMAI, ICAI, etc.
    - Some words which have a different meaning if written with a capital letter as in - State (organized community with Government), state (condition or plight), Government (governing body), government (governing function), East/West (countries in globe) east/west (direction), Board of Directors (collective decision-making body), board of directors (administration).
21. **Abbreviations:** Use of a shortened or contracted form of a word or phrase for representing the whole is called **abbreviation**. Abbreviations are useful for writing notes, memos of inter-office and other informal papers; but always pronounced in full. For example, Prof. is always read and spoken as Professor and Dr. as Doctor. The use of these words saves time while writing.

    Abbreviations like (i) Mister (Mr.), Doctor (Dr.), (ii) symbols like dollar ($), rupee (Rs.) and (iii) words like Ltd., Inc., Co., Pvt., are common. Every organization has its abbreviations. The use of them in document is meant for public, the layman may not understand them properly. An accepted way is to write the word in full the first time it occurs in the document with abbreviation in brackets and use its abbreviation in the subsequent occurrences. Abbreviation is also used in weights and measures when it follows a figure as: Write 40 kg, and 10 m. When written without figures, it is: forty kilograms and ten meters respectively.

22. **Acronym:** Forming a word from the initial letters of words in a set phrase is called **acronym**. The initial letters of words are written in capitals without full stop as: United Nations Organization (UNO), National Bank for Agriculture and Rural Development (NABARD), Reserve of Bank of India (RBI), International Monetary Fund (IMF), Indian Bank Management (IBM) and World Bank (WB). Some commonly used abbreviations are given as:

Before names:

Smt.	Shrimati
Mr.	Mister
Ms (Messer's)	Messieurs
Mrs.	Mistress

For units of measure:

Cal	Calories
hp	Horse power
hr	Hour
mg	Milligram(s)
mm	Millimeter
min	Minute
sqft	Square foot/feet
doz	Dozen
lb	pound (weight)
Oz	ounce
sec	Second
km	Kilometer
Kw	Kilowatt

Miscellaneous:

a/c	account
ad/advt.	Advertisement
approx.	Approximately
arr.	Arrival (in time tables of railways, etc.)
ave.	Avenue
bldg.	Building
B.F.	Brought forward (in accounts books)
Bros	Brothers (in names of business firms)

C.	Centigrade/Celsius
C.F.	Carried Forward
cf.	Compare
do	Ditto
E. & O.E.	Errors and omissions expected
G.P.O.	General Post Office
ht.	Height
Inc.	Incorporated
MS	Manuscript
Mt.	Mountain
N.B.	Please note (Latin: nota bane)
pl.	Plural
P.T.O.	Please Turn Over
qr.	Quarter
R.S.V.P.	Please reply (Latin: repondez s'il vous plaît)
sec.	Secretary
viz.	Namely (Latin: videlicet)
wt.	Weight
yr(s)	Year(s)

(Please refer to a good dictionary, if necessary, for more abbreviations)

5.1.5 Appearance of Business Letter

A business letter covers various accepted parts with external and internal features by custom that are convenient to handle and process the correspondence in the office of organization. Parts of a letter are outside, inside, top, bottom, middle, left, right, first page, second page, enclosures and annexure. Each one has certain significance and carries a definite place in letter writing. A letter must impress visually before it is read as the first impression is the best impression. It is just like a person's clothes and general appearance to create first impression which is likely to be long lasting, so also the paper and envelope used in correspondence certainly produce an initial effect. Letter appearance hinges upon all the things that make up the letter. Some are:

1. **Stationery** must be of good quality preferably using white paper with black print for the heading. Typing must be neat with equal spacing between words, between lines, double spacing between paragraphs and between different parts of the letter without corrections or cancellations. Leave margin one-and-a-half inch on the left, one inch on the top and right, and at least one inch at the bottom.
2. **Paragraphing** is pleasing appearance necessary for breaking a composition into readable, logical and progressive units. It is important for appearance and composition. Usually, a letter must have three to four paragraphs. They are:

- ➢ A short opening paragraph may have only one or two sentences
- ➢ One or two longer middle paragraphs carrying the main message or text of the letter
- ➢ A short closing paragraph may be only one sentence

3. **Folding** of letter must be neat. If it is badly folded, it makes a poor impression. The folded letter size must be such that it fits in the envelope leaving enough space for cutting the envelope open by the receiver.
4. **Envelope address** is typed half-way down and one-third inward on the envelope from the left to ensure the post-office franking or stamping. The appearance of address is as important as that of the letter because it is first seen before the letter.

5.1.6 Parts of Business Letter

Customs and convenience have laid certain requirements and specifications as parts of a letter. Different locations are fixed for different parts on the sheet and a slight variation from left to right in the different layout styles and order of appearance from top to bottom is the same in all styles. The main parts of a letter are heading, date, inside address, salutation, complimentary closure and signature. Reference number, delivery mode, subject line, attention line, enclosures, courtesy, sender's and typist's initials are also included for serving the needs of a letter.

1. **Heading:** Heading announces the name and conduct of business, whether a college, bank, company, transport agency, trading firm, building construction, Department of State or Central Government, an insurance company, etc., and constitution (public or private). Also mention the line of business, period of establishment, location of Head Office or Registered Office, telephone number, branch, zone, Section, Fax number and e-mail address on the top of letter pad along with a logo of business. Details will be furnished in bilingual if it is a public sector undertaking as per the Official Language Policy. Generally, the name and logo are covered at the top and the address, etc., are given at the bottom. Much thought and efforts are involved in design and selection of letter head as it has a potential to create favourable impression.
2. **Date:** Every letter must have two lines space below the heading on the right for date. It is an important point of reference for further correspondence. Usual practice of placing date is as: 16-05-2017 or May 16, 2017 or 16 May, 2017. Writing sequence of date, month and year in figures varies from country to country. In United States of America, the practice is to write month first and then date and year written as 05-16-2017. In India and United Kingdom, it is understood as May 16, 2017.
3. **Reference Number:** Reference number gives the letter number, file number and other filing details with which it can easily be located among the office records. It is placed on the left opposite to date. Usually, it is written as:

   Your reference
   Our reference
   Reference number

4. **Inside Address:** Receiver address by name or by designation is placed inside the letter without the full postal address. The word 'To' before the address is outdated and avoid it for greater elegance. When the letter is addressed by name, it is essential to write the name exactly as the person spells it. If the person has a title such as Professor, Doctor, Father, Revered, Justice, Captain, Brigadier, etc., the same is to be stated correctly. If no such title, write the word, Mr. or Sri in case of male and Ms (Ms now used for both Miss and Mrs.) in case of female.

   In addressing the letter to the dignitaries like the President, the Governor, the Chancellor, the Ambassador, the Pontiff, or to a religious head, use an appropriate title like His Excellency, His Highness, His Holiness, etc., after ascertaining the same from the appropriate authority. Any mistake in addressing a person inside the letter certainly distracts the impact from an otherwise well drafted letter. The form of inside address is as:

   The Secretary
   University Grants Commission
   Bahadur Shah Zafar Marg
   New Delhi – 110 002

5. **Attention Line:** Attention line in a letter is used to draw the attention of a specific person in an organization who is handling the matter. This is needed in case the letter is addressed to the firm but directed to the attention of individual, by name, so that the letter is sent to that person without delay. If the letter is addressed by name to an individual in a organization, there is no need for the attention line. This attention line functions to ensure that the letter reaches the particular person whose response is essential. It is placed between the inside address and salutation. An example for attention line is given as:

   Kind attention: Ms C. Ravali Reddy

6. **Salutation:** Salutation is at the margin followed by a comma with two lines below the inside address. It matches the first line of inside address. Use Gentlemen or 'Dear Sirs' or 'Sirs' if the letter is addressed to the officials in business organization and the salutation is plural while in singular, use 'Sir', 'Dear Sir' if it is addressed to the official by designation say, The Finance Manager in singular salutation. If the official is a lady, the salutation is Madam or Dear Madam (Mesdames plural for madam). The business letters are, now, quite commonly addressed to an official by name on designation, e.g., Mr. C. R. Krishna, Finance Manager. In such case, the salutation is Dear Mr. C. R. Krishna. Use Ms before a lady's name as Dear Ms C. R. Krishna.

7. **Subject Line:** A line giving brief and quick indication of the subject of letter is referred to as subject line. It ensures clarity and contents of the letter in brevity. It is placed either above or below the salutation at the centre of the letter. The subject line is placed after the salutation if there is an attention line.

   Dear Sir,

   Sub: Your deposit a/c no. 128510100134234

8. **Message:** The body of letter contains the message to be conveyed. Arrange it so as to retain the essence of communication and the very reason for writing the letter in appropriate paragraphs covering the related thoughts and facts sequentially. The message extends over several pages, mentioning clearly the page numbers and pins properly.

   Closing Line: Closing line is two line spaces below the last line of the text of letter at the right side before the signature. It is mentioned with a comma using the word's first letter as capital letter; it is also referred as complimentary close. Good writer takes pains to make the closing line as effective as possible. The most common form is: Yours Faithfully and Yours Truly while other forms are: "Faithfully yours", "Truly Yours".

   If the name of addressee is used in salutation, the closing line is: "Yours sincerely" or "Sincerely Yours". When the salutation is Dear Sir, Madam, the closing line is "Yours faithfully" while the salutation is Dear Sri or Dear Mrs. the closing line "Yours sincerely". "Respectfully" is used only when writing letter to a high public official.

9. **Signature:** Just below the complimentary close follows the signature. Below three or four line spaces of the complimentary close, type the signatory name in brackets and the designation below it. The signature includes the name of the firm, either above or below the name and designation of person who signs. Signature has legal implications and effects, and owes responsibility to the contents of a letter. The style that follows in practice is as:

Yours faithfully	Yours faithfully
RR Publishers	(C.R. Krishna)
(C.R. Krishna)	Finance Manager
Finance Manager	RR Publishers

   In case of the person whose signature is not personally liable but has given power of attorney to sign on behalf of the person or firm who will be responsible, the words **per pro** or **p.p**. (per procurationem) are used. The words are placed before the name of person or firm on whose behalf the letter is sent.

10. **Postscript:** The word, postscript (PS) is derived from a Latin word 'PostScript' meaning written afterwards. Additional information is typed or written after the letter is fully completed; it is known as postscript. It is a bit of friendly personal note writing in a line used for conveying information as an extra but not related to the main message of letter. It can establish successfully the personal contact with reference to common experiences or friendly personal enquiry. For instance, 'it was nice meeting you at the last conference held on July 10, 2016' or 'there is an early bird prize for the first five orders'.

11. **Window Envelope:** Superscription refers to all that is written on an envelope, i.e., name and address of the person or company to whom the letter is directed (centered on the envelope) and the name and address of the sender (at the bottom left on the envelope). Indicate the type of delivery service to be used as: Registered

Post, Air Mail, Certificate of Posting, Hand Delivery, Courier, Fax, etc., on the top centre or top left of the envelope. A window envelope is a transparent paper on the centre of envelope through which one can read the 'inside address'.

12. Other Aspects: Some other related aspects of business letter are enclosure or annexure, continuation of page, spacing, folding, outside address, envelope and window cover. These too call for adequate attention in order to ensure the elegance of the letter. Enclosure is written on the left below the signature and contains the related relevant information and accompanies the letter. It is used like this:

Encl: 1. Copy of draft agreement

2. Mark a courtesy copy also called carbon copy (or simply c.c.) of the letter to other person or party for whom the matter is concerned

For future reference in the sender's office and the person who prepares or dictates the matter of letter, the dictator's and the typist's initials called reference initials (either capital or small letters or combination of both) with date are placed at the bottom of the authorized signatory as: SKU/tk

08-01-2019

Specimen Form of a Letter–Parts:

1. Head Address
2. Date:
3. Reference
4. Inside Address
   ....
   ....
   ....
   ....
5. Attention Line
6. Salutation Line
7. Subject Line
8. Body of the letter ....
   ____
   ____
9. Complimentary close
10. Signature (name)
11. Reference initial
12. Enclosures
    1.
    2.
13. cc
14. Postscript

13. **Use of Abbreviations:** Often use abbreviations or acronyms while writing letters in communication of messages. They serve a useful purpose as long as they are understood as what they are intended. However, it is true that some abbreviations with which the writer is familiar may not be readily comprehended by the reader while some of them may convey different meaning depending upon the context. Hence, it is necessary that the writer clarifies what he means at the first instance. A typical example of 'GP' abbreviation can convey different meanings to different persons as given in Exhibit 5.4.

Exhibit 5.4 A Typical Example for 'GP' Abbreviation Conveys Different Meanings

- Gross profit to the financial analyst
- General Practitioner to a medical representative
- Government paper to an investment banker
- Golden Peacock to a film director
- Greek Philosophy to a student
- Garden Path to a city planner
- Grand Prix to a race enthusiast
- Gram Panchayat to a block development officer
- Government Press to a printer
- Grid power to the electricity department
- Gross product to an economist

5.1.7 Layout of Business Letter

The design in different parts of a letter placed is known as **layout**. Letter's overall effectiveness is being enhanced by layout. The parts of letter are placed in the same order from top to bottom in all layouts except indention and paragraph styles wherein variation occurs. The layout styles are:

1. **Indent Layout:** Every paragraph starts three to five spaces away from the left margin. In inside address, the subsequent lines begin two spaces away from the beginning of previous line; a comma follows each line and a full stop is placed at the end of last line. This layout is the oldest style and not used today. An example for indent layout is given below.

M/S Pinto Exporters Limited
Global Mansions
Tirupati -517502

September 10, 2018

The Chairman,
Bajaj & Co.,
Mumbai - 400004

Sir,

Sub: Your letter dated August 25, 2017 and received the contents.

This has reference to you letter dated August 25, 2017 for the supply of fans. Today, we received fans and I am directed to convey the approval of purchase of fans. As per our company, a provision of 10 per cent discount must be provided to pass the bill. Kindly make this provision in the bill and send it for us to take action for payment.

Yours faithfully,
Sd/-
(Jaya)
Purchases Manager

2. **Full Block Layout:** This is modern style and every line including the date and the closing line begins at the left margin without indention. The address has no punctuation at the end of the line and the salutation and closing line do not have a comma at the end. A double line space is followed between the parts and between the paragraphs. An example for full block layout is presented below.

M/S Rinto Imports Limited
Aravind Mansions
Hyderabad -500003

January 12, 2019

The Finance Manager
Syndicate Bank
Shop No. 4
Pondicherry

Sir

Sub:

This has reference to your letter dated January 1, 2017 for the supply of fans. Today we received fans and I am directed to convey the approval of purchase of fans. As per our company, a provision of 10 per cent discount must be provided to pass the bill. Kindly provide this provision in the bill and send for us to take action for payment.

Yours faithfully
Sd/S. NIRVI
Managing Director

3. **Modified Block Layout:** In this layout, some parts are placed on the left, some in the middle and some on the right. The place, the sender's address, salutation and each paragraph may be aligned to the left. Closing line and signature may be either centered or aligned to the right.

4. **Modified Block with Indentation Layout:** It has the inside address in block form but the beginning of every paragraph is indented. The date and closing line are on the right side; and the salutation and closing line are followed by a comma as in the traditional style. For making it effective, the letter writer should ensure that the layout is modern and elegant.

5.1.8 Types of Business Letter

Business is big or small, old or new, local or national, public or private, proprietary or partnership, monopolistic or competitive, manufacturing or service and alike. It has certain common features and approaches within the given environment. Internally as well as externally, it deals with stakeholders, i.e., owners, employees, customers and the community. Further, business is organized into various functional areas of personnel, marketing, inventory, finance and accounts, administration, secretarial and so on. Letters of business are of various types and emanate from all these sources. The persons who deal with these different types of businesses as well as various functional areas are also correspondent at one time or the other and in one form or the other. To make effective correspondence, one has to familiarize oneself with various types of business letters in both ways. Some specific types of letters are presented below.

1. **Enquiries and Replies:** Letters of buyers' enquiries about goods and services and sellers replies giving information and quotations are common in business. Though telephone or e-mail or fax has become modes of enquiries and replies today, the letter mode is effective communication. With no formalities, the letter is short and straight to the business. For example, you can begin with a question like:

   Could you give us the following?

   Or

   Please send us the following.

   Or

   I would appreciate to receive the following from you.

   (a) ***Enquiry letter:*** The letter may begin with an explanation of the need given as:

   We intend to set up 10 laboratories with a capacity of 50 students each to work at a time in college. These are to be set up in 8 × 8 meters with granite tiles. This information is put forth in a letter form as:

   Dear Sir,

   I saw some samples of your granite tiles for flooring in a recent trade fair held here. I would like to make use of them in designing a room of 8 × 8 meters. Please provide the following information:

   1. In what size, colours and designs can you supply the tiles?
   2. Are the tiles likely to be affected by rising moisture?
   3. Is any special processing of the under-flooring needed?

I shall be most grateful if you could send me answers to these questions within a few days.

Yours faithfully,

In the above letter, the points covered are (a) courteous request for information, giving its purpose, (b) statement of what is wanted and (c) request that the information may be provided in a definite period.

(b) ***Reply to enquiry:*** Give prompt attention to an enquiry and make every effort for the order. Your letter is a business letter. Tell the potential customers what he wants to know the exact details. Reply by presenting facts to the customers, the benefits of buying the product. The letter given below illustrates the reply to an enquiry.

Dear Sir,

Thank you for your request for our catalogue and price list. They are enclosed.

You will find models shown on page 10 for your purpose. We have supplied these desks to many schools and colleges. The schools and colleges found them highly satisfactory as they required little maintenance and are easy to clean. The pleasant appearance and variety of colour add to the attractiveness of the classroom and advantage.

We shall be very happy to discuss your requirements personally. Please call us at any of the numbers given above for an appointment for our representative to meet you.

Yours truly

2. **Orders and Reply:** Business organization places orders for purchases of inventory and commodities, rendering of services, installation and maintenance or any such activity. An order is a request, not a command. Hence, effectiveness of an order depends upon the accuracy and precision of details. The following points cover placing an order.

- **Order request** – Pleased to place an order with you for the supply of ....
- **Order description** – State clearly the type and number of items or material, make, capacity, quantity and other related details unambiguously
- **Rate** – Mention clearly the specific details such as rate per piece, per metric ton, per 1000 ml box of 20, etc., including tax or packaging charges, if any
- **Packing** – State the specifications of packing say, tablets come in strips of 10 or bottles of 50 or 100
- **Delivery schedule** – Clearly specify when, where and in which lot the items ordered, etc., are to be delivered. In case of carriage forward, the mode of transport.
- **Mode of payment** – Mention the mode of payment (by DD, cheque) while placing the order
- **Validity** – State the validity of order within which goods must be delivered
- **Other terms and conditions** – Specify, if any, the other terms and conditions like discount, insurance coverage, conformity to samples, etc.

Orders can be grouped into three: (a) first or trial order, (b) repeat order, and (c) routine order. All the details remain the same in all these orders except opening and ending sentences.

(a) ***First order:*** Placing an order to check the efficiency in terms of price conformity of samples, packing and delivery of goods in time, prompt receipts for payment, etc., is called first order; it is also called trial order. This trial order may emanate from any of the following: (i) Seller's sample or approval of quotation, offered substitute product in a new area. (ii) A retailer may also place a trial order to find out the demand for a new product. (iii) Only small quantity is ordered for trial. See Exhibits 5.5 and 5.6 to place trial order and reply to the trial order.

Exhibit 5.5 First Order

Dear Sir,

We have tested your samples of adhesive paste of large tins and found that No. 24 is suitable for our requirement.

We are glad to place an order for 1000 large tins of this paste. Please deliver the tins at our factory at Kachiguda. Our cheque of 25000 for advance payment and our Sales Tax Declaration Form are enclosed.

The material supplied should be of the same quality as the sample and we reserve the right to reject material of any other quality.

Yours faithfully,

Exhibit 5.6 Reply to First Order

Assure the customer that every attention has been paid to the order and the future orders will receive the same careful attention. The points taken into account are:

- Expression of thanks for the order
- Statement of terms, etc.
- Assurance of satisfactory goods and services and expectation you will deserve further orders

Dear Sir,

Thank you for your order for 1000 large tins of adhesive paste. We shall deliver you goods within time as required. The bill will be sent with the goods; payment within seven days entitles you to a discount of 2%.

You will find that our goods and services are of a high standard. We are looking forward to a standing contract for regular supply of these goods.

Yours truly

(b) ***Repeat order:*** If buyer is satisfied with goods bought on a trial consignment, he may place a repeat order. This repeat letter opens with a reference to the first order. We are glad to say the adhesive paste you supplied last month has been found suitable for our purpose and we would like to have another similar consignment. See Exhibit 5.7 for placing repeat order and reply to it.

Exhibit 5.7 **Repeat Order**

Dear Sir,
We are glad to say that the large tins of adhesive paste purchased a month ago have proved popular and are sold out. We need another similar consignment immediately. Please supply 500 large tins of adhesive paste and deliver them at our factory at Kachiguda. A cheque of Rs. 10,000/- as advance payment and our Sales Tax Forms are enclosed.
Please dispatch immediately.

Yours faithfully,

Exhibit 5.8 **Supply**

When the customer repeats his order, it can make a more definite attempt to win his confidence. Given below points are taken into account.

- Appreciation for success of the first order
- Statement of terms, etc.
- Expectation of regular business that will follow

Dear Sir,
We are glad to learn your letter of the 20th the first order lot of adhesive paste large tins sent on the 4th is suitable for your purpose.
We are sending with this letter, the consignment of 2000 large tins of adhesive paste you have ordered. Our bill of Rs. 1,00,000 is enclosed; cash payment within seven days will entitle you to a discount of 2.50% per cent.
We are looking forward to supplying our products to you on regular basis.

Yours truly,

(c) ***Routine order:*** This order is usually placed by filling in 'Order Forms' accompanied by a letter containing details of requirements. This letter opens with a courteous request for goods to be sent as: Please send the enclosed order on your regular terms. If there is any special requirement, state it at the beginning or at the end as: The customer for whom we are ordering the products is to leave town on the 15th and hence send them by 12th. Please ensure delivery in time. See Exhibit 5.9 for routine order.

Exhibit 5.9 Routine Order

Sir

Please send the following goods according to your usual terms.

Catalogue No.	Description	Price ()
155 A	1 Wall cabinet sky-blue	–
22	1 Computer table-cum cabinet, brown	–
33	1 Poly-sink cabinet, light blue	–

These products are required urgently as the customers for whom we want them have already removed the cabinets and need immediate replacement. Please arrange them for quick delivery.

Yours faithfully,

3. **Quotation:** The intending purchasers seek competitive offer from the intending suppliers of goods and services is called **quotation**. Each quotation has two parts; first part is when the buyer calls for quotation from the seller and second part is when the supplier responds and sends the offer with all the relevant details. Business organizations are sought and sent quotation as regular correspondence. While inviting and sending quotation, the following is worth considering:
   - Description covering quantity and quality
   - Rates and discounts for bulk orders, etc.
   - Mode and terms of payment
   - Delivery time
   - Taxes, duties and charges
   - Transportation and delivery
   - Samples and approval
   - Insurance, breakage allowed, etc.
   - Guarantee period and after sales service
   - Annual maintenance contract (AMC) details

   The management of organization has to be paid due attention for all the points above to ensure clear and mutual understanding and avoid different interpretations or expectations. The letter writer is well versed with some common areas of business correspondence which are presented in Table 5.1.

Table 5.1 Common Areas of Business Correspondence

Department	Letter
Purchase	Calling quotation for products and services. Inviting tenders for jobs and supplies. Asking for samples and drawings. Placing test orders, status enquires, technical and commercial bids
Sales	Dues collection from various agencies and customers Follow-up letters Correspondence with financial institutions Opening/closing of accounts Overdrafts, cash credit and current accounts Stop payments instructions Issue of letter of credit (LoC) Protesting wrongful dishonour of cheques Concerning interest payment and service charges Complaining wrong credit, debit and delay in realization Payment of insurance premium, renewal of policy, claims, settlements Department of Post and Telegraph, Telephone, Provident fund, Income tax, Commercial tax, etc.
Personnel	Calling candidates for written tests and interviews Offering appointment Confirming the service Changing emoluments Disciplinary matters Leave and travel concessions Training programme and deputation
Secretarial	Change in management Change in business hours Opening and shifting of branches and offices Corresponding with directors, shareholders and debenture holders Company meeting with agenda Transfer and transmission of shares Declaring dividend Corresponding with agents and transport companies Representing the trade associations, chambers of commerce and others
Other	Job application Preparation of bill of exchange, promissory note, hundi, etc Legal correspondence Newsletter and house journals Preparing charts, graphs, stickers, etc. Inviting a guest Congratulating on achievements Condolence Introduction Goodwill messages Press releases, publicity, etc. Appeals Saying 'thank you' Appreciation

Communication which is as old as human beings has evolved over centuries and gained sophistication in line with the progress of civilization on achieving a breakthrough to learn, speak and develop language as a vehicle of thought followed by reality of the printed word and development of technology in 20th century turned into a new dimension in the field of communication. Mass communication and visual communication seem to be increasingly emerging as preferred course among the youths in the urban areas. Mass Communication is an exciting field and growing rapidly at it throws up more job opportunities.

5.2 INTERFACE OF MEDIA AND BUSINESS

The scenario in today's business world is ever-changing in the complex and competitive environment. Business needs effective and good communication with capability to communicate anything or everything to anyone, anywhere and in any form – voice, data, text or image at a speed with accuracy, focus, elegance and appeal through letters, circulars, reports and statements. Towards this, new skills have been supplementing to the conventional skills and becoming increasingly relevant. In other words, the conventional skills are by 'no means' sufficient, but one must learn additionally new skills for appropriating to meet the business conditions. The new skills are necessitated to patronage the old ones in the context of new millennium where the persons are speaking more of global language in changing environment as the globe has become reality of a village. It is appropriate to quote Bill Gates who said this: "Business is going to change more in the next ten years than in the last fifty years. 1980s were about quality, 1990s were about re-engineering and 2000s will be about velocity. Information access will alter the lifestyles of consumers and their expectations of business. Very soon, people around the world will be living the web-lifestyles."

The major trend across the business world is to produce better quality products or services at low cost to survive and continue the prospect of business in the competitive environment; and its transactions in terms of procuring and selling goods and services at '24 × 7' availability through the network of communication with modern technology. It resulted in a philosophy of lean management which certainly needs to enhance the use of communication technology in all the functions of modern-day industry and commerce.

The means of transmitting or conveying a message is called **media** (medium is singular). Some media carry written words (say mail) and other carry the voice (say telephone). Business is more oriented towards high Information Technology as the electronic media can carry the written material and voice as well. The use of electronic media enhances people to speak more of global language. As a result, it has reflected in slow demise of manuscript and handwritten correspondence (letters and memos) with e-mail messages.

Access to knowledge and information, and speedily reaching the destination and cost-effectiveness have become a big push towards the electronic gadgets and new media like internet, websites, online connectivity, automated teller machine (ATM), customer terminals, short messaging services (SMS) and alike. All these together are pushing up and placing a greater mechanization approach in the communication system with an element of dehumanization. The system and strategies of business communication are strengths of organization internally as well as externally. (Table 5.2).

Table 5.2 Strengths of Communication

Strengths	Services
Speed	Need for swift, online, real-time communication across all target groups
Convenience	Access, retrieval at the users' convenience
Cost	Making communications reach vast sections at affordable prices
Information technology	Communication system in tune with the IT enabled environment
Global	Develop the skills and languages of global relevance

5.2.1 Choice of Medium

In selecting a medium for the communication purpose, one has to consider several aspects. First, the choice of decision is related to which media – verbal (written and oral) and non-verbal (body language and visual presentation) to be used for sending messages. Next, the choice of decision pertains to the mode to be used for sending the messages. The message to be sent is required to:

- Convey urgently
- Cover distance between the sender and the receiver
- Safeguard and ensure secrecy (in cases like warning memo, appraisal report)
- Ensure accuracy without the loss of message
- Guarantee of delivery
- Get immediate feedback
- Carry emotional content and the like

Conveying information face-to-face is the best method to provide an instant feedback and allow a satisfactory closure. Since, face-to-face conversation may not possibly cover a large number people; the next best thing is to choose such a medium or a combination as personal as possible. Mail, courier, telex, telegraph, fax, e-mail, notice boards, bulletin boards, newspapers and magazines are used in transmitting written communication while telephone, cellular phone, voice mail and radio in oral messages. Cinema and television are the most powerful media as they can transmit all types of messages. However, the following aspects are considered while choosing a medium for sending the message. These are:

- Type of audience the message wants to reach
- Speed of message to be conveyed – time, pressure and distance
- Need of confidentiality

- ➢ Need of accuracy in transmission
- ➢ Need of reliability
- ➢ Cost effectiveness
- ➢ Availability of medium
- ➢ Need of copy for record
- ➢ Feedback necessity
- ➢ Intensity and complexity of message

5.3 TRENDS IN BUSINESS COMMUNICATION

An account of new communication technology development, the scope of information transmission on mechanical devices has widely been enhanced. Messages sent through media are classified into (a) conventional mode and (b) modern mode. There is another mode of communication called mass communication that is explained ahead.

5.3.1 Conventional Media

The use of media on the basis of traditional carriers is called **conventional media**. The process of communication under the conventional media came into being in the modern civilization when the birth of language and progressive use of spoken words saw the light of the day in the society. The existing printing press and printing technology has boosted the business communication. The trends in conventional media are discussed hereunder.

1. **Mail:** Usually, a postal service is a major government owned network with links within the country as well as among the countries of the world by using the services of rail, road, air, sea, etc. Mail services are ordinary mail, registered mail (with or without acknowledgement), quick mail, express delivery mail and under certificate of posting mail. A special mail service offered by the post office is termed Speed Post to ensure delivery of letters and parcels on the same day within the city, within 24 hours to certain cities in the country and within 48 hours to the cities in other countries. Now, the post office offers the electronic media for new services in some cities.
2. **Courier:** The courier services are the modernized and sophisticated forms of delivery of messages at the door steps of recipients. It is just like the messenger or runner used in the olden days with messages before the postal service came into being. The courier service is private network which collects and delivers letters/ packets door-to-door. Delivery of letters and packets with quick service is a great advantage. However, the courier service is costly and available to limited cities where it maintains its network.
3. **Hand Delivery:** Delivery of letters, documents or parcels within the city is referred to as hand delivery. This method ensures prompt delivery and acknowledgement from the receiver. This method is most useful when proof of delivery is required for record as the messenger can bring back a signed copy or an official receipt or

a signature in the sender's book. But, the speed and reaching of message under this method depends on the effectiveness of messengers. As it requires a number of employees for outdoor work, it may cost more.

4. **Telegraph:** Message transmitting through sounds in Morse code is termed telegraph. It gives an impression of urgency and, therefore, gets immediate response. The telegraph office registers special telegraph address in 'one word' to the interested companies to register this facility and the pin code number is added. A facility for reply-paid telegrams is available; a person can send telegram and pay for the other party's reply telegram at message sender's office itself. This creates an impression in the mind of receiver to reply immediately.

5. **Telex:** Telex, introduced in 1958 (abbreviation of teleprinter exchange), is a worldwide teletype service in instantaneous messages sent through a direct dial of teleprinter-to-teleprinter system. Telex connection can be obtained through the post office; each subscriber has an identification code for connection. It works 24×7.

   Telex comes with a keyboard for typing messages to transmit and receive. A roll paper is fitted to the telex machine; messages can be typed continuously. When the message is typed on the sender's machine, the same message gets typed at the same time on the receiver's machine too. A two-way dialogue can be carried by typing out in turn, if the receiver's machine is attended.

   Telex is an excellent international network. Telex messages are charged on the basis of the time taken for transmission and the distance. This mode of communication was used by the railways, airports, stock exchanges, banks, etc., to relay on a screen where moment-to-moment information is required to convey to the concerned people. Teleprinter is now outdated.

5.3.2 Modern Mode

The communication channels and media of yesteryears have been efficient, even today, in terms of range, speed and media of communication of both personal as well as business through the support of internet, laptop, mobiles and computer. John Nesbit and Patricia Aberdeen have said about modern media of communication in their book entitled *Mega Trends 2000*: "In telecommunication, we are moving to a single worldwide information network, just as economically we are becoming one global marketplace." Thanks to globalization and cross-border flow of ideas and resource development in one place are reaching other parts of the world; even impacting rural areas. A wider choice of channels and media has been impacting effective communication to the stakeholders in the society.

The new concepts of e-mail, e-governance, e-commerce, e-business, m-marketing, e-banking, e-tender, e-bay, e-signature, internet, networking system, data warehousing, teleconferencing, video conferencing and short messaging system are playing a key role in the field of sending messages from any source to any destination in the world. The modes of modern communication are discussed below.

1. **Telephone:** Telephone is an electronic form of communication, useful and universal medium of oral communication with person who is far away. Over the years, telephone has developed many new facilities like intercom, Subscriber Trunk Dialing (STD), International Subscriber Dialing (ISD) and Cellular Phone in communication system.

   An internal telephone system allowing communication between the persons in different parts of a building or a campus is called **intercom**. Intercom eliminates the need of visiting another part of the office and passes on the information quickly to the intended person. A phrase appropriately suited in this context is "If you want to talk, you do not have to walk." It even has a facility of broadcasting messages to the entire office over all the internal lines or a particular section on one line.

   Contacting a person through his personal telephone number is referred to **local dialing**. Contacting a person through his personal phone number with a code number of the place without access to the telephone exchange is called **subscriber trunk dialing.** Every city or town or place has a code number which you dial before dialing the personal telephone number. Contacting a person through his personal phone number in another country without calling the operator at the telephone exchange is called **international subscriber.**

   Dialing: Every country has an international code number which you dial before dialing the required person in the city of another country. For India, it is 091. Both STD and ISD have the facility of locking system. One can lock, if he desires, with a number code on telephone attached to the electronic exchange. Advancement of technology has brought in much sophistication in telephone facility in providing better services to the people. These are:

   - A cordless telephone frees the hand set from the hand-out and allows the user to take it around within a range of 100 meters away from the hand-hold.
   - Caller identification device attached to the telephone can show the number from which the call is being made.
   - Answering machine can take a message in the absence of the receiver or if he cannot answer it.
   - Three or more persons from different parts of the world or different cities in the country can talk/discuss through telephone conference.

2. **Cell Phone:** Cell phone also called **mobile phone** evolved on the fixed radio signal receiver/transmitter and telecommunication technology. It operates through airways (much like radio) but the receipt of communication gets affected by weather conditions, underground parking or passages and fortified buildings. Further, it does not work outside the jurisdiction of network signals. The numbers storage with names, record of missed calls, text messages and information given by the network about the weather and other vital news, etc., are the service provided by a cellular phone. It also offers additional services like:

   - Voice mail (which is a personal answering machine service)
   - Call conferencing (which allows user to connect up to five parties in a discussion)

- Ask me (services of food and flowers ordering, airlines and railways information, restaurant bookings and alike)

The cellular phone has freed managers and others from their confinement to the office. They can be in touch with the office from wherever they are. A good example is that a manager talking about business on his cellular phone while relaxing on a beach may be a depressing sight; but then, he might not have been relaxing on the beach at all but for it, which allows him to stay in touch.

3. **Fax:** A device for transmitting copies of printed matter/images over telephone line is known as **fax**. The machine is connected to the telephone through a modem (modulator-demodulator, abbreviated as modem). The sender has to dial the receiver's fax number, insert the document into the machine and 'press' the start button. The machine scans the page and makes an electronic representation of the text and graphics, compresses the data to save transmission time and transmits it to the dialed fax machine. The printout contains the time, date and fax number of the sender's machine and the sender also gets a confirmation printout showing the fax number of receiver machine, the date and the time of transmission and the number of pages transmitted.

   The receiving machine decrypts the signals and uses its in-built printer to produce an exact photocopy of the original page. Information can be quickly exchanged between or among the offices and organizations and individuals; conveying the information to the concerned persons quickly.

   A computer with required software, installed modem and connected telephone line can be used for sending fax. In recent times, computers have the facility of an in-built modem and software for fax. Fax through computer can transmit only the messages created on computer. Usually, fax is used only for sending information which is not confidential. Fax provides benefits compared to others (Table 5.3).

Table 5.3 Benefits of Fax

In comparison	Benefits of Fax
Post	Much faster More secure
Telephone	More economical No language problem Permanent record
Telex	Faster No special preparation No operating skills More economical
Courier	More secure More economical Faster

4. **E-mail:** Messages and whole document on computer is communicated instantaneously on availability of a computer, a telephone line and a modem. E-mail technology is much faster in communicating message to destination and provides the recipient with text.
5. **Video Cassette:** Audio means sound or hearing and video means seeing. Its use is gaining importance throughout the world as a tool of self-learning. The learner can listen to the cassette along with observations of body language according to his/her own convenience; and use it again and again. In recent years, the audio-video cassette is used in teaching.
6. **Internet**: Multiple data developed independently sent through satellite links and telephone wires with the help of computer networks are referred to as internet. It is a world-wide network.

5.4 MASS COMMUNICATION AND ITS TYPES

Carrying out the activities and communicating from many to many for the purpose of promoting good progress of public in the society is called **Mass Communication**. In fact, mass communication aims at reaching out to a well-defined target group which is not confined to any known address; and ensures that information reaches the group and also attracts their attention. It is a method of reaching a large, varied and well spread out audience. Mass communication focuses on acquiring the mind and market share. The specific goals include:

- Building and maintaining awareness
- Achieving acceptance
- Winning trust, cooperation and recognition
- Cultivating understanding

Every organization, be it a business firm, an educational institution, a public service, a club, a hospital or a department, is a member of the society that came into existence and functions to enshrine the motto towards the society's progress. This needs effective communication. The public relations can be simply put as: "The inward and outward seeing eyes." The media used towards this mass communication reaching out to public are: press, radio, television, films, word-of-mouth, books, literature, internet, etc. Communication with a wide-cross section of literate and illiterate audience takes place through the methods given below.

- Advertisements through print and audio-visual media hoardings and bill boards
- Posters and banners
- Exhibitions and trade fairs
- Sponsorships and events
- Pamphlets and brochures
- Gift articles (diaries, calendars, key chains, etc.)
- Press conferences and press releases

- Publicity
- Newsletters
- Web sites
- Questionnaire
- Direct marketing
- Literature
- Competition and sports
- Public relations

Some important types of mass communication media used in sending messages are discussed here.

1. **Board:** The commonly and popularly used method of pictorial presentation in earlier days was boards. In the past, the board was available in black colour only, hence it came to be called **blackboard**. Today, it is available in different colours with a beautiful glass top. Advancement in techniques led to emergence of a variety of boards in use which are: (a) plastic board, (b) magnetic board, (c) electronic board, and (d) hand-worked mechanical board. The boards need care and attention in their layout to carry no stale notices and look attractive.
2. **Radio:** Radio as an apparatus is used for sending messages in the form of voice communication with the help of electromagnetic waves in open space without connecting wire. Its frequencies are below 1000 MHz. The merits of radio include being more flexible, less expensive and permitting portable work stations. Its demerits are limited data transfer rate and very low security. The standard broadcasting radio is amplitude modulation (AM) and frequency modulation (FM). Based on the use of electromagnetic spectrum, radio ranges are classified into:
    - Very low frequency (VLF)
    - Low frequency (LF)
    - Middle frequency (MF)
    - High frequency (HF)
    - Very high frequency (VHF)
    - Ultra high frequency (UHF)
    - Super high frequency (SHF)
    - Extremely high frequency (EHF)
3. **Film:** Film as an audio-visual is more useful for instruction, information, education and entertainment. Events like conference, demonstration, experiment, work study motions of machines, topic of interests, animation and alike can be used as the best medium of communication. Film for public exhibition is subject to film censorship by the Central Board of Film Censors. Animation in film imparts the impression of life and movement to the static images. A factionalized film exceeding 2000 meters long in 35 mm is referred to as a **feature film**. This feature

film with format is a story woven around a number of characters wherein the plot is revealed mainly through dialogues. A specific focus or theme on certain subject is shown in documentary film.

Like TV, film is a direct contact with the facts and ideas through sight, hearing and action for making a direct impact on audience. In business communication, films can be used for a variety of purposes to inform or motivate the employees about the activities of programmes, philosophy; or consumers about the goods or services. It is the best medium to present work study operations of machines, equipment, etc., and topics of social interest. The most powerful medium of communication with all the possible forms among the written, oral, visual and auditory is film. It can be shown in a cinema theatre or projected on a small screen in room with a film projector or projected on television screen through a video player or transmitted by television. Entertainment films of different kinds are a powerful medium for employees' education and relations (Exhibit 5.10).

Exhibit 5.10 **Out-of-the-Box Thinking**

All human beings are born with an equal level of intellect. But then, how is it that one succeeds while the rest do not or get stagnated at a particular level. Experts who deal with human intellect say, "The one who succeeds is among the ones who learn and practice the concept of 'out-of-the-box thinking'. Even Nobel laureate Albert Einstein once said "An average person uses only five percent of his brain in his entire life." A lot can be learnt from the film *3 Idiots*. This movie is a contemporary idea which has a strong message, especially for the students and the parents who believe that there is nothing beyond the professional courses of engineering and medicine. The movie subtly explores the idea of freedom for children.

The film titled *3 Idiots* definitely gives enough thought to the intellectuals and academia to ponder upon especially when it comes to higher education and career choice in the present scenario of competition nationally and globally.

4. **Public Relations:** A deliberate and organized effort of an organization for building and maintaining a beneficial relationship with all the stakeholders (i.e., target groups and the cross section of the community) within which it operates is termed as public relations.
5. **Advertisement:** Any paid form of non-personal presentation of ideas, goods or services by an identified sponsor is called an advertisement. It is effective in reaching out across the target audience and conveying the message. The press and print media, radio, television, cinema slides, newspapers, magazines, souvenirs, hoardings, sign boards, etc., form advertisement
6. **Publicity:** An organization makes constant efforts for publicity; for which it may not be paid anything. It is an important facet of promotional strategy and sustains the image as well as marketplace of organization. Publicity includes demonstrations, seminars, exhibitions, bus panels, posters and banners, sports events, stickers and

balloons, neon lights, pamphlets and brochures, press conferences and meets, gift articles, trade fairs and competition.

7. **Press Release:** Announcement of important message or development concerning to an organization that wishes to convey to the public at large through the press and other media is referred to as **press release**. It includes financial results, product launches, performance highlights, new branches and offices, changes in management, benefits to the customers and shareholders, community-oriented initiatives, tie-ups and joint ventures, cessation of business, awards and achievements, ratings and rankings, research findings, meeting, and conferences, etc. As a means of cost-less communication, press releases cover both literate and illiterate audience. However, the message is to be brief and with minimum text.
8. **Hoardings and Bill Boards:** Hoardings and bill boards are used for posters conveying simple ideas but short messages including pictures. Usually, they are placed high up, so that can be seen from a distance at important locations.
9. **Newspapers and Magazines:** Newspapers and magazines are used for inviting tenders, providing information on employment opportunities, public notices and advertisements.
10. **Television:** Television is audio-visual and transmits live events. A news reader say, in Hyderabad can take the audience to a view of what is happening in America or hold a live discussion with a reporter in China.

5.5 INTERPERSONAL COMMUNICATION

Interpersonal communication is used for personal selling. The qualities of AIDA (Attention, Interest, Desire and Action) model are only desirable in an advertisement copy as a communication tool. Though advertising has the capacity to generate highest awareness and arousing interest too; but is not so effective in leading the consumers to action. Personal selling is the highest in creating a desire for the product and making people buy it. But, it is low in generating awareness. The summary of interpersonal communication and mass communication is presented in Table 5.4.

Table 5.4 Distinction between Interpersonal and Mass Communication

Factor	Interpersonal Communication	Mass Communication
Speed with a large audience	Slow	Fast
Cost of reaching large audience	High	Low
Attention arresting capability	High	Low
Message flow traffic	Two-way	One-way
Feedback	High	Low
Market coverage	Large	Less

Advertising mass communication, as the name itself suggests means that the message is sent to a large audience with great speed. Salesman's presentation about sales is interpersonal communication; each time he adapts the message to his prospective buyers. Mass communication is cost effective, but one-way communication feedback is not reliable. Interpersonal communication provides immediate and accurate feedback, and is expensive. It is much more effective than mass communication as the buyer gets immediate response from the sales person. Though mass communication has some demerits, it enables to reach a large market economically. Mass communication leads to a paradox that advertising is efficient promotion but inefficient communication.

QUESTIONS

1. What are the essentials of a good business letter?
2. Discuss punctuations of a business letter.
3. Describe the appearance of a business letter.
4. Discuss the parts of a business letter.
5. What is the layout of a letter? Discuss layout styles of a business letter.
6. Write an illustrative letter about enquiry and reply.
7. Illustrate a model letter of ordering and reply.
8. What do you mean by media? Discuss media and communication interface.
9. Write a note on conventional media communication.
10. Write a note on modern media of communication.
11. Discuss telephone and cellular mobile phone.
12. What is fax? State its benefits compared to other media of communication.
13. What is mass media communication? Discuss its types.
14. Explain the following:
    (a) ABCD letter
    (b) Use of capital letter
    (c) Abbreviations
    (d) Salutation
    (e) Complimentary close
    (f) Window envelope
    (g) Quotation

6 CHAPTER Business Report Writing

"Writing is the best way to talk without being interrupted."

— **Jules Reynard**

LEARNING OBJECTIVES

This chapter will enable you to

- to learn the meaning and purpose of a business report;
- to write and summarize the skills of a report; and
- to learn the essential qualities and documentation style of a business report.

INTRODUCTION

Everyone in the management of an organization has to do some form of report writing for taking decision on its progress and understanding problems faced in the conduct of business activities. In the business hierarchy, the higher the employee goes, the more he has to write reports. No easy path is available for writing a good report on the issues of business but its writing is an arduous task which intelligently does serve the purpose. Likewise, writing a good report is an evidence of good documentation with intelligent vocabulary, grammar, rhetoric, punctuation and presentation of facts, analysis and reasons logically in lucid approach. Anyone who is keen on developing varied business communication skills with an acquired good insight artistically, it certainly helps to write a good report. Knowing the cause-effect development or effect-cause relation is possible through the means of an effective communication.

Writing of a report is the final and important step after the detailed study of an issue or problem undertaken on conduct of business with suggestions for its future course of action. Report writing contains the statement of investigation or analytical study process with its nature for drawing logical conclusions with solutions. A report contains the description of:

- Issue or problem of study
- Adoption of methodology in arriving at the conclusions
- Making worthy suggestions for implementation

Writing of report is a means of communicating investigator's or committee's experiences to the intended ones which add to knowledge. How brilliantly the collected material is analyzed, how meaningfully conclusions are made and how precisely suggestions are put forth add a little value. Resources of money, manpower, material and time spent in analysis or investigation become mere waste, if the reported results are not comprehensive. Therefore, the report should be carefully worded with thought provocation and made understandable clearly. Simple, legible and accurate form of communication document to the targeted audience presented aesthetically is the nature of a report. All these elucidate the significance of writing business report.

6.1 MEANING OF REPORT

The meaning of the word, report as per English dictionary, is thus, (i) bringing back the account of information, (ii) stating ascertained facts, (iii) narrating, describing or repeating the interrelated sequence. Each interpretation has its relevance in the context of report writing. Account or experience expressed after investigation would be the most appropriate. A report contains communication describing the problem studied, methodological presentation of all the information in arriving at the conclusions and making worthy suggestions logically.

Results of a survey or investigation recording and communicating to the intended person in the society are the fundamental characteristics of writing a report scientifically. Define every term carefully, its adoption procedure, recognize the limiting factors, document references and logical conclusions arrived at cautiously with due consideration in practice. Simply, science is a public institution and scientist must oblige to communicate comprehensively the logical conclusions and suggestions made to others. Thus, the business in a communiqué is a means of presenting the results of a problem studied effectively and creatively. One who has effective skills of business communication acquires a good insight in writing a report. He has the power of knowledge to make 'new things familiar' and 'familiar things new.' Therefore, it can be said that communication has become an integral part, not only for academic pursuits but also for all the areas of human activity to 'upkeep' social values and social life with economic facets of people in the society.

6.2 PURPOSE OF REPORT

A report provides a feedback to the business management on various working aspects of enterprise. Documented information would serve as feedback to the target group. For instance, the glory of the bygone era (Chanakya Accounting for Economic Administration) can be known by inscriptions which serve as authentic and documented source of information. Every organization has been conducting periodical reporting on its various activities towards the progress of business. Writing of business report is for varied purposes given below:

- Review of performance
- Keep a check on continuing activities
- Plan for future requirements
- Conduct market survey/investigation
- Submit standardized information

6.3 FUNCTIONS OF A GOOD REPORT

Communicating information in the form of business report is highly specific for the designated audience. Hence, a well communicated message performs several functions, such as

- Present the nature of and the reasons for the study of problem and all methodology
- Provide reference material for future use
- Judge the quality of contents of the report
- Evaluate the ability and competence of person(s) who conduct survey or investigation
- Provide systematic knowledge on the issue and analysis
- Provide the factual base in framing policies and strategies

6.4 TYPES OF BUSINESS REPORT

Business reports may be special or routine. The former refers to presenting a decision on a special problem-situation being investigated by an individual or a committee of persons who have knowledge and understanding on the subject constituted specifically for the purpose whereas the latter refers to periodical (regular interval or completion of a task), in nature, that conveys information about the progress or status of task by filling in the form of print. Chart 6.1 gives an idea of various types of business reports.

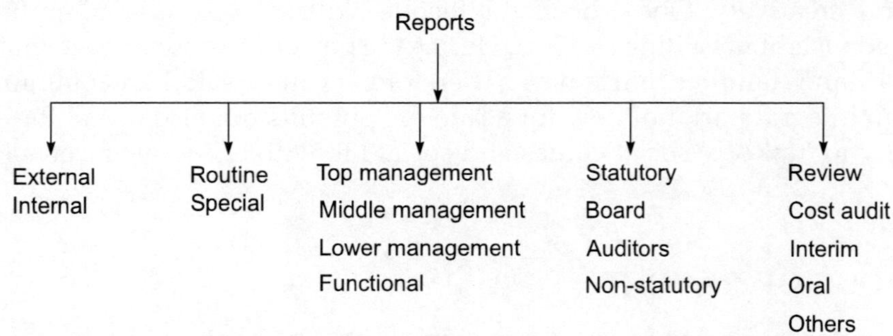

Chart 6.1 Types of Business Report

6.4.1 External Report

Preparing report on the business affairs in compliance with the provisions of Companies Act, 1956 for the use of external parties like shareholders, debenture holders, investors, financial institutions, financial analysts, stock exchanges, government, researchers, etc., is called an external report. The annual report containing Auditors' Report and Board's Report, Income Statement and Balance Sheet is meant for the shareholders as public document and also filed with the Registrar of Companies and Stock Exchanges. The final statement of accounts is expected to conform to certain minimum standards of disclosures. Though, the company is not answerable to anyone other than the shareholders, still the report is useful and meant for the public.

6.4.2 Internal Report

A report containing preparation for the use of various persons at various levels of management in the company is called an internal report. In other words, it is the medium of written communication to transmit the information for various levels of management in the organization keeping in view the recipient level to make decision at his level. As such, it is a private document and does not conform to certain statutory standards.

6.4.3 Routine Report

Routine report is of various types:

1. **Progress Report:** A progress report contains organization's information on its project progress which is in the process of being completed. Construction of works or manufacture of products or implementation of a programme are examples included in the progress report.
2. **Inspection Report:** This report contains information on the matters with regard to irregularities or deviations from the fixed standards (quality) in day-to-day work, internal audit, audit and inspection of works, products, construction works, machinery and property, and surprise check in order to ensure whether proper initiation is taken on the work. For this purpose, a printed form containing checklists is used. Wherever needed, the remarks on specific observation are to be provided to the auditor on financial matters. In such cases, the inspection authority uses its own format for the inspection report.
3. **Appraisal Report:** A report of superior on his subordinate's work performance is prepared (usually filling a format) as is required by the management is called an appraisal report. On this basis, the management takes a decision for the deserving employees towards promotion or sanction of additional increment or other benefits. This helps employees get feedback on their performance.
4. **Periodical Report:** Report is prepared with needed information in routine nature at regular intervals on the working of a section or department. It is prepared by filling a printed or a typed form.

6.4.4 Special Report

Special report is of various types:

1. **First Information Report:** In business organization, the preparation of first information report (FIR) required to be submitted to the higher authority by a responsible person or person-in-charge on the spot when a disaster like fire, robbery or accident or collapse of building occurs is called special report. It contains all the available information such as what happened, how and at what time, who first noticed it, what steps were taken immediately, extent of destruction or loss of life or property or important papers, etc., pertaining to the incident. The first information report is always written by an individual appointed for that purpose.

2. **Investigation Report:** After making a thorough and diligent study or critical inquiry on the issue/problem undertaken, the investigation report is written. When the management so desires to find out the causes or reasons for problem/situation and also needs suggestions for solving it, investigation report is made. Facts of information are to be collected and the collected facts analyzed for inferring logical conclusions and thereon making suggestions or solutions in the report to be submitted to the management. Such an investigation report requires high thinking and better skills, innovative approach, discussion and presentation to draw logical inferences. Usually, this nature of work is assigned to a committee consisting of competent and experienced persons. Financial intricacies, falling sales, incurring loss, sickness of firm, mounting bad debts, declining deposits, customers' complaints, labour unrest, etc., are good examples for investigation and thereupon calling report.
3. **Research Report:** When an organization is interested to launch a new product or service in the market or make any major changes that affect the company's fortunes, an in-depth study like research is proposed. The field or area is to be surveyed, data to be collected (responses of households) and compiled (data available in reports, etc., including policy matters), data organized, analyzed and interpreted; and deductions drawn logically and worthy suggestions made. Financial viability, commercial feasibility, launch of a new product or service, suitability of a site for factory with facilities, etc., are good examples for research report.

   An individual or a committee conducts investigation depending upon the size of survey. For example, estimation of loss due to damage to a machine. An engineer may conduct a survey on factory location as it involves a great deal of work and hence, a committee would be required.
4. **Project Report:** After completion of a proposal undertaken, the project report is made. After the completion of preliminary and main surveys, a project report is to be written focussing it on the future with the expected results. Generally, the project report is used for planning the funding of enterprises by the authorities, financial institutions, government, etc. It is prepared by an individual on his own for getting his proposals approved or sanctioned. Many entrepreneurs prepare project reports on their proposal to start industries and submit it to the authorities concerned.

6.4.5 Business Report

Report according to the levels of management is of various types as discussed below.

1. **Report to Top Management:** Board is the top management, mainly concerned with formulation of policy; and planning and coordination at various levels in the organization. Hence, the functional heads need to provide detailed data and information on the financial statements like Profit and Loss Account, Balance Sheet, statement of funds flow, cash flow, capacity utilization, cost of production, sales, credit collection, research and development, etc., to the

Managing Director/Chairman who, in turn, submits the same to the Board for taking appropriate measures in the form of policy, planning and coordination.

2. **Report to Middle Management:** The middle management is functional management which is concerned with the task of implementing goals and objectives set by the Board. The matter of report for implementing depends upon the degree of centralization and decentralization of authorities. Various types of reports relating to the functional level are (a) production report, (b) sales report, (c) purchase report, and (d) financial report.
3. **Report to Lower Management:** This report is also called supervisory level management report, mainly concerned with the actual execution of policies.

6.4.6 Functional Report

The functional report is classified according to the functions of business management. They are categorized as internal reports with broad categories. These are: (a) operating report (control report, information report and venture measurement report), and (b) financial report (statistic report and dynamic report). The former deals with the operations of a company at various divisional or branch levels while the latter deals with the financial position.

6.4.7 Statutory and Non-statutory Reports

Corporate report is broadly classified into statutory report and non-statutory report. According to Section 165 of Companies Act of 1956, preparing a statutory report containing the Auditors' Report, Board's Report and Annual Accounts is related to the Statutory Report of company and sent to the members for the benefit of getting information clarification.

1. **Annual Report:** Annual report besides being mandatory is also relevant and contains the information sharing on image building development. A well brought out annual report can help create a favourable image or impression about the organization with its progress during the year.

   A business organization brings out a report regularly on business transactions covering progress during the reporting period of a year; this is called annual report. Banks, educational institutions, charitable institutions, regulatory bodies, associations, trusts, non-governmental organizations, etc., bring out annual reports. The motto is to inform its stakeholders and public in general about the progress achieved and performance highlights.

   Every registered organization is required to comply in conformity of the provisions of the Companies Act. For instance, banks are required to publish their Balance Sheet and Profit and Loss Account within six months of the year-end as part of the Annual Report and distribute to all the concerned people. The Balance Sheets and Profit and Loss Account are figure-oriented which follow the accounting principles and accounting standards whereas the annual reports additionally contain the narrative statements, comparative analyses, charts, pictures; all such presentations aim at putting the Balance Sheets and Profit and Loss Account figures and ratios in proper perspective. Further, a well brought out and widely distributed annual report builds up favourable image or impression about the organization.

Realizing and recognizing the significance of annual reports, the organizations devote considerable time, effort and resources in bringing their annual report with substance or content as well as good design, printing, layout, pictures, charts, etc. A typical annual report of a large sized business organization covers all the details. There may be some additions or deletions to the list.

- Board of Directors
- Top Management Team
- Names of Auditors
- Progress at a Glance
- Performance Highlights and Working Results
- Directors' Report
- Accounting Policies adopted
- Profit and Loss Account and Balance Sheet
- Schedules attached to Balance Sheet
- Notes on Account, wherever necessary
- Auditors' Report
- Commentary on Financial Statements
- Ratios and Statements
- Remuneration paid to the Top Management
- Changes in the Board
- Acknowledgement

2. **Board Report:** Board of Directors' annual report contains information on the state of affairs of the company, dividend proposal, proposal on reserves, material changes and commitments, if any, resources conservation like technology, energy, foreign exchange earnings, etc., need to be attached to every balance sheet.
3. **Auditor Report:** Auditor, on behalf of the share holders, scrutinizes and checks the correctness or otherwise accounts of the company and submits a report which is called auditor report. It is attached to the Balance Sheet including auditors' separate, special or supplementary note, and the Profit and Loss account.
4. **Non-statutory Report:** The report that is not required to be prepared under the Companies Act is known as non-statutory report. It includes the directors' report to the shareholders on certain special proposals or problems, and the committee report on special matters like finance committee, allotment committee, standing committee and special reports of the Company Secretary.

6.4.8 Other Reports

Other reports contain review report, cost audit report and interim report.

Any report must have utility and use for decision-making and formulation of a plan. As such, an executive who receives the report should examine it and decide its usefulness. Such report is called review report. Preparation of report by examining the cost accounting records is called cost audit report. Every company prepares report to examine the cost accounting system, financial position, capital employed, net worth, profit after depreciation and other expenses, process of manufacturing, consumption of raw material in quantity and value, wages and salaries of employees, stores and spare parts, capacity utilization, income, etc. If in a report, only a piece of information on the subject matter is contained, then a committee is constituted to submit its report clearly with financial needs before submitting a final report is called interim report. The contents of this report are incorporated in the final report.

6.5 STRUCTURE OF BUSINESS REPORT

The format of business report consists of three patterns. These are:

- Letter form (written in first person, i.e., I am personally of the opinion or we are personally of the opinion, I suggest or we suggest, etc.)
- Letter-text form (written in both letter and text form)
- Memorandum form (This form is usually adopted avoiding the formalities followed in letter form and followed the printed memorandum report form ensuring uniformity, clarity and simplicity)

A structure or pattern of report contains various parts enabling to present all the needed information in an easy-to-read form. However, there is no defined form containing all the parts; each part's size and nature is determined by the parts of report form. The structure of business consists of Preliminary and Text sections. These are discussed below.

6.5.1 Preliminary Section

The preliminary section contains all the informal materials disclosing the need for and identification of a report. It covers the following aspects:

1. **Title:** The report must have a full title page covering the title, the name(s) of the person(s) or committee who prepared it with month and year of submission of work report, subject title, period and location of the study. The title appears at the top-centre of the title page as:

   International Financial Reporting System – A Comparative Study
   by
   Sai Krishna

2. **Terms of Reference:** The report of a committee or an individual begins with the letter of authorization and terms of reference on which the report is to be made. The terms of reference provide authority with legal sanction and substantial powers to the committee or an individual to collect data, summon witnesses and

interview people, and lay down boundaries of the study in clear terms. Thus, the report covers the terms of references outlining the other important aspects of the study namely (a) details of assessment, and (b) purpose and scope of the study. The details include:

- Who assigned the report
- On what date
- How the committee was appointed (by a resolution at a meeting or by office order as given below in Exhibit 6.1)
- By what date report is to be submitted
- Whether report is expected to make suggestions
- Names of committee members in case of committee

In the case of company, the Board may appoint a person or a group of persons to prepare report. In the case of Government, the Ministry concerned or Parliament may appoint committee and authorize it to report. The research institutes or Universities may permit eligible and qualified persons to investigate on the researchable problems and report the findings of the study with suggestions.

Exhibit 6.1 Resolution Pertaining to the Committee Composition

Andhra Bank
Registered office: Hyderabad

The committee was appointed by the following resolution adopted at the meeting of the Board of Directors held on 16, May 2016 as:
Resolved that a committee consisting of Mr. A. Arya (convener), Mr. B. Yara (member) and Mr. C. Arya (member) are hereby appointed to study the trend of NPAs in Andhra Pradesh between April 2004 and March 2014 and to submit a report with recommendations in one month's time.

Officer Order

According to the D/O letter No. 125 dated 26-12-14 from Ms. Chowna, Managing Director, a committee consisting of Mr. A. Arya (convener), Mr. B. Yara and Mr. C. Arya were formed to examine the complaints of customers of Andhra Bank in Andhra region. The committee was asked to report with recommendations in two weeks time.

3. **Preface:** Preface contains the author's or committee's opinion on the report and a statement on the report, objectives, circumstances leading to write a report, etc.
4. **Acknowledgement:** The author of a report should express proper acknowledgement to all source-materials cited in the report. It is a matter of intellectual honesty and validation of his work. For permitting to use ideas, tools, thoughts, etc., of authors, the writer expresses his indebtedness to them.
5. **Page of Contents:** It simply consists of the contents of report – chapter/ unit titles, synopsis under each chapter/unit with sub-titles, appendices, bibliography, etc.

6.5.2 Body of Report

The body of report contains classification, organization, analysis and interpretation of data with suggestions at the end. This section contains all the issues in detail pertaining to the investigated/surveyed research problem. These are discussed below.

1. **Purpose and Scope of Study:** The background of problem covering geographical area surveyed, methodology, definition of concepts, statement of problem, aspects of problem examination and the limitations of the study with the time and finance factors. An example: owing to constraints of time, the committee limited its study to four districts in Andhra region on the aspects of mobilization of deposits.
2. **Presentation:** Presentation is the second section of the report and covers the method used for collection/compilation of data. It begins with the meetings held by the committee as: The committee met four times, on 4th and 24th December 2016, 10th and 25th January 2017.

   The terms of reference of the study determines the nature of data required: secondary data or primary data. If the required data is secondary, it can be compiled from annual or administrative reports and other published sources. On the other hand, if the required data is primary, then collect either through questionnaire or interview schedule through closed-ended or open-ended questions administered on the sample-respondents selected through appropriate random or non-random sampling. In both cases of data compilation and collection, it is pertinent to the various issues covered in terms of reference. Record the collected data by holding the meetings with the officers of bank and interview with selected households. Process the collected data properly which follows classification, tabulation, and analysis with visual aids to make logical findings.
3. **Findings:** In the third section of the report, findings are made on the basis of logical conclusions. The findings and conclusions depend upon the thoroughness of investigation, data classification, organization, tabulation, analysis and interpretation. This section ends up with a brief summary of findings and conclusions. Exhibit 6.2 focuses on the essentials in writing a report.

Exhibit 6.2 Essence in Report Writing

"Sometimes, too many meetings create confusion. There are many changes in business conditions, so decisions cannot be made theoretically. You must have the feel and smell of each situation plus experience to get the right information and make the right decisions. Meetings are justified for obtaining information. But I don't think you need that much detail. Whenever I get a three-page report, I feel that half a page would be enough. In written report, managers often go in for two or three pages where one sentence would be enough. The top executive needs only the key things to make a decision."

4. **Recommendations:** Recommendations are made on the basis of findings and conclusions, if the entrusted task intended suggestions to the problem to be investigated. They are meant for actions by the appointing authority as remedial

measures to solve the problem. The suggestions should be written in the same order as the problems stated in the findings. In case, the entrusted assignment is only fact-finding, then the report ends with logical conclusions drawn. The recommendations start with an introductory sentence like:

The committee makes the following recommendations or the committee recommends the following steps or the following steps are recommended. The steps are:

1. Deployment of funds should be purpose-oriented linked with social aims like family planning, no default in the past, etc.
2. Monetary mechanism should be enforced continuously and vigorously.
3. Recovery should be linked with the marketing services.

5. **Signature:** A committee report should be signed by all members of the committee. The signatures are affixed on the right side of the report at the end. The Chairman of the committee signs the report supported by the signatures of all the members. The signature to the report signifies their acceptance or consent to its contents. If any member(s) disagree(s) with some of the points in the report, the member(s) sign it with a note of dissent.

   The place and date (date of submission of the report) are on the left of the report. For instance,

   Place: Hyderabad
Date: May 16, 2016

   A. Arya
(Convener)
B. Yara
(Member)
C. Arya
(Member)

6.6 DOCUMENTATION OF REPORT

In written communication, documentation has evolved as a subject of growing significance with well defined profession especially in the globalization scenario where business transactions are abound both in scope and wider area of geographical space. Therefore, documentation of a report is a nature of technical writing with offshoot of knowledge. The writer of business report should have specialized knowledge with writing skills who can translate the working of business houses into user-friendly content. Here, communication needs the services of technical writer, curriculum developer, technical publication specialist, technical editor and even graphic designer. To sum up, documentation calls for an insight into business knowledge and excellent communication skills with command over English or relevant languages and being well-versed in techniques of writing too. Notwithstanding any features of the report, the writing style of a report is presented below.

1. **Organization:** Clear organization is one of the canons of writing a good report. Each chapter or unit may be divided into appropriate number of sections with

suitable headings. Heading serves as pointer to where the discussion is made. The standard usage of paragraphs and giving headings to the topics and sub-topics should be followed. Generally, the grouping is from 'centered' section headings to 'marginal' headings to 'paragraph' headings and then to individual paragraphs. The physical presentation is another aspect of organization.

2. **Heading:** The centre heading is placed in the centre of page and is usually in bold capital letters. It is separated by two or three lines space from the text material. Heading is used on the left-side margin without leaving any space. No punctuation mark like full-stop or colon or semi-colon is used at the end of the heading.

   The paragraph heading is used to head an important aspect of the subject matter discussed in the section. No space is left between the margin and the heading; and the matter is presented in continuation of the heading along the same line. The matter presented under each paragraph may be grouped into several sub-paragraphs without separate heading, each sub-paragraph with a unified idea. Thus, a chapter/unit contains centre heading(s); each section contains several marginal headings; each marginal heading may have two or more paragraphs. The writing of a report, therefore, needs a plain discourse with accuracy, clarity of ideas and sequence of sentences, coherence of writer's thought smoothly and naturally from one to another statement, conciseness and readability.

3. **Punctuation:** The punctuations in writing a good report are:
   - Use correct spelling and sentence grammatically without errors
   - Avoid the first and the second pronouns (I, me, we, our, your, etc.) and use the third pronoun
   - Use active voice preferably
   - Use male and female pronouns when references made pertaining to male and female respectively
   - Use 'words' when the number is in single digit, and fraction (one-sixth) and at the beginning of a sentence
   - Use the word per cent with a number and percentage without reference to a number
   - Use the word per cent symbol (%) only in tables and graphs
   - Use the number even if it is a single digit in figures and tables
   - Present all tables and visual aids as near as possible to the text to which they refer

   Table and visual aids are used to provide a basis for discussion or points made in the text. They help the reader to understand properly and recognize them meaningfully as self-contained and self-explanatory.

   The margin on the right and top is one inch, and the margin on left and bottom is one and half inch each. Textual material is used in double-space. A paragraph is indented by seven spaces. Words should not be divided at the end of the line.

4. **Summarization:** The business executives of a unit, be it business organization, corporate sector, political institution, an individual or a group of individuals

need a summary of discussion or precise presentation in order to absorb quickly important information aspects for making sound decisions. What you read and how you express yourself concisely are two essential skills required in summarizing. A summary is a concised written or oral original passage containing no special expressions but the sentences are from the body of text. The utility of summarizing skills are in the following cases.

- Composing a telegraph or telex message
- Writing minutes of a meeting
- Drafting an advertisement copy for press
- Writing synopsis of a report
- Adjusting desired information on a package
- Saving a sheet to fax
- Storing information for future use

5. **Footnote:** Footnote is explanatory and explains accurately the idea without making it unduly long. If it is too long, it is better to provide the same in appendix. Footnotes are single-spaced with double spacing between two consecutive citations and are given consequently within each chapter or on each page. Footnote citations for references should contain indentation of full information. Footnote serves the following purposes:
   - Acknowledges indebtedness
   - Clarifies the information given in the text
   - Establishes the validity of evidence
   - Provides sources of information on the subject
   - Provides cross-reference to material appearing
   - Explains upon a point in the textual discussion
6. **Writing Style:** The report should be authoritative and appealing yet precise. It should:
   - Be a good piece of composition, presenting ideas logically and concisely
   - Maintain the original point of view
   - Be in the same tense as in original
   - Contain no examples or quotations
   - Not make use of first person
   - Make no comment on the views expressed in the original
   - Always have a title indicating text of report

6.7 QUALITIES OF GOOD BUSINESS REPORT

A good report must have certain qualities. They are:

1. **Clarity of Problem:** The report needs to indicate the clarity of problem, and avoid the use of jargons, terminology and phraseology so that the reader can understand meaningfully the scope and focus of the study.

2. **Clarity of Thought:** Clarity of thought as well as language is the most essential quality of the research report. The sentences should be simple without involving complicated clauses and long paragraphs so that the important points are sufficiently highlighted, with which the reader grasps easily what the report writer wants to say.
3. **Use of Concepts:** Appropriate use of concepts in terms of operations should be explained clearly in the context of inferring logical conclusions and generalizations thereon. Avoid the use of terms of contradiction as well as confusion which affect the report itself.
4. **Method of Presentation:** Perhaps, the most difficult part of report is the way in which it is to be presented. Opinions are sharply divided. The preparation of good report is scientific and should be up to the taste, expectations and understanding of readers keeping in view their degree of standards.
5. **Language Flow:** The language should be free-flow; avoid errors in spelling, use appropriate punctualities with standard rules, use present tense rather than past, and use direct and positive sentences. These are obvious ingredients in presentation of a report to be stated as a good report.
6. **Unity:** The condition of being one is referred to as unity. Each sentence must contain a single idea expressed clearly. All such individual sentences relating to the matter constitute a unified individual paragraph. Each paragraph in a section constitutes a unit of thought. The unity of principle is an aid to coherence which applies to the (i) individual sentences, (ii) individual paragraphs, and (iii) totality of the subject.
7. **Inclusion of Data:** The collected data and compiled data may contain non-essentials. Hence, the investigator should use only essential data ignoring non-essential data so that report may lend to quality of analysis. Essential data, whether more important or less important, should be used as per the need. The investigator can also attach the less important data as appendix.
8. **Chapter Plan:** A report should have separate chapters assigned to the objectives, introduction, conclusion and suggestions. Further, chapters must contain sections, sub-sections, tables and visual aids.

   Size of Report: The report must be reasonably sized covering the essence of investigation in compliance to the objectives.

6.8 SPECIMEN REPORTS

1. Drafting of Telegram

The drafting of a telegram contains clearly understandable message of essentials only conveying the main point without using punctuation. Incorrect use of punctuations in a telegram can dangerously mislead. For instance, No Price is too High which means that "No, the Price is too High" or "No price is too high." It is not clear whether a person is unwilling to pay such a high price or is willing to buy at any price. Some words should be added or it should be redrafted making the meaning clear.

The contractions like can't and don't are common which are easily recognized without an apostrophe. Others like I'll or we'll are common in everyday usage, but can mislead as the words have different meanings without the apostrophe (say Ill or well). Keep the number of words minimum. Words like Mr. or Mrs. for a person and Messrs, Co., Ltd for companies can be avoided. Use telegraphic address if the receiver has it. For example, the Institute of Chartered Accountants of India has the telegraphic address as ICAI. It is enough to write the telegraphic address and the pin code. The signature can also be in one word; the company's name or personal name can be used as signature. The obvious words that are not necessary while sending a message are:

Articles a, an and the

Personal pronouns like I, you, us, him

Obvious prepositions like on, in, of, by

Helping verbs used in the present and past participles like is, are, has, have

2. Report on Surprise Visit of Branch

Date: May 10, 2018

To

The Chairman

ABC Foods Limited

Sir,

Ref: Office Letter No. 468 dated April 08, 2017

Sub: Report on Working of Hyderabad Branch.

In accordance with your letter directions as referred above, I visited the Hyderabad branch on April 20, 2017. I observed the working of this branch office for four days and also inspected the office and the records. I am sorry to report that the branch office is run in the most unsatisfactory manner.

I reached the branch office on April 20, 2017 at 10.20 a.m. which is 10 minutes after opening time. I found that there were only a peon and two clerks. Taking me to a client, they informed me that office work starts only at 11.00 a.m. The manager Mr. Koushik arrived at 11.30 a.m.; lacking discipline himself. He is unable to maintain any discipline among the staff.

The stock register and account books have not been properly maintained for the last four months. It appears that office stationery and small articles are freely used, and taken away by the staff. The general indiscipline, if not controlled at once, is likely to result in heavy losses. Already the business is in loss since many of our clients have turned to our competitors owing to the poor service rendered by our branch office.

Recommendations: Since, the situation is quite bad, it will be necessary to take drastic measures to restore discipline in the branch office. I recommend that Mr. Koushik should be transferred to the Head Office and be placed in a subordinate position. Mr. Gemini, Assistant Manager of Pune branch has proved himself quite able; he may be promoted as Manager and posted at Hyderabad which is a potential centre of business.

Yours faithfully,

OM RAM

Secretary

3. Report on Decline of Sales

To Date: ....

The Managing Director,

ABC Tiles Ltd.

Ref: Your letter dated ....

Sub: Report on decline of sales

As per you instructions, I have enquired fully into the causes for decline in business of company in the last two years till May 2016 and submit my report which is as follows:

Several new companies have put out glazed tiles in the market; some of which have introduced artistically designed tiles in a variety of colours. Besides, most companies make square tiles in four sizes and rectangular tiles in two sizes. The production of tiles of our company has limited to six standard colours without design and to only two sizes.

Tiles are used extensively in kitchens of homes and hotels but the demand is for designed tiles and for sizes other than those we make. Hence, while the market for tiles has gone up, we have not been able to keep our share of the business.

Recommendations: An experienced designer should be appointed to create new designs for our tiles.

A colour technician should be appointed to assist the designer.

Some more popular sizes and shapes should be introduced.

An intensive advertising and sales campaign should be launched in order to win back the lost market.

Follow-up correspondence should be maintained with all former customers in order to regain and build-up old contacts.

Yours faithfully,
HONEY
Secretary

4. Auditors Report on Incurring Loss

The Directors Date: ....

Food Processing Works Pvt. Ltd

Tirupati

Sub: Submission of Report on incurring loss

As per your directions stated in your letter dated 1st January 2016, I observed the working of your company for ten days to investigate the methods of running the business and the daily conduct of the staff. From observation, the following defects were noted.

The Secretary loses interest because of age and poor health. The Registrar is too indecisive to control the office staff that disobeys his instructions. As a result, the work is not carried out according to the instructions of the Managing Director and is often seriously delayed. Customers complain about delays and some even cancel their orders owing to the delays in delivery.

The Managers-in-charge of Departments except the Department Stores have become too friendly with the workers. Their authority is thus weakened and the workers have wasted a great deal of time. The production has seriously gone down and the goods are not finished to the needed standard. This has resulted in rejection by customers and general loss of business apart from the loss of man hours, power and raw material. This matter has been reported twice to the Secretary by the Works Manager but no action has been taken.

Owing to ill-health, the Accountant has not kept his professional knowledge up-to-date and has made no effort to find out the best costing system to suit the business of company. Prices quoted for some contracts have been far below the cost and some of the carried out contracts have resulted in losses. When an attempt was made to correct this, unreasonably high prices were quoted leading to the loss of business.

Recommendations: The Secretary should be superannuated and the Registrar be demoted to the position of superintendent; and these positions should be filled with competent and efficient men who are able to impose discipline on the staff.

All the Managers of Departments except the Manager of Stores should be dismissed immediately with one month salary.

The Accountant should be suspended and a person with up-to-date knowledge should be appointed.

A staff meeting should be called to explain the need for discipline and to point out that disobedience to orders of superiors will be punished with immediate dismissal. Notices announcing this warning should be put up in all the Departments of the Offices and the Works.

Yours faithfully
BRAHMA
A G V REDDY & Company

5. **Report on Workers Unrest**

Date: ....

Terms of Reference: The work was assigned by Board of Directors at its meeting held on December 15, 2016 with terms of reference being the causes of workers' unrest and making recommendations to remedy the situation.

Procedure: The Manager of Works was met twice and detailed discussions were held; once alone and the second time in the presence of his assistants. Further two meetings were held; one with the foremen alone and one with the foremen in the presence of the assistants. Works Manager and 20 workers selected at random were interviewed personally and their views ascertained.

Findings: The discontent, apathy and unrest followed were observed among the workers in the month of January 2017 for the first time. To begin with, there were only signs of occasional outbursts of ill-temper or lack of interest in work. These were followed by group meetings and discussions of workers. Finally, at the end of February, meeting of all the workers was held and a memorandum was presented to the Works Manager. A report was sent by the Works Manager to the General Manager but the workers' representation was not sent.

Several foremen felt that unless remedial measures were taken, the situation might get out of hand, with a possible strike.

Causes of Unrest: Workers felt resentment at the insistence of the new Works Manager on punctuality and greater efficiency while the conditions in factory have become too uncomfortable for efficient functioning. Complaints were made by workers that:

There was no suitable bus service available from bus station to the factory. Even a slight delay in starting the machines was ticked off by the Works Manager.

There was not enough room in the canteen; workers strength has doubled during the last two years.

Machines were kept too close to each other and workers were unable to operate them with ease.

Conclusions: The complaints made by the workers seemed just:

Workers find it difficult to reach office in time as transport service is many a times irregular. However, the delay has never been more than ten minutes.

Workers have to spend part of their lunch hour waiting for a seat in the canteen as the canteen lacks space. Sometimes, they are often forced to eat hurriedly to be in time after the lunch hour.

Additional machines installed have been in violation of the Factories Act which lays down the minimum space between machines.

Recommendations: A bus service should be operated between the factory and the bus/railway station, to be run four times daily to coincide with the two shifts.

The store-room adjacent to the canteen should be cleaned up and handed over to the canteen for additional space.

The work should be suitably rescheduled until the machines are moved to the new premises.

The Works Manager should be advised to take a more humane view of the problem until the conditions are made more comfortable.

RISHI
Secretary

QUESTIONS

1. What is a report? State its purposes.
2. Explain types of business report.
3. Explain the structure of business report.
4. Discuss the documentation of business report.
5. Write a note on annual business report.
6. Explain the qualities of a good report.
7. Explain the punctuation of a quote and its citation.

7 CHAPTER

Marketing Service Communication

"How can we reach our customers, and how can we find ways to let our customers reach us."

— **Author**

LEARNING OBJECTIVES

This chapter will enable you to

- understand the relevance and role of communication in marketing;
- develop advertising message; and
- learn transaction of business electronically.

INTRODUCTION

Information spread about the features of product or services of an organization to the end-users in the market is referred as **diffusion**. Diffusion is the process by which the message is communicated within the members of the social system over time. In conventional marketing, communication is one-way through media. A sale is not just the end-transaction, but it is just the beginning of a long-term relationship of marketing. Relationship marketing, therefore, opens a two-way communication channel with consumers in the market. Consumers collaborate with the management of manufacturing to generate new products or new services by providing feedback as well as ideas. This guides the company about the products or services how customers think, what and why they prefer, and how they rate the company. If a customer repeats buying the product for a life-time, it makes up a tidy sum.

For instance, Hindustan Tobacco Association, 2010 research has shown that the life-time value of one cigarette smoker amount spent is ₹ 1.6 lakh over a period of ten years. It amounts to 70,000 times the value of a cigarette pack approximately. Retaining the existing customers against onslaught of competition is important and the reasons, if any, for desertion are monitored. Winning the loyalty of customers does obviously depend upon the relationship marketing; thus intertwined the communication and the collaboration as a marketing strategy. This kind of relationship marketing and trust between the organization and its customers benefit mutually. Hence, effective marketing communication is a key aspect in retention index of consumers.

For the purpose of marketing, a manufacturer has to communicate with the sales staff, delivery staff, servicing experts, wholesalers, agents, importers, exporters, and overseas agents, various kinds of retailers like chain-store owners, departmental stores, cooperative stores, supermarkets and down to the smallest road-side stall-keepers. Besides, distribution success or failure also depends on packaging, printers and transporting, advertising agents and media owners. To this list may be added people concerned with testing and approving, various officials of government, opinion of leaders and consumer organizations. Yet, marketing is not the only activity of manufacturing organization but building a strategy of it.

The business management is always involved in carrying out its functions – planning, organization, direction, staffing, coordination and control by communicating with others. The first step of a sound business management begins with communication. Thus, management and communication are intertwined; hence the management functions cannot be accomplished without communication. Modern marketing is the management of four 'P's namely (a) product, (b) price, (c) promotion and (d) place or distribution channel. Marketing communication, in corporate sector, is the most important part.

For example (i) the product communicates a distinctive image such as youthfulness, glamour or prestige, etc., (ii) the brand name communicates physical and psychological attributes of the products like dream flower talc, (iii) the package communicates what the manufacturer thinks of his consumers' convenience and sense of beauty, and (iv) the price communicates the quality of product. Further, there may be communications between the seller and the buyer for strengthening their relation. Therefore, each element of marketing-mix either helps or hinders communication and consequently the goal of ultimate sales. Therefore, marketing communication is a broader term than a promotion strategy. However, the latter is the most important element of the former.

7.1 MARKETING COMMUNICATION PROCESS

Figure 7.1 illustrates the process of marketing communication as applied to the product promotional strategy.

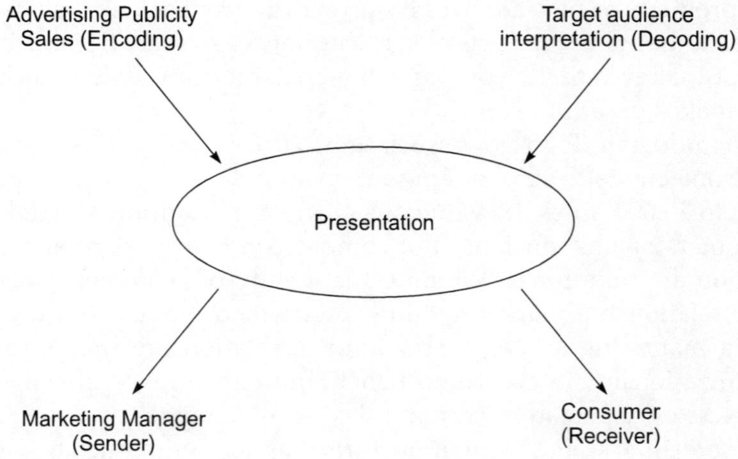

Figure 7.1 Marketing Communication Process

The marketing manager is the sender of the message. This message is encoded as advertising copy and publicity material, sales promotional displays or sales presentation by the sales personnel. The media for delivering the message may be the print like press and magazine or the electronic media like television, radio and films or a salesman who makes a presentation. The decoding step involves the consumer's interpretation of message. This is often the most challenging aspect of marketing communication as consumers may not always interpret the message the way the sender wants them to interpret. A major difficulty in communication process occurs in encoding and decoding. This may happen because the meanings attached to various words and symbols which may differ from consumer to consumer depend upon the frames-of-reference and the field-of-experience between the sender and the receiver.

7.1.1 Integrated Marketing Communication

Modern marketing calls for more than just developing a good product, but pricing it attractively and making it available to the customers. Business firms must communicate. Like good communication is important in building and maintaining any kind of relationship in business organization, it is a key element in a firm's efforts to build profitable customer relationship. In the modern era, the business organizations are facing some new marketing communication because of shifting to targeted marketing from mass marketing. They are adopting the concept of integrated marketing communication so that no one person or department is responsible for thinking through communication roles of various promotion tools and coordinating the promotion-mix. In a way, an integrated marketing communication builds up brand identity and strong customer relationship by tying together all of the firm's messages and images through interactive communications technologies.

7.1.2 Marketing Communication-Mix

A business organization's total marketing communication-mix, also called promotion-mix, consists of the specific blend of promotional tools such as (i) advertising, (ii) sales promotion, (iii) public relations, (iv) personal selling, and (v) direct marketing. These are used to pursue the set objectives of marketing. Description of these promotional tools is discussed hereunder.

1. **Advertising:** Advertisement can reach masses of geographically dispersed buyers at low cost per exposure and enable the seller-company to repeat the message many times. Television advertising can reach huge audiences. "If you want to get to the mass audience," says a Media Services Executive, "broadcast TV where you have to be." To introduce anything to a huge audience in a hurry – say a new product, a service, a new campaign, a new movie – the networks are still the biggest show. Media of advertising includes print, broadcast, internet, outdoor and others forums.

   Beyond reaching, advertising is positive about the seller's size, popularity and success because the consumers tend to view the advertised products as more legitimate. It builds up a long-term image for product or service (say, Coca-Cola) and triggers fast sales.

2. **Sales Promotion:** Sales promotion includes a wide variety of promotional tools like coupons, discounts, premium, point-of-purchase displays, etc., which have unique qualities such as attracting consumers, offering strong incentives to purchase, dramatizing product offers, boosting sagging sales and alike. All these stimulate as early as possible and build up a stronger market response. In other words, sales promotion consists of short-term incentives to encourage purchase or sales of products or services. Advertising says "buy our product,' while sales promotion says "buy it now." Simply, it is a short-term incentive for encouraging the purchase or sale of product or service.
3. **Public Relations:** Public relations are the major mass-promotion tools. The message through public relations reaches the audiences as 'news' and is easily believed the readers. A well-thought-out public relations campaign is effective and economical compared to other promotional tools. In reality, the marketers tend to the under-use public relations as an afterthought. Press releases, sponsorship and special events fall under public relations. Public relations are used to promote (i) product, (ii) people, (iii) places, (iv) activities, (v) organizations, and (vi) even nations. Nations have used public relations to attract more tourists, foreign investment, international support and alike.
4. **Personal Selling:** Selling is the oldest profession/job in the world. People who sell are known by many names: salespeople, sales representatives, account executives, sales consultants, sales engineers, sales agents, sales district managers and sales account development to name just a few.

   In building buyer's preferences, convictions and actions, personal selling is the most effective tool at certain stages of buying process. It is because of personal interaction between two or more people so that each person observes the other's needs and characteristics and makes quick adjustments. The effective salesman keeps the customers' interests at heart in order to build a long-term relationship. It includes sales presentations, trade-shows and incentive programmes.
5. **Direct Marketing:** Direct marketers communicate with customers, often on a one-to-one and interactive basis. Various forms of direct marketing – telephone marketing, direct mail, online marketing, kiosks and others – all share four distinctive features viz., (i) specific person, (ii) immediate, (iii) customized, and (iv) interactive. It allows a dialogue between the marketing team and the consumers; the message can be altered depending upon the consumers' response. Direct marketing, thus, is well suited to the highly targeted marketing efforts as it obtains an immediate response and cultivates lasting one-to-one customer relationship, for example, Dell Computer interacts directly with customers, by telephone or through its website, to design the systems that meet customers' individual needs. Buyers place order directly with Dell, and Dell quickly and efficiently delivers the new systems at their homes or offices.

7.1.3 Ethics

1. **Meaning:** The word, ethics derives from 'ethos' which means character. Peter Drucker defined it as: "Ethics is more important to do the right things than do

things right." Roger Devlin has defined ethics as: "If you can tell the difference between good advice and bad advice, you do not need advice." Most people have no difficulty in understanding the spirit of ethics and do not question or argue about the axiom that ethics is not a matter of choice. Just as you do not question the right of other people to live, you do not question their right to expect ethical behaviour from you. In literature, ethics means a set of principles or morals. Good words and nice phrases are pre-requisites for ensuring communication purposefully and for building-up organizational relationship meaningfully to achieve the purpose. More than this, today's business being affected critically depends upon one important aspect namely ethics. Ethics is always an add value, concerning communication with honesty in the life of human beings.

2. **Honesty:** The noblest word among the social virtues is honesty. It essentially binds people together in the family, community and society. Nevertheless honest communication involves an obligation to one's self, and to other people. With intuition in the mind, rightness is known with respect to expertness in living. Under the cordial virtue, honesty may be taken 'justice.' It does not only mean being faithful to contracts and carrying out the duties needed by the Law of the society, but also means loyalty in all of one's relationships with others including the obligation to speak honestly. Honest communication is for everyone. It is the most essential tendency to apply rigorous ideal of honesty in communication for goodness and progress of the society. Honest communication with value-orientation is most needed in political environment to realize that every proposed Law is an alternative safeguarding interests of people in the nature.

7.1.4 Marketing Ethics and Communication

Marketers are, sometimes, accused of deceptive practices which lead consumers to believe they will get more value than they actually do. Deceptive practices are of (i) deceptive pricing (say, wholesale price or large price reduction), (ii) deceptive promotion (say, misrepresenting product's features), and (iii) deceptive packaging (say, exaggerating package contents through subtle design, using misleading labeling). These deceptive practices have led to the formation of legislation and consumer protection in guiding and governing the principle of societal marketing service. The business organizations should develop marketing ethical policy covering the following aspects in conduct of business.

- Distribution relations
- Advertising standards
- Customer service
- Pricing
- Product quality and development
- General ethical standards

All these are essentially needed to integrate in marketing-mix which would develop good relationship marketing (GRM). See Exhibit 7.1 for morally difficult situations in the arena of marketing.

Exhibit 7.1 **Morally Difficult Situations in Marketing**

You work for a cigarette company. Public policy debates over the past few years now leave, no doubt, in your mind that cigarette smoking and cancer are closely linked. What would you do?

The Research and Development Department has changed one of your products slightly. It is not really "new and improved" but you know that putting this statement on the cigarette package and in advertising will increase sales. What would you do?

You are interviewing a female applicant for a job as salesperson. She is better qualified than the men just interviewed. Nevertheless, you know that some of your important customers prefer dealing with men, and you will lose some sales if you hire her. What would you do?

Honesty is the hallmark in one's self to other people. Respect to rightness gives one an expertness and esteem in living. It is an essential quality of people in binding together either in the family or community or society. In fact, it is a fundamental rule of conduct. How honesty aids, see Exhibit 7.2.

Exhibit 7.2 **Be Honest in Communication**

Transparency in communication is the best tool to motivate people or employees. By being honest and realistic, the management gives good reason to be loyal and productive employees. If the organization is going through a bad phase, it may be tempted to suggest employees that everything is going to be okay. Attempts to sugar coat or gloss over bad news does not help in any way to keep employees engaged during uncertainty. Instead, prepare people or employees by truthfully describing what they are facing. The key to success lies in communicating messages which are hopeful yet realistic. This involves understanding the organizational pulse and the feelings of employees. This, in turn, helps the employees or people to even keep at distant locations in the loop.

Ethical practices should be instituted by the companies to flow from the top and percolate to all the levels below. For instance, a lofty statement about ethics in the company's 'vision' statement is good but not enough. Companies should constantly practice ethics, question themselves periodically and take the course of corrections to travel in the right direction as ethics is not a destination but it is a journey. Such significance of ethics being honest, truthful and fair in the marketplace becomes a cushion for sound business strategies. Unethical practices do immense damage to relationship marketing in the long run. Therefore, the success of business heavily depends upon effective communication with an inbuilt mechanism of ethics.

7.1.5 Rationale of Ethics in Business

The measures compelling in today's business need to go beyond good words and nice phrases. The spirit in which communication is a effected and relationships addressed is ethics or values concerning communication in business. The operational scenario of today's business is described as: The marketplace of today's competitive business can be described as a battleground and marketing a civilized form of warfare in which most battles are won with words, ideas and disciplined thinking. The spirit behind the words counts much.

In this type of scenario, every business has its set of principles or code of conduct. This code often outlines the do's and don'ts of its approach to business and customers; and articulates its duties and responsibilities as well. Every profession including business in the society has ethical values governing its business conduct. Value refers to a certain intrinsic quality or worth whereas ethics refer to the treatment of morality or duty. Hence, values and ethics often go together. The progressive business makes it a point to articulate values and lay emphasis on the ethical aspects in transacting business. Emphasis is on the need of ethics in business organization in respect of the following aspects explained below.

1. **Competition:** In competition beat, business often does not have much choice except to use flashy words and ideas to penetrate the markets to win over and retain customers. The bottom line is to sustain business; the governing of which needs the rules that a business follows in pursuing communication and customer relations. It is well known fact that business decisions are taken more with the head than with the heart. A business, which really endures, is one that shows commitment to the values following ethical dimension with pecuniary objective.

2. **Perpetual Entities:** Business organizations are perpetual entities in the corporate world; for which much significance is being attached to fulfill the specific needs of people in the society. They will continue to thrive and survive as long as they strive to meet this specific need in the manner which is acceptable to the customers or service seekers. In other words, they must earn and sustain people's trust and confidence on an ongoing basis as business cannot exist and operates in vacuum. Communication as an effective tool has to take cognizance of this phenomenon between them.

3. **Principles:** The progress of business organizations are value driven and affirm their commitment to the core principles of business in order to earn and retain customers' trust and confidence. Good governance needs effective communication and a good congenial atmosphere should adhere to the committed business principles. For instance, the vision document or the mission statement with words and deeds should clearly reflect the value system of business when an advertisement comes into being. Some business principles that should be adhered to, in conduct of business are that the organization may decide not to:

   - Make any adverse comments, implicitly or explicitly about its competitors and their products
   - Advertise in any politically affiliated newspaper or journal
   - Pass on to the customer any loss arising out of mistakes committed by its employees

- ➢ Finance (bank or financial institute) speculative or activities which are not in the best interest of the society
- ➢ Go against products which are eco-friendly and promote environment protection

4. **Caveat Emptor:** The sense of a fair play in buying goods or services is an important value which should permeate communication and customer relations. It is appropriate to note that in early part of the nineties, many companies came up with their initial public offers (IPO), deliberately carrying vital information in fine print and the gullible investor was taken for a ride. Some companies made a quick buck and vanished; in the process, the investor's confidence eroded in the primary market activity. At that time, a growing realization came up among the market leaders to follow the best practices in investment so that the investors' confidence is not eroded. A value driven approach is must, if the faith in the market is to be kept up. Everyone associated with communication should make every effort to abide by such values. The caveat emptor means to be aware of the purchaser. This term is popularly applied in marketing parlance.

5. **Corporate Governance:** The term corporate governance has a wide connotation. It supports the business ethics to shun short-cuts and unethical practices; and to bring out accountability of the management to the stakeholders. It means the corporate governance strives to ensure three cardinal principles of communication, viz., (i) **adequacy** (relevant information made available to all concerned ones), (ii) **transparency** (openness without hoodwink), and (iii) **consistency** (business conduct that reflects core principles and performance claims which stands over a period of time) of business organization while dealing with its stakeholders, viz., shareholders, creditors, the state, employees, suppliers, etc.

   Through advertising, the marketer, for example, communicates information about his products or services. There is widespread research on how the advertisement will be prepared, when it will be presented, what will be its principal appeals and so on. Advertising research is, in turn, preceded by research on consumer behaviour. What are the motives or purposes for which consumers buy a product, what are the feelings which actuate them to purchase and so on. See Exhibit 7.3 for ethics in operation in a real-life story.

Exhibit 7.3 Ethics in Operation: A Real Life Story

The focus is to create, maintain, develop and constantly improve the quality of relationship between the business and the customers leading to a durable and long-standing bond of friendship, trust and quality. This ultimately develops customer loyalty.

ABC Company at its highest level has considered the position deeply with the following commandments. These are:

- Invest and develop quality equipment
- Do not quote opportunistic prices
- Do not lower tendered prices to bag orders
- Indulge in ethical marketing and never bribe
- Do not use agents to do the dirty work while pretending that the company is clean
- Accept delays and disappointments
- Do not blame others for failure in winning contracts or getting the equipment passed
- Make sure that everyone in the company sends the same signal that it wants business only on merits

The company was struck by the policy. There were denials and the company management might have looked like a fool in the eyes of some people. But slowly and steadily, the word went around that the company is not interested in bribing or dining for winning contracts. Hints and approaches were stopped from corrupt quarters. The company got invited for only official techno-commercial negotiations. A joke erupted among the competing bidders that ABC Company is philosophical and the best loser. It continued to lose orders in many tenders, big and small; even when its prices were lowest on some pretext of deviation brought up by someone in the chain of authority.

Within a year, the situation started changing and very senior officials started suspecting something amiss. They saw the confidential notes and reports which showed that the ABC Company is not showing interest. It was invited once, twice and again to the special negotiation meetings by the highest authority who always asked if it was really interested in business and if so, why it was so rigid. The company politely and firmly used to convey that it offers right qualities and prices, and is prepared to wait to take orders based only on merit. Enormous goodwill was generated and across the line went a word that the company's price should be treated as benchmark. It started getting business and educational orders to start with. Orders were won sometimes even when its prices were marginally higher.

By the second year, the position of ABC Company changed dramatically. Most offices in the line of authority started recommending its tender with signal that it is upright and honest. Within a period of three years, ABC Company not only prospered image-wise but commercially too in a difficult field by following steadfastly the ethical value. Thus, ethics is about honouring the human spirit, honouring the people who are 'business' and honouring the consumers who become a foundation for success of business.

7.1.6 Cross-Culture Communication

In the lives of members of organization, culture plays a key role. Organizational theorists, in the recent past, have begun to focus on the significance of culture which occupies a crucial role. Apart from the members, organizations which are institutionalized take on a life of its own and get value support and immorality.

A shared value system of member of organization which distinguishes itself from other organizations is referred to as culture. The communication pattern is a feature of organizational culture; the degree to which organizational communication is restricted to the formal hierarchy of authority. Every business organization has a dominant culture and a number of subcultures; the former being referred to, by a majority members of an organization and the latter refers to the core values of the dominant culture plus additional values which are particular and peculiar to the members of that sub-group. A subculture reflecting common problems – situations or experiences of the section or department employees' is a limitation in large business organization. The subculture is being aroused by department delegations and geographical separations. For instance, a production department may have a subculture, i.e., uniquely shared by the members of that department only. Nevertheless, culture of organization has common properties which does not mean without subculture. Maintenance of an effective communication in business organization in a situation or prevailing dominant sub-cultures seems to be difficult.

Cross-culture communication can pose trouble during interaction. Different individuals in business organizations may possess different cultural backgrounds. Perception or meaning of message is not the same for each person due to difference in perception and degree of understanding makes difference in encoding the message by the sender and decoding of message by the receiver into subjective symbols. If the degree of difference in the background of members' organization is greater between the receivers, the greater is the difference in the meanings attached to it by particular words or behaviour. People from different cultures see, interpret and evaluate things differently; consequently act upon it differently. Misperception, misinterpretation, misevaluation and misunderstanding are the results of cross-culture communication. Guidelines to improve cross-culture communication are given below:

1. **Maintain Similarity:** Until similarity is established it is always desirable to guess the existence of difference in communication. It is a fact that people think the others are similar to them working in the organization. In practice, it is not a fact! Until similarity is proved, assume that difference exists.
2. **Emphasis Description:** Emphasize description rather than its interpretation or evaluation as another rule. It is always advisable to delay the judgment description until the observation and interpretation of situation from the point of different perspectives of all cultures is involved completely.
3. **Empathy:** Empathy is considered a primary prerequisite for a satisfying experience in any relationship with the degree of depth of understanding. The sender should put himself in the recipient's shoes before sending a message. He is supposed to understand values, experiences and frames of reference of the recipient. In brief, he has to see and understand the other person as he/she is.
4. **Working Hypothesis:** Treating interpretation of assumption is considered a hypothesis for improving the cross-culture communication with further testing is another rule in cross-culture communication.

7.2 COMMUNICATION MODEL

Marketing communication especially through advertising meant for a group of end-users of products or services is called target audience. Of course, buying of a product or service is the ultimate response of buyer being expressed by 'desire to buy' and 'ability to buy'. The receipt and acceptance of advertising message by the target customers is core issue dependent on the effectiveness of advertising appeal. Attention, Interest, Desire and Action are being formed as acrimony of AIDA which is a sound model of communication in capturing a better market share. This is a solitary reason behind the great divergence between the number of people exposed to the advertisement and those who ultimately take the decision to purchase their desired goods or services. The elements of marketing-mix become crucial at this stage of advertisement. AIDA is explained below.

1. **Attention:** The focus of advertisement must be on how to attract the attention of targeted customers; for which the size of advertisement with typography and use of colours compel them to be attractive. In other words, advertisement must be in a position to add its attention value. Using celebrities in advertisement, dramatization, model selection and illustration contribute to attract good attention.
2. **Interest:** Advertisement seen does not mean advertisement read but people see the illustrations. So, illustrations have to work hard together with headlines provoking further reading. For interest creation, the format of advertisement copy either scientific or humorous to consider the situation, illustrated selection and its integration to life are the basic issues that must be considered while preparing an advertisement copy. This stage affects the attitude to buy.
3. **Desire:** Function of advertisement is to motivate people or create desire in them physiologically as well as psychologically for product or service through appeals. The advertisement copy must kindle the motives. People become prone to buy products only when their reservation about product quality, price, durability, after-sales service, etc., is supported by giving evidence, testimonials, endorsements, facts and figures.
4. **Action:** End of desire is to buy the product. It is behavioural stage.

7.3 MESSAGE DEVELOPMENT

Many media carry the advertising messages for so many products for which advertising is necessary. A number of organizations advertise their products or services. Therefore, there is a lot of communication in all directions with message development being direct, indirect and zigzag.

Advertising objectives can be achieved through a creative strategy of message describing what to say (content) and how to say (style) and the media strategy describing which media and what time the message is to be put across in the society. Basically, advertising strategy is a creative mix of advertising message and communication media focusing on the target audience and the product concept. The advertising message appeals have three features: (i) meaningful – making the product desirable or interesting with benefits, (ii) believable – the product will deliver the promised benefits, and (iii) distinctive – tell how the product is better than the competing brands (examples are (a) Timex has been an affordable watch that takes a "lickin" and keeps on "tickin"; (b) Rolex stresses luxury and status). Thus, developing an effective message strategy begins with identifying customer benefits which can be used as advertising appeal.

A message is to structure keeping in view the broad objectives of communication and the audience. The format of advertising message is characterized by the type of media in which it is used. In radio advertising, the elements are words, voice qualities (speech rate, rhythm, pitch, articulation) and vocalization (pauses, sighs, yawns) while in print advertising, the message format elements include: (i) size of letters in headline and body of message; and (ii) position of picture with colour. Appeal messages influence buying behaviour needs of buyers by developing a creative advertising copy as it involves time, money and energy. The message development copy synthesizes the purpose of creative strategy (induces direct action and influences the attitudes of customers) and compels the readers or audience 'to stop, look and listen.'

The features of a good advertisement copy are that it must (a) be thematically sound, (b) be interesting, (c) be communicative, (d) have credibility, (e) be complete and (f) contain truthful information. However, the well governing aspects of advertising message presentation are:

- Drawing conclusions: Message should enable consumers to draw definite meaning. To promote the use of eggs among vegetarians, a poultry farm gives advertisement with a new name an 'Veggs'. The baby firm gives an advertisement as 'Your baby is born with a 3-month gift of iron.' After 3 months, milk alone cannot give him the iron he needs.
- Repetition: Improves audience attention and increases awareness and knowledge on the part of prospect of products or services.
- One-versus-two-sided communication: One-sided message tends to work best with the audiences which are initially favourably predisposed to the claims made in advertising message while two-sided message tends to be more effective with knowledgeable audience capable of sound reasoning when exposed to counter propaganda.
- Comparative advantage: Parallel categories of products or services are compared with each other to get the competitive advantage. Examples are Captain Cook Salt and Tata Salt, Johnson & Johnson Stayfree Napkins and Whisper Napkins, manufacturer free-service and private-service.

7.4 E-MARKETING

The products fit for the online world are the ones that do not need to be seen, touched or tried by the consumers. Examples are books, music, office products, etc. But, shopping a car or a shirt is still a distinct possibility for people in India. Change is the law of nature. Organizations are developing new relationships with customers, distributors, suppliers and partners. With this perception, the key for survival and growth is changing.

E-commerce is such change happening today. It has given birth to interactive marketing. The four major e-marketing domains are given in Table 7.1.

Table 7.1 E-Marketing Domains

Initiation by	Targeted to consumers	Targeted Business
Business	B2C	B2B
Consumer	C2C	C2B

Supply chain is the entire process of accepting a customer's order through internet to deliver the ordered product to him inclusive of procurement and production of product. It is a collection of interdependent measures, following them give rise to meeting the customers' needs. In other words, it is a generic term which covers the coordination of order generation, order taking and order fulfillment and distribution of products, services or information. The goals of supply chain management are to: (i) reduce cost, (ii) increase profits, (iii) improve relationship performance with customers and suppliers, and (iv) develop value added services to provide a competitive edge. The supply chain management goals and benefits are given in Table 7.2.

Table 7.2 Supply Chain Management

Management	Goal	Benefits
Supplier	Reduce the number of suppliers. Let suppliers become partners	Reduce purchase order processing costs per employee and increase processing order Reduce order processing cycle time
Inventory	Shorten the order bill cycle	Information can be sent immediately, inventory levels reduced, improved inventory turns and eliminates stock occurrences. Equips to receive documents
Distribution	Move documents to shipping	Fast paper work with more accuracy
Channel	Disseminate information on changing operational conditions quickly to trading partners	Instant access on pricing, product and technology requirement Linking production with international distributors which eliminates reselling network
Payment	Payment can be sent and received electronically	Invoices can be computed at increasing speed, errors can be reduced, less transaction fee and increased number of processing invoices.

7.4.1 E-Business and E-Commerce

E-business is transactions of a business organization and functional process enhancing organizational competitiveness through the application of technologies whereas e-commerce is only the 'front-end' of e-business which is a generic term that encompasses all forms of business transactions executed over the internet. In other words, e-business goes beyond e-commerce by integrating it tightly with business operations to improve performance, create value and enable new relationships between the customers and the business. Thus, e-business is a marketplace carrying out business through internet technologies and network computing to securely transform the following:

- Internal business processes via intranets
- Business relationships via extranets
- Trade (buying and selling of goods or services) via e-commerce

E-commerce is a way of executing business transactions like ordering, invoicing and paying, shipping of products and producing of financial statements through an interactive electronic media (i.e., internet). In other words, it helps the business to expand, strengthen and access the new markets as an alternative to paper-based methods of communication and storage of information. Simply, it is 'doing business online.' Thus, both e-business and e-commerce are a natural evolution of current business and technology trends, which have now, become new paradigms of the new digital economy. The reasons of using e-business are to:

- Attract new customers
- Build loyalty among the existing customers
- Improve customer services
- Streamline business processes
- Increase sales to existing customers
- Grow market share
- Enhance communication among customers
- Enhance employees communication

The growth of e-commerce heavily depends upon the communication infrastructure. For conducive and healthy environment, the Government of India passed the Information Technology Act, 2000 by the Parliament on May 17, 2000. It is the second cyber laws in the whole of Asia after Singapore providing a legal recognition for transactions carried out by means of electronic data interchange.

The functions of e-commerce are broadly grouped into (i) online point-of-sale and transactions processing, (ii) web wholesaling and retailing, (iii) electronic data interchange, (iv) electronic funds transfer, (v) electronic banking, (vi) interactive marketing and (vii) supply chain management. Chart 7.1 explains obviously the scope of e-commerce.

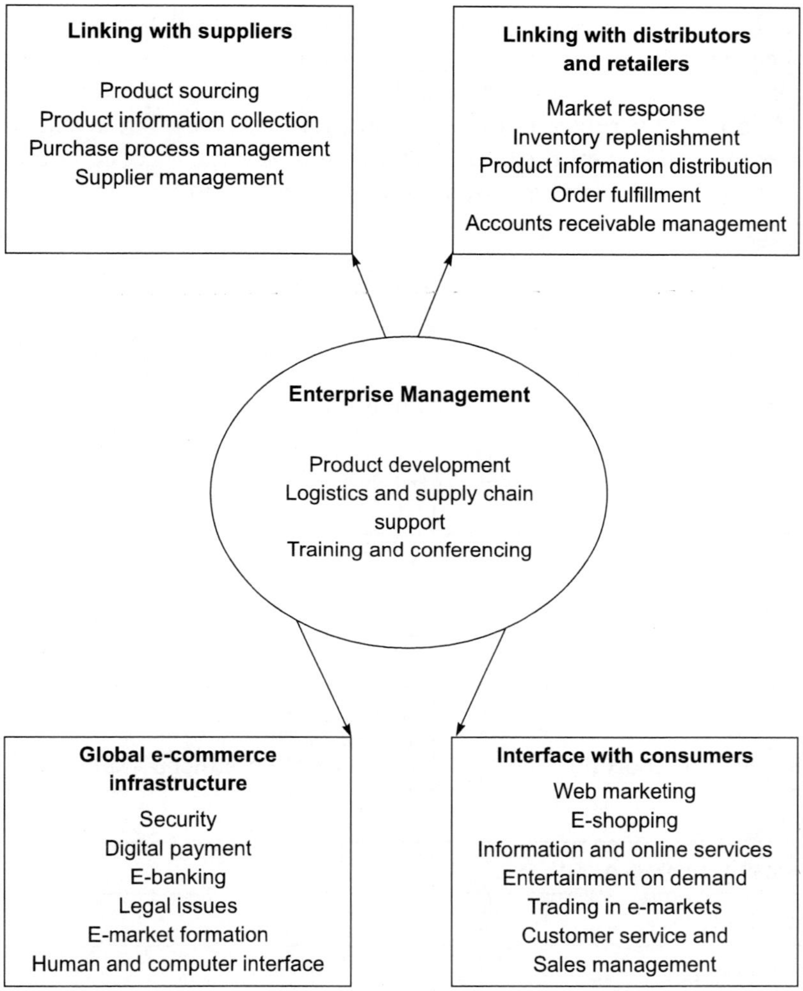

Chart 7.1 Interface of e-Commerce

7.4.2 Scope of e-Business and e-Commerce

The internet automates the processes and hence business is able to resolve the delays involved in supplies and delivery of products, keeping the cost at bare minimum. Human beings cannot vanish either in functional process or trade of an enterprise but move to other tasks for generating the real value such as:

- Personalized customer service
- Sales
- Business development
- New product research

It is perceived that e-commerce is a (a) strategy, (b) technology, (c) system, (d) business, (e) sales approach, and (f) mastery in modern business methodology addressing the needs of business enterprises, consumers and management for improving add value to the quality of goods or services with speed and reduced costs. In a way, the digital economy is spreading and becoming global in view of the demands of customers and the imperatives of business. Specifically, e-business and e-commerce include the following issues (Table. 7.3).

Table 7.3 Scope of e-Business and e-Commerce

e-business	e-commerce
Merchandise planning and analysis	Suppliers
Order entry, order tracking, order fulfilment	Distributors
Warehousing	Dealers
Inventory	Vendors
Shipping	Suppliers sourcing
Returns	Selection
Pricing promotions	Post-sales support
Financial accounting and reporting	Awareness to product research
Customer service	
Customer relationship management	
Knowledge management	
Supply chain management	

Further, e-commerce through internet enables to contribute to the rapid internationalization of the services sector. Internet makes e-commerce a separate larger package of production and consumption of information-intensive service activities. Thus, e-commerce plays a fundamental role in service industries and primary industries which are as follows:

- Computing
- Accounting
- Human resource: knowledge management
- Marketing: supply chain management and customer relationship management

7.4.3 Online Shopping

Shopping through use of credit or debit card without leaving house is termed as online shopping. It is a gateway for consumers and merchants to link up quickly and securely over the worldwide web. Today, it has become a popular internet activity. Malamaal.com stated that "we offer products from unorganized sectors, which do not have means to reach various parts of the globe. These products, from a particular city or region, can be purchased through our site." This online shopping provides sheer convenience, wider choice, better value, unique gifting opportunity, saves time and strain, micro-targeting, mass personalization, know customer preferences and integrate source of information.

E-commerce is the most remarkable facet of the emerging digital economy. It ensures not only radical changes in business service and communication with the customers but also the way it manages their relations with supplies and partners. This drive reduces cost, improves efficiency and has an edge over competition. This enables the business enterprise to adopt a new methodology for doing business termed business-to-business (B2B). The present-day business enterprises carry out good work and link stakeholders in supply chain, taking out existing inefficiencies which are time-consuming and tedious tasks for cutting down costs as a primary goal. The stock exchanges, banks with credit, debit and smart cards, payment and delivery system (B2B), etc., are working online.

For making Indian business, more competitive at the global market is at rapid strides and e-commerce offers considerable opportunity. Even considered the most pessimistic projections with regards to the expected users of internet at 300 million people in availing e-banking, e-broking, e-reservation, e-money transfer, e-procurement, e-marketing, e-tender, e-learning, e-health care, e-processing and production quality, e-couriers, etc., indicate that e-commerce is a boom.

India with a population of nearly a billion, not even a million (12 per cent) having access to computer as well as internet is a primary cause of e-commerce which is still in its infancy. Most people are not comfortable with the idea of credit cards itself; let alone using them on the internet. There is no direct impact to generate desire as well as no bargaining which trigger the consequence of no purchase. Security and safety remain worrying issues in the minds of users. India will soon become a major player in e-commerce provided that the government should integrate the computer network with safe measures as an integral part of the economic infrastructure and become an asset for common people.

Though convenience at any place and anytime shopping online with variety of products and wider choice, but absence of (i) making sure of product quality, (ii) providing an opportunity of negotiation, (iii) insuring security of transactions without misuse, (iv) ensuring a touch-feel-try of product, (v) e-billing universal trademarks, etc., are the issues that need to be addressed immediately. At the national level, the Government of India and at the international level, the World Trade Organization and International Chamber of Commerce have to evolve an inbuilt mechanism for development of e-commerce. For this purpose, a regulatory authority should be developed. Further, the government should take steps to arrest online frauds or bad trade practices polluting the online environment and ensuring e-commerce's inner beauty – 'simplicity and security' of transaction.

QUESTIONS

1. What is marketing communication? Explain the marketing communicating process.
2. Write a note on communication model.
3. What is cross-cultural communication? Explain
4. Distinguish between interactive and mass communication.
5. Explain the role of marketing communication

8 CHAPTER

Communication and Listening and Speaking Skills

"When you are listening to somebody completely and attentively, then you are listening not only to the words, but also to the feeling of what is being conveyed, to the whole of it, not part of it."

— **Jiddu Krishnamurthy**

LEARNING OBJECTIVES

This chapter will enable you to

- master skills in communication; and
- understand the listening skill and its importance.

INTRODUCTION

In the modern days, changes have progressed in communication style due to advanced technology. Its influence is being seen in the spheres of governance, management, business, education, transmission of noble thoughts and diffusion of innovative and invention results and daily lives. Persons in every field need to acquire knowledge and skills for being successful in their field. The aim of communication is not achieved completely till the receiver receives the message which the sender intends to send.

Communication is an important skill. Communication skills are not only needed in daily personal life, but also required in the profession, workplace and in business. Depending on the nature of profession, working in a team or interacting with customers or other people, often find certain situations which are challenging to handle. Here it is an area where having best communication skills becomes handy.

Good listening is as much hard work as good speaking. Good listening leads to proper understanding of the message while poor listening can lead to misunderstanding and incomplete understanding. In other words, a receiver becomes the sender and the sender becomes the receiver and communication becomes a complete two-way process. Therefore, good communication calls for listening skills and a good speaker must necessarily be a good listener. Davis K says that "Nature gave persons two ears but only one tongue which is a gentle hint that they should listen more than they talk. Listening requires two ears, one for meaning and one for feeling. Decision-makers who do not listen properly have less information for making sound decisions."

A listener receives message, decodes and interprets it. Communication may be oral, written, visual and non-verbal comprising interchange of opinions, ideas, reactions and information, and alike to fulfill the goals of an organization. In a progressive organization, feedback from the concerned persons receives equal importance. Reading is the basic source of knowledge. Listening and discussion supplement reading in the pursuit of acquiring knowledge. Knowledge is more precise and effective, developed through writing than either teaching or discussion alone. Therefore, one would need to speak, make presentations and write examinations or assignments to demonstrate knowledge. This would make him master language skills to read, write or speak. To work effectively with other(s), communication skills and strategies are the need of the hour. All the three, namely: (a) reading and writing, (b) language and expression, and (c) speaking, listening and presenting constitute communication skills.

8.1 CORPORATE EDUCATION

An aspect that possesses knowledge for developing human resources lies on the skills of know-how and do-how to sustain life-living and improving the socio-economic growth and development is called education. Exposure of students to the practical aspects and skills is most essential. It means a shift from just acquisition of textbook knowledge to all important aspects of acquiring skills. This ensures students' communication and interpersonal skills by interacting with people and also fair performance at the interview being conducted by the corporate executives.

There was a time when teaching was considered precious and free from buzzwords like work-life balance, target achieving, conflict handling, crisis management, etc., But today, the scenario has totally changed because the corporate sector felt that a change is required under global scenario. This transformation should be change-prone in both industrial and service sectors. In the past, much importance was given to traditional tools of teaching whereas it is, now, time to move towards corporate education under ever-changing environment nationally and globally in the competitive era. As a part of this change, the students are required to expose to the respective field rather than a classroom session. Even the faculties are motivated to concentrate and focus more on their personality development and relevant administrative skills leading to students' purposive-orientated coaching. In other words, weight must be given to assess the quality of education imparted to the students for proper decision-making in job selection and enriching the jobs.

An effective communication in an interactive process depends upon the basic thread of communication skills and listening skills. So that, the sender has a thorough evaluation of the choices available and their relative advantages of media and modes in making good communication; and the listener (receiver) comprehends the message received. In other words, the message reaches the intended audience with the meaning of sender and the receiver prompts to reply the phenomena of communication which does come to, is an end with purpose. The skills of communicating the messages and the skills of listening are, therefore, a coin with two sides which add value to communication. The skills of communication and listening are discussed in the following pages.

8.2 COMMUNICATION SKILLS

The means employed for taking the message to the target audience is called communication skills. They are a focused thrust in communication with a fundamental and dynamic activity for upkeeping pace progress of people, business and occupation in the society. It is seen in the earlier chapters that communication is so effective to work and work-life situations but identified as complex due to interplay of human beings, organizations and electronic devices. Communication process is, thus, complex due to diverse human skills, attitudes, aptitudes, behaviour-styles and socio-cultural background. Notwithstanding this complex situation, the process of communication must strengthen self-development and career development indeed a *sine-qua-non* for achieving excellence in the sphere.

Communication begins with what we intend to communicate and how detailed it is. Is it a stray thought, idea, concept, event, achievement or development? Can we encode and transmit the message? But, the essence and core of communication must be clear with simplicity of facts, events, inventions, innovations, concepts and expectations leading to well-being and welfare of people in the society.

1. **Objective to Communicate:** Communication is objective-oriented to reach a person with a meaningful message. Whether communicating the message is only to inform or analyze, reiterate, caution, report or remind. Is it to motivate and win over, influence, inspire and seek response? Thus, communication has varied objectives of reaching information, analysis, persuasion, negotiation, detailing, motivation, counseling, developing, educating, imparting and enlisting action with different implications helping learn different skills of communication.
2. **Form to Communicate:** The mode and media, channels and alternative approach determines the form of communication. Will communication be oral, written, non-verbal, audio-visual, and electronic or a mix of these? Is communication is a formal or informal channel? Is it direct (face-to-face) or indirect? Will it be through letter, telex, fax, e-mail, internet, telephone, short message service? Besides, time availability, speed and cost also constitute the determining factors of communication form. The choice is determined on the basis of skills of communication, relative costs, merits and demerits.
3. **Whom to Communicate?** The sender of message should be clear about the target audience and how to reach them. The target audience are (a) dispersed across different functional, hierarchical and geographical areas; (b) spread across different market segments or different units and regions; and (c) have different motivation levels. Considering all these, will it be direct or indirect communication? Will it be open or confidential? Will it be general or personal? 'To whomsoever it may concern.' In view of fact that all these have limited use, good communication skills make communication specifically to address.
4. **When to Communicate?** Communication must take place at the right time; but neither too early nor too late. While sharing of information about the events, developments, achievements, etc., the scheduled time ensures receptivity in important meetings.

5. **How often to Communicate?** Timing, intensity and frequency are necessary for effective communication. Is one-time message enough or is it necessary to follow up? One should remember that too many reminders without appreciating the underlying factors would serve little or no purpose; and undermine the person's (sender's) authority.
6. **How to get Feedback?** The final step in effective communication is feedback. Feedback is not as easy as sending information. It involves considerable skills. Good communicating skills involve understanding what makes people respond to questionnaire, get back to the sender and provide the desired feedback. (Exhibit 8.1)

Exhibit 8.1 Skill of Feedback

Swami Chinmayananda was well known for his discourses on Bhagavad Gita. He was also known for his wit, wisdom and command over the English language. In one such discourse, Swami attended and brought out very eloquently the difference in meaning of seemingly identical words.
Swami remarked as: "Before marriage, life is incomplete." Then, he said that "After marriage, life is ....?"
He paused, waiting for the audience to supply the missing word. As expected many in the audience shouted 'complete.' Swami smiled and said 'Finished.' "After marriage, life is finished."
Not that he really meant it, but the difference a word can make was crystal clear.

8.3 SOFT SKILLS

Soft skills, which complement core competencies, are in great demand particularly in the era of competition and globalization. In order to survive and thrive in the present-day competitive environment, an organization helps people to adapt, be creative at problem solving and good at relation building. For this, one needs not only career functional expertise alone but also expertise to build an equally strong competence in soft skills to become a much sought-after employee. All the personal qualities and attitudes which make an employee compatible and resourceful are referred to as soft skills. Here is a list of soft skills that are most preferred by employers across the globe.

1. **Positive Attitude:** Employer prefers those who can generate lot of positive synergy and spread goodwill within the teams and in the organization as a whole. Getting such upbeat mood persons into the organization keeps off worries. Muster as much optimism as you can. After all, your success hinges on it!
2. **Communication:** Communication is essential to build a necessary rapport with colleagues, superiors and clients. Articulate as much as possible about work while expressing thoughts, ideas and needs. Also the key to mastering communication skills lies in developing good listening skills. By listening attentively, one can understand speaker's perspectives better. This will help the presenter to present messages better.

3. **Problem Solving:** Technical knowledge, no doubt, provides an edge in problem solving. In growing complexities of the business environment, the issues which are less and less familiar may emerge; for which a creative flow is needed. The survival directly correlates with one's own creative abilities.
4. **Management:** A person is expected to consistently produce more in less time as the modern period is lean and mean. While working on multiple activities, learn to prioritize. The one who is wise in time usage, the more successful he will be.
5. **Team Spirit:** In business, success depends on team spirit. To be a good team player, one must be willing to cooperate and share knowledge. The most important aspect is putting team goals above personal goals. "More of us and less of me" a phrase that fits well here.
6. **Self-confidence:** A person can perform well only when he has a strong belief in his abilities. Always display the courage to ask the right questions and also to express views candidly. Updates knowledge on continuous basis via learning from experiences to maintain a high level of confidence.
7. **Handle Criticism:** To grow professionally, one must be open to criticism. Learn to take criticism well. Gain as much from others' inputs. This will help to meet the expectations of people who matter in a better way.
8. **Flexibility:** To possess in an uncertain world, flexibility is an asset. In ever-changing business scenario, put forth demand to adapt quickly to the new situations. The clue for developing greater flexibility lies in becoming a quick learner.
9. **Withstand Pressure:** In the fast paced work setup, the unexpected crises generate tremendous stress. If anyone is buckled under pressure, he will lose the battle. The knowledge with panic only makes matters worse while it helps a person to try and keep cool with perception.
10. **Good Work Ethics:** The honest will gain the trust of the employer. Focus on building a good reputation certainly protects career in the long run. Good work ethics are highly valued by employers especially in times of dwindling morals.
11. **Humour in Communication:** Humour, as skill, plays an important role in the life of human beings and so also in communication. When an opportunity is available, let us make use of it as a winning edge on which depends, how effective the humour is. In other words, it gains attention, creates rapport, makes a message more memorable, relieves tension, enhances relationships and motivates people. An eminent psychologist Robert Baron said "confrontations at work often depend on how you say things rather than what you say. A good laugh cuts across organizational boundaries." Effective speakers are known for their humour, 'wit and wisdom' which calls for the presence of mind and relate events in a pleasant and appealing manner. A wrong kind of humour can cause damage rather than earn goodwill and understanding. So, cultivate and find expression of humour as effective communication suitably with the context, area and consideration. Humour differs from joke. A joke has a time and a place while humour can be used even in business scenarios (Exhibit 8.2).

Exhibit 8.2 Humour Punctuation

An English professor wrote the sentence on the blackboard and directed his students to correct it. The sentence is this: "Woman without man is nothing."

Boys wrote: "Woman, without her man, is nothing."
Girls wrote: "Woman! Without her, man is nothing."

If a person already has the skills, he sharpens with some amount of perfection. Suppose, some of them make every effort to fill the skill gap at the earliest because soft skills are just as important as hard skills for professional excellence. Therefore, soft skills are as valuable as core skills.

8.4 LISTENING SKILLS

Comprehending a speaker's full meaning of a word is called listening. Mutual understanding is possible with listening only. Therefore, good communication calls for listening skills; a good speaker must necessarily be a good listener and a good listener must necessarily be a good speaker. Good listening leads to proper understanding and motivation whereas poor listening can lead to misunderstanding and incomplete understanding.

Research has shown that the human mind can process words at the rate of about 500 a minute while a speaker speaks at the rate of about 150 words a minute. The difference between them is quite large, i.e., 350 words a minute. Therefore, listening, usually, requires self-discipline, and sometimes, it requires self-examination to be said well. See Exhibit 8.3 to understand the difference between hearing and listening with a simple example.

Exhibit 8.3 Hearing but not Listening

Shyam : Ram, is the message clear?
Ram : Yes, Mr. Shyam the message was clear but I could not comprehend it.
Shyam : Ram you said "the message was clear" and in the same breath you say that you could not fully comprehend it. That means you have been only 'hearing but not listening.'

Listening which is an intellectual activity depends upon the success of the ability to listen. The kind of listening required is based on the following occasions: Listening to (a) music needs the appreciative listening, (b) lectures, presentation and instructions require attentive listening and (c) political speeches, sales talks, judging contests resorts to critical listening. K. Davis defined listening as: "Listening is a conscious and positive act, requiring will power. It is not simple, but passive exposure to sound."

A major problem in the communication process is lack of or ineffective or inactive listening. In the listening process, everyone is involved but everyone is not listening as attentively as needed. Myers and Myers have described 'not listening' beautifully as:

Supervisors complain that subordinates do not listen!
Subordinates complain that their bosses do not listen!
Parents complain that their children do not listen!
Children complain that their parents do not listen!
Teachers complain that students do not listen!
Students complain that teachers do not listen!
Somehow everyone is not listening!

A good listener is one who possesses the following features:

- Looks at the speaker
- Seeks clarifications by asking questions
- Repeats some of the things of replier
- Does not rush the speaker
- Is poised and emotionally controlled
- Reacts responsibly with a nod and a smile
- Does not interrupt
- Pays close attention
- Sticks to the subject till completion of speech

8.4.1 Importance of Listening Skills

Listening is an art. A good listener knows how to prompt and persuade but not cut or interrupt what the other person is saying. At times, speaker has the message thought in mind but fails to use the right words while communicating. Nevertheless, a good listener puts such a speaker at ease, helps articulate and facilitates the speaker to get across the complete message with clarity. Hence, there is every need in the organizations at various levels that the concerned persons should develop listening skills for success. It is noticed earlier, that every business organization has its stakeholders and communication taking central place. For purposeful listening, people need to listen to each other attentively.

Modern business organizations are in an information era and people associated with them in whatever form or type of business or profession need to develop listening skills. There is so much sharing between the organizations and the stakeholders; to deal with each other, each other have to become good listeners. The sales force and the people at the counter made contact; and everyone concerned with understanding the customers' needs should actively and sincerely listen to the customers. Organizations making conscious efforts in this direction are described as listening organizations.

Research studies show that a rough estimate of an executive's commutation time (in percentage) is spent as: Writing 9% reading 16%, speaking 30% and listening 45%. Though listening is quite critical, less focus has been given to listening compared to that of other three basic communication skills in teaching and study namely reading, writing and speaking.

Good listening skills are needed in dealing with customers' complaints, employees' grievances, hearing the voice of dissent, seeking suggestions from customers, employees and others. Discussing and resolving issues in the meeting and other interactive forums of business organizations always depend upon good listening skills, i.e., lending a patient ear. Making sense of an event shows how important the listening skills are in arriving at a correct decision. See Exhibit 8.4.

Exhibit 8.4 Making Sense of an Event in Decision-Making

It is known that perception is the process of making wise decisions. A classic example is that of two salesmen of a shoe company who visited a remote village and made the following observations.
Salesman Ramu: "There is absolutely no scope for shoe sales. No one wears shoes here."
Salesman Gopi: "No one wears shoes here. There is a tremendous scope."
It is noted that though the information base is the same, the inferences are quite different with sense of perception.

8.4.2 Listening Process

Listening is a process that calls for concentration. It begins with hearing, interpretation, evaluation and ends with response. Listening is done not only with ear but also with the other sense organs such as the eyes and mind. Therefore, listening is intellectual involving both the body and the mind with attention and making interpretation whereas hearing is a physical act with perception of sound with ear. A good listener helps the speaker in establishing a wavelength through which communication traverses smoothly. Listening encompasses five steps namely (i) hearing, (ii) decoding, (iii) comprehending, (iv) remembering, and (v) responding so that a communication process becomes meaningful and purposeful. The process of listening is explained in Table 8.1.

Table 8.1 Listening Process

Components	Purpose
Hearing	First step in listening relates to receiving words of the speaker with the sensory perception of sound.
Decoding	As a conscious exercise, it involves sensing and filtering of verbal messages received and considers all the useful ones and discards the useless. A sense of appeal and sense of judgement are the factors which play during sensing and filtering the messages.
Comprehending	Filtered messages are comprehended with a meaning by knowledge, experience, perception and cognitive power of listener.
Remembering	Messages received are meant not only for immediate consideration and action but also for future use. Though absorption takes place in the present, its use may take place, sometime, in future. Remembering is a process wherein the assimilated message is stored in memory for facilitating future call.
Responding	Sent message intended for feedback to the sender. Develop response towards the end in the form of prompting or reassuring that the message is well received.

8.5 TYPES OF LISTENING

Good listening passes through five steps, namely, hearing, decoding, comprehending, remembering and responding (Table 10.1) with positive results. Based on the effectiveness of listening, it is classified into four types namely: (a) passive listening, (b) selective listening, (c) active listening, and (d) poor listening.

1. **Passive Listening:** Receiving and absorbing a message with inert or no conscious effort is known as passive listening. In this, listening stops at hearing itself and there is no effort to further process the message. In other words, the listener is present physically but does not participate actively in the process of communication. It is just like hearing a tape recorder. This listening is said to be insufficient listening where the listener will not recall or remember the message in the future. The factors responsible for this state of affairs are physiological and psychological that may be due to fatigue, ill-health, and disregard for the speaker or lack of interest in the subject. It is also due to the speaker's failure to reach the receiver's wavelength.
2. **Selective Listening:** Selective listening is quite common and is done selectively. People listen to only that speech or information they want to hear. The listener is not focused in his attention, allows the mind to wander and the message is not thoroughly processed. This happens due to the fact that the receiver has no concentration or he considers the speaker not so well informed or he considers himself to be better informed than the speaker or such other reason which hinders active listening.
3. **Active Listening:** Communication is not always about sending messages across. It is also about active listening. In this active listening which is also called emphatic listening, the listener makes conscious efforts to listen attentively, decodes the message and absorbs it which certainly removes roadblocks to successful performance. Especially in today's business world which is characterized by widely dispersed teams, listening assumes even greater significance. The listener shows regard for the speaker, concentrates on what is being conveyed, motivates and prompts the speaker and shows empathy. Listening skills relate to the ability to listen effectively. Active listening means that one not only comprehends the message but also remembers in the future and recalls the same as and when required.

   In listening process, we come across different types of listeners which are portrayed as: The poor listening habit affects accomplishing effective listening and improving listening. A person who seeks a relatively quiet, with no intentions and blissful repose is referred to as sleep listening. One who keeps smiling and nodding, impressing the speaker is called eager listening. A listener is said to be a tiger listener if he is ready to pounce on everything the speaker says, occupied with creating trouble.

8.5.1 Hearing and Listening

Often people get confused with the terms, hearing and listening; may use them synonymously. Listening is concerned with making meaning out of what is heard and needs attention and concentration towards the subject matter for interpretation. Though listening first uses hearing which does not mean just hearing into the ears but is a process of conscious thought and understanding. The word, hearing is physical which involves just simple reception of message or sound in the ears. Thus, listening is active while hearing is passive. Effective listening comes from hearing with ears and evaluating and judging message received with the mind. There is no effective listening without hearing. Hence, effective listening is a coin with two faces; one is hearing and the other is listening.

Exhibit 8.5 Understanding is more important than Being Judged

Rupa met her classmates, Riya (dancer) and Reha (musician) in the school who were in grief. At that time, Rupa asked them what happened at the competition. Riya replied, "I danced and Reha sung a song." The judge remarked that we were not good and hence were eliminated. While they were upset and sad, the TV channel captured them.

Rupa, on hearing this, took them to the school garden. She picked up the water can and began watering the plants. She sang while watering, praising the plants. This made Riya and Reha realize that the judge was trying to tell them that they required practice to perform better than taking his remark as a judgement.

Therefore, understanding what someone is trying to say is more important than relating it to a judgement.

8.5.2 Listening Barriers

It is unfortunate that listening is not provided any specific training and as such its significance is not realized. To overcome defects in listening, every person should make a sincere effort. Apart from defects, there are some barriers to listening. These are:

- Distracted mind
- Wandering attention
- Lack of motivation
- Absence of planning to present a good argument
- Jumping to conclusions
- Failing to understand what is being/was said
- Criticizing tendency
- Emotional excitement
- Impatience
- Excessive note-taking
- Noise
- Selective listening
- More thinking than listening
- Poor perception
- Lack of interest

8.5.3 Improving Listening Skills

Though people use listening skills more than any other communication skill, it is rarely taught. To listen effectively, one needs to maintain a considerable amount of self-control and concentration as the human brain (in listening) works about four times more than the mouth (in talking). It is little wonder that a student found himself nodding off in class or wondering why he seems to gain very little from attending lectures.

Delivering message in a listenable talk will command and hold an audience's attentive listening. Good listening is one's own training effort. One who has positive habits can cultivate to improve listening. One can improve his listening skills by practicing the following techniques and principles.

- First, pay complete attention to the speaker with concentration.
- Second, a clear understanding of the spoken message does not come only through words but is supplemented by signals too. So, use both eyes and ears.
- Third, give full attention to aspects such as (i) making and maintaining comfortable eye contact, (ii) reflecting appropriate feelings in facial expression, (iii) sitting/ standing in an attentive posture, (iv) tuning in to the speaker's line of thought and seeking clarification, and (v) maintaining silence. It is good culture that one must be silent and attentive while the other is speaking. One's self-confidence and maturity of mind depend upon the status of silence.

8.6 PUBLIC SPEAKING

Public speaking, also called oration, is the process or act of giving a performance focused around an individual's speech to a live audience. This speech is structured and deliberate with three general purposes, namely: (a) to inform, (b) to persuade, and (c) to entertain. Public speaking is commonly understood as formal, face-to-face talking of a single person to a group of listeners. Along with the basic elements of public speaking, the general purpose can range from transmitting information to telling a story to motivating people to act. Public speaking can also be considered a discourse community where the audience and speaker are working to achieve a certain goal or find a purpose.

Public speaking and interpersonal communication have several common components including motivational speech, leadership, personal development, business, customer service, large group communication and mass communication. It can be a powerful tool to persuade, influence and inform the audience. It utilizes ethos or character also.

Public speaking can be done by professionals in the present scenario. Either through independently speakers' bureau or via other means they are contacted. An early evidence of training in public speech in ancient Egypt, the first known work on oratory, written over 2000 years ago, came from ancient Greek. Based on this, principles are drawn from the practices and experiences of orators. In classical Greece and Rome, the main component of composition and speech delivery was rhetoric which was a key skill in public and private life. The art of public speaking developed by the ancient Greeks is called **classical antiquity**. Any citizen who wished to succeed in court, politics or in social life had to learn techniques of public speaking.

With the emergence of the scientific method after World War II, there began gradual depreciation of the Latin style of oration, the emphasis laid on a plain style of speaking and writing. A good example of public speaking is Mahatma Gandhi's message of non-violent resistance in India.

The presentation of public speaker's main motto can range from telling a simple story to transmitting important information. Professional public speakers often engage in ongoing training and education to refine their craft and improve their skills. This may include seeking guidance from others to improve such skills like learning better story-telling techniques or learning how to effectively use humour as a communication tool. They also engage in continuous research in their topic area of focus.

Professionals in public speaking are not hesitant to share tips and challenges they come across, but great public speaking comes from their heart for persuading the audience into believing what one is saying. The public speakers follow some of the tips which are: how to engage the audience, how to prepare for a long speech, important things to remember when speaking and things to avoid and the importance of a backup plan.

Speech of credibility or ethos is an important feature to be followed in public speaking. This is essential to establish audience with reliable and informed subject at hand. Thus, public speaker must establish credibility. Good sense, good will and good moral character are three essential features that help one establish good ethos. The training centers of public speaking promote the idea of adapting certain life-stances to become a growing orator. The life-stances are called the 12 'E's as presented in Table 8.2.

Table 8.2 12 'E' Life-Stances

'E' Life-stances	Explanation
Examine	Examine how one's life process is (SWOT analysis)
Exchange	Let go of small conveniences as an exchange for greater good
Exercise	Exercise skills and widen depth of information to address areas
Express	Express one's belief in his/her dream through integrity in oration
Expect	Expect oppositions and failure
Expose	Expose one's way of ability in oration and use of opportunities for it
Extract	Extract and personalize every positive principle and knowledge
Exclude	Exclude negative thinkers that oppose orator's ambition
Exceed	Exceed normal exceptions through review and restructuring
Exhibit	Exhibit confidence in your objective and areas of oration
Explore	Explore all possibilities and different fields of oration
Extend	Extend a helping hand to those in the field of oration

8.6.1 Tools of Public Speaking

The technology and methods of public speaking have traditionally been through oratory structure and rely on an audience. However, culture evolving over time, the tools used in public speaking has undergone some modifications. New advances in technology have allowed for sophisticated communication for speakers and public orators with rostrums to hold their papers. For large gathering, the speaker can speak with the aid of a public address system of microphone and loudspeaker. Public speakers may also use audience response system.

Today, the technology and media sources aiding the public-speaking atmosphere include both video-conferencing and telecommunications. The former is one of the more recent technologies which are revolutionizing the way public speakers communicate messages to the masses. David M. Fetterman of Stanford University (1997) wrote in his article, *Videoconferencing over the Internet*: "Videoconferencing technology allows geographically disparate parties to hear and see each other usually through satellite or telephone communication systems." This technology is helpful for large size conference meetings and face-to-face communication contexts, and is becoming more widespread across the globe. The use of head-mounted displays such as Google Cardboard, a virtual reality platform in which the users immerse in a variety of realistic environments and can train accordingly, is a new approach used in public speaking. The tools of public speaking are discussed below.

1. **Speaking Out:** Everyone has good ideas and strong opinions but, a few of them have confidence or experience to communicate to others. Jointly commissioned with the Southbank Centre, Sam Lawlor said that speaking provides a 15 minute introduction to the basic skills required to speak confidently and effectively in public. Featuring the experiences and advices of a range of performers, campaigners, artists and politicians, it encourages that every one used to take the next opportunity to have their say! "With what a wonderfully composed, measured and sensible film, I really enjoyed its flavour and its practical but informative approach. By arranging for so many people to share from different perspectives/experiences, it gives to all viewers real encouragements. Vaclav Havel, playwright, former President of the Czech Republic and Founding Patron of Speakers' Corner Trust said: "Freedom of expression is the cornerstone of democratic life. It is free exchange of ideas among citizens about how they should live together and how they should govern that create and sustain the democratic society. So, the rights to free expression are scarcely less important than the right to live in peace and free from want."
2. **Better Public Speaking:** Whether people are talking in a team meeting or presenting in front of an audience, all have to speak in public from time to time. People can do this well or people can do this badly, and the outcome strongly affects the way that audience thinks about them. That is why public speaking causes so much anxiety and concern. Good news is a thorough preparation and practice; the speaker can overcome his nervousness and perform exceptionally well.

3. **Magnitude of Public Speaking:** Even if one does not need to make regular presentations in front of a group. But, there are plenty of situations where good public speaking skills can help speaker advance his career and create opportunities. For example, a speaker might have to talk about an organization at a conference, make a speech after accepting an award, or take a class for new recruits. Speaking to an audience also includes online presentations or talks. For instance, when training a virtual team or when speaking to a group of customers in an online meeting is sending information. Good public speaking skills are important in other areas in speaker's life too. The speaker might be asked to make a speech at a friend's wedding, give an eulogy for a loved one or inspire a group of volunteers at a charity event. In short, being a good public speaker, one can enhance his reputation, boost his self-confidence and open up countless opportunities. However, while good skills can open doors poor skills can close doors. For example, the manager of business might decide against promoting employee after sitting through a badly-delivered presentation. Make sure that speakers learn how to speak well!

8.6.2 Strategies of Better Speaking

Good news speaking in public is a learnable skill. As such, the speaker can use the following strategies to become a better speaker and presenter.

1. **Plan Appropriately:** First, make sure that speaker plans his communication appropriately. Use tools like the rhetorical triangle. The 7 'C's of communication is about how speaker will structure what he is going to say. When he does this, think about how important a book's first paragraph is. If it doesn't grab him, he is likely to put it down. The same principle goes for speaker's speech from the beginning; he needs to intrigue his audience. For example, he could start with an interesting statistic, headline, or fact pertaining to what he is going to talk about and resonate with his audience. Planning also helps one's own thinking. This is especially important for unpredictable question and answer sessions or last-minute communications.

   Remember that not all occasions available for speaker to speak in public will be scheduled. You can make good impromptu speeches by having ideas and mini-speeches pre-prepared. It helps to have a good and thorough understanding of what is going on in preparation.
2. **Practice:** There is a good reason that one says that practice makes one perfect! You simply cannot be a confident and compelling speaker without practice. To practice, seek opportunities to speak in front of others. For example, **toastmasters** are a club geared specifically towards aspiring speakers, and one can get plenty of practice at toastmasters' sessions. One could also put himself in situations that require public speaking, such as by cross-training a group from another department, or by volunteering to speak at team meetings. If he is going to be delivering a presentation or prepared speech, create it as early as possible. The earlier he put it together, the more time he will have to practice. Practice it alone plenty of

times, using the resources he will rely on at the event, and, as his practice, tweak his words until he flows smoothly and easily. Then, if appropriate, do a dummy run in front of a small audience; this will help him calm his jitters and make him feel more comfortable with the material. The audience can also give him useful feedback both on his material and on his performance.

3. **Engage with Audience:** When the speaker speaks and tries to engage his audience. This makes him feel less isolated as a speaker and keeps everyone involved with his message. If message is appropriate, ask leading questions to the targeted individuals or groups, and encourage people to participate and ask questions. Keep in mind that some words reduce your power as a speaker. For instance, think about how the following sentences sound: "I just want to add that I think we can meet these goals" or "I just think this plan is a good one." The words, 'just' and 'I think' limit your authority and conviction. Do not use them.

   A similar word is actually, as in, 'actually', I like to add that we were under budget last quarter." When you use the word, it actually conveys a sense of submissiveness or even surprise. Instead, say what things are. 'We were under budget last quarter' is clear and direct.

   Also, pay attention to how you are speaking. If you are nervous, you might talk quickly. This increases the chances that you will trip over your words, or say something you do not mean. Force yourself to slow down by breathing deeply. Do not be afraid to gather your thoughts; pauses are an important part of conversation, and they make you sound confident, natural and authentic. Finally, avoid reading word-for-word from your notes. Instead, make a list of important points on cue cards, try to memorize what you are going to say – you can still refer back to your cue cards when you need them.

4. **Pay Attention to Body Language:** If one is unaware of it, his body language will give his audience constant, subtle clues about his inner state. If he is nervous, or if he does not believe in what he is saying, the audience can soon know. Pay attention to his body language: stand up straight; take deep breaths, look people in the eye and smile. Do not lean on one leg or use gestures that feel unnatural. Many people prefer to speak behind a podium when giving presentation. While podium can be useful for holding notes, it puts a barrier between you and the audience. It can also become a crutch, giving speaker a hiding place from the dozens or hundreds of eyes that are on him. Instead of standing behind a podium, walk around and use gestures to engage the audience. This movement and energy will also come through in his voice, making it more active and passionate.

5. **Think Positively:** Positive thinking can make a huge difference to the success of speaker's communication, because it helps him feel more confident. Fear makes it all too easy to slip into a cycle of negative self-talk, especially right before he speaks. The self-sabotaging thoughts such as 'I will never be good at this!' or 'I am going to fall flat on my face!' lower your confidence and increase the chances for one not being able to achieve what he is truly capable of. Use affirmations and visualization to raise his confidence. This is especially important

right before your speech or presentation. Visualize giving a successful presentation and imagine how speaker will feel once it is over and when he has made a positive difference for others. Use positive affirmations such as " 'I am' grateful that I have an opportunity to help my audience" or " 'I am' going to do well!"

6. **Cope with Nerves:** How often have you listened to or watched a speaker who really messed up? Answer is not very often. When we have to speak in front of others, we can envision terrible things happening. We imagine forgetting every point we want to make, passing out from our nervousness or doing so horribly that we will lose our job. But those things almost never come to pass! We build them up in our minds and end up being more nervous than we need to be. Many people cite speaking to audience as their biggest fear, and a fear of failure is often at the root of this.

   Although the symptoms can be annoying or even debilitating, the Inverted-U Model shows that a certain amount of pressure enhances performance. By changing the mindset of speaker, he can use nervous energy to his advantage. First, make an effort to stop thinking about him, his nervousness, and fear. Instead, focus on audience: what speaker is saying 'about them.' Remember that speaker is trying to help or educate them in some way, and his message is more important than his fear. Concentrate on the audience's wants and needs, instead of ones's own. Crowds are more intimidating than individuals, so think of speech as a conversation being had with one person. Although the audience may be 100 people, focus on one friendly face at a time, and talk to that person as if he or she is the only one in the room.

7. **Watch Recordings of Your Speeches:** Whenever possible, record your presentations and speeches. You can improve your speaking skills dramatically by watching yourself later, and then working on improving in areas that did not go well. As you watch, notice any verbal stalls, such as 'um' or 'like:'

   - Look at your body language: are you swaying, leaning on the podium, or leaning heavily on one leg?
   - Are you looking at the audience?
   - Did you smile? Did you speak clearly at all times?
   - Pay attention to your gestures. Do they appear natural or forced?
   - Make sure that people can see them, especially if you're standing behind a podium.
   - Last, look at how you handled interruptions, such as a sneeze or a question that you weren't prepared for.
   - Does your face show surprise, hesitation, or annoyance?
   - If so, practice managing interruptions like these smoothly, so that you're even better next time.
   - The more you push yourself to speak in front of others, the better you will become and the more confidence you will have.

QUESTIONS

1. What is communication skill? Discuss mastering communication skills.
2. Explain how listening skills are important with an illustration.
3. What constitutes the listening process? State the types of listening.
4. What is public speaking? Explain 12 'E' life-stances.
5. Explain what are the public speaking tools.
6. Describe the strategies of better speaking.
7. Explain the following:
   (a) Humour in communication
   (b) Good listener
   (c) Barriers to listening
   (d) Improving listening skills
   (e) Classical antiquity

9 CHAPTER

Electronic Communication

LEARNING OBJECTIVES

This chapter will enable you to

- understand the scenario of modern communication trend;
- know development of e-communication; and
- identify the relevance of social media.

INTRODUCTION

Information is wealth. Effective creation of wealth heavily depends upon how effectively information is utilized for the purpose of achieving the defined goals of business. Effective use of information depends on effective storing, organizing, retrieval and analysis for final decision-making. The splendid endeavours of veterans and researchers have resulted in new technologies in the field of communication. Gillman J. A. has defined new technologies as: "Micro-electronic system, incorporating computers and telecommunications." The new technologies based on the silicon chip and fiber optics have made a remarkable development having a dramatic impact on marketers and buyers. The specific features of new communication technology are as follows:

- Equality in reaching
- Quality accuracy in quantity of message-load
- Efficiency in cost reduction
- Speed in message being delivered
- More areas being covered in terms of population and location

The new communication technology can replace the predominant traditional manual methods of communication involving high cost, much time, inaccuracy and inability in communicating message load. The corporate sectors such as financial institutions, banking, insurance, education, transport, manufacturing, services including innovative research and development, etc., have been installing new communication technologies to realize their potential and usefulness. As a result, rapid progress in terms of growth and development has emerged in various issues of expanding the economy and enhancing life, i.e., living quality of people. The new communication technology is so indispensable in the context of globalization with a vast coverage of geographical territory. The enterprise resource planning (ERP), today, has become a buzzword in the corporate sector. Perhaps, the development and deployment of information technology has been an immediate and strongest source responsible for such a rapid shift.

Tremendous importance has been attached to the prudence of business management worldwide. Every business organization is discovering and devising new paths of cost, time and energy with means of insulating the operational execution of projects while enhancing the internal efficiencies for robust progress. Clarity of information with quality and receiving (feedback) at an increasing speed and optimal efficiency, there is every use of modern network to attain the goals of business.

Modern business organizations are doing business operations in a highly competitive and ever-challenging market environment. To develop the competency and value based human assets, business management selects the best, develops the best and provides the best of communication network.

Technology developments towards the end of 20th century have brought out new dimensions in range, speed, methods and modalities of communication in business. Internet, laptop, mobiles, modems and computer based message operating system have begun impacting in every sphere of communication activity in business. Ideas and resources flow across the border and the development in one place is rapidly reaching the other parts of the world. Hence, it becomes necessary to keep abreast of technology developments, appropriate its merits and use it for improving the effective communication within and outside business organization. During this time, the technology revolution has begun impacting in rural areas too.

9.1 EVOLUTION OF MODERN NETWORK

Telephony since its inception in 1876 had facilitated the transmission of speech enabling dissemination of information and knowledge rapidly while telegraphy helped transmission of written messages instantaneously. Beginning of 1930s, radio broadcasting of messages over wide areas was established. Onward of this radio broadcasting, the sending of messages were based more and more on electronic-based approach. Broadcasting of pictures along with voice had begun in 1950.

Television, as colour transmission, has been increasingly affordable by more people as it became cheap with every succeeding decade. With the modes of telephony, telex and television, the communication satellites have helped instantaneous transmission of news and views of events happening in the country and also across globe. The electronics, computers and telecommunication are enabling simultaneously printing of newspapers from several distant centers in the nation. Thus, satellite has reduced distance; and time has shrunk in transmission of message/information.

Intensive exploitation of economic resources for optimum production and increase of consumption of goods/services are accountable and responsible for the sustenance of big companies in the society to attune the economic efficiency. It is but for the efficient management of these companies that owe to inform complete and contended information to all the stakeholders on issues like: How they are performing and how best their services could be provided to the consumers? It is here that the communication system does not only help the organizations but also become significant and noteworthy serving means to all the concerned individuals in the society. Accordingly, all this is affecting to achieve the goal of progressive transformation of the society at large. Communication evolution has revolutionized over the centuries and gained sophistication in line with the progress of civilization. Access to knowledge and information has become easier and speedier.

9.2 CLASSIFICATION OF COMMUNICATION

Modern-day communication is broadly grouped into two: (a) electronic communication, and (b) non-electronic communication. Electronic communication with modern technology – computer with network has been widely used due to emancipation of information technology at the beginning of the new millennium. The use of computer devices facilitates 'ease' and 'spread' of communication with the help of computer network and other means which is called e-communication. It refers to transfer of writing, signals, data, sounds, images, signs or intelligence via an electric device. E-communication carries in a variety of forms by the use of communication technology tools like computer, telephone, fax, mobile pager, smart phone, radio, audio-video and teleconferencing. Thus, it is an efficient way of delivering messages to the intended persons and a fast way of communication to the people across the world.

As a result of revolution in electronic communications, gigantic rise in its use has occurred in some organizations surprisingly. Now, it is commonplace for people to utilize e-mail as easily as computer. The government is committed to promote the aspect of learning and developing communication with the intention that everyone ought to access internet. Good number of businessmen are conducting their business online via Internet access. Thus, e-communication offers unique benefits and challenges. The non-electronic communication comprises verbal, face-to-face interactions which play a larger role in daily business affairs. Non-electronic communication has been discussed in the earlier chapter and electronic communication is being discussed here.

9.2.1 Electronic Communication

Computer mediated communication (CMC) with internet and e-communication has become the means to send messages. Today, business organizations interact with their various constituents – employees, board members, customers, partners and others based on the nature of message and goal to achieve on available communication media of telephones, voice mail, fax machine, print, etc. Electronic communication is a powerful new channel which not only changes how one can use the option, but also creates new ways to interact. For instantce, electronic communication combines numerous media such as text, graphics, sound, video, etc., into a single message.

Electronic communication is the transmission of information using the advanced techniques such as computer, facsimile machines, voice mail, electronic mail, teleconferencing, audio-video cassettes, and private television networks. It can be said that e-communication means conveying information through the use of information technology devices.

Communication does require processing the information in the departments of accounting, finance, personnel, establishment, public relations, sales, market research, production, purchase and so on. For day-to-day functioning of a business concern with its multi-dimensions, e-communication is required. So, the modern communication technology is the call of the day to emerge for meeting a varied need of modern business enterprise.

Merits

- Speedy transmission: Electronic communication requires only a few seconds to communicate through electronic media.
- Wide coverage: Communication coverage is wide and even sending messages across the globe requires only a second.
- Low cost: E-communication saves time and money. For example, SMSs is cheaper than traditional letter.
- Exchange of feedback: E-communication allows instant exchange of feedback with perfect use of electronic media.
- Control operations: Management can easily control the operations across the globe due to advancement of electronic media.
- Share: One can easily share conversation, picture, image, sound, graphics, maps, interactive software and thousands of things due to electronic communication.

Demerits

- Volume of data: Increasing volume of communicating information at such a fast rate unable to absorbs within the relevant scheduled time limit.
- Cost of development: Huge infrastructural development and frequent change of technology certainly create more cost demand in electronic communication.
- Legal status: Data or information, if faxed, may be distorted and will cause zero value in the eye of law.
- Undelivered data: Data may not be retrieved due to system error or fault with the technology. It causes delay of undelivered data.
- Dependency: Technology is changing everyday and the poor countries cannot afford to adopt new or advanced technology. So, they too depend on developed countries for sharing global network.

9.2.2 Types of E-Communication

Electronic communications are broadly grouped into (i) one-way (simplex), (ii) two-way (full duplex or half duplex) transmissions and (iii) analog or digital signals. These are as:

- **Simplex:** The one-way e-communication is referred to as simplex. Radio, TV broadcasting are examples.
- **Full Duplex:** The two-way e-communication is referred to as duplex. If people talk and listen simultaneously, it is called full duplex. Telephone is an example.
- **Half Duplex:** In two-way communication form, only one party transmitting message at a time is known as half duplex. Radio transmission, Amateur radio, etc., are examples.
- **Analog:** A smooth and continuous varying voltage signal is termed as analog. Examples are Sine Wave, Voice Video.

9.2.3 Terms of Electronic Communication

New concepts are noteworthy to the progress of business communication. The concepts are web, computer, e-mail, e-commerce, e-business, internet, network systems, data warehousing, teleconferencing, videoconferencing and short messaging system (SMS) are certain concepts often been used.

1. **Web:** In modern days, the communication technology has a wider access to regional, national and global in the matters of business operations towards (i) resources management, inventory, production, sales, etc., (ii) monitor of progress, price trend, market position, etc., and (iii) proper up-keep of finance and accounts. In all these, web has become a key source on which lies satisfaction of human beings and the fortunes of entire business worldwide.

   The purposeful use of five M's, namely, money, machine, material, manpower and management revolve around on the aspect of effective and good communication system in transmitting messages. Bill Gates makes the observation thus: "Business is going to change more in the next ten years than in the last fifty years. If 1980s were about quality and 1990s were about re-engineering, 2000s will be about velocity. The access of information will alter the lifestyles of consumers and expectations of their business. Very soon, people around the world will be living in the web lifestyle." In the context of globalization, the business communication system and the strategies of tomorrow necessarily reckon with the core strength of corporate communication, both internally and externally pertaining to the aspects of:

Speed	: Need for swift, online, real-time communication across the target group
Convenience	: Access and retrieval at the convenience of users
Low Cost	: Reach of communication at affordable price
IT Enabled	: Tune with new information technology environment
Quality	: Accuracy in message transmission
Global	: Develop skills and languages of global relevance

2. **Computer:** An electronic machine device using the language of strings of binary numbers with a set of rules to store, process, analyze and retrieve information is called a **computer.** It is a system of communication through the use of symbols, characters and rules that can be used in sending messages. The New Webster's

Dictionary defines computer as: "An electronic contrivance which solves problems and does complicated calculations by processing data according to the prescribed instructions, and then produces and/or retains the outcome of the processes." Computer is a versatile electronic instrument combining various media functions. It is a single multi-stage equipment for all kinds of transmission of information. The software development of computer takes over more and more tasks: both functions in place of business and at home.

3. **Networking:** In 1980s, India developed the internet under a joint venture of the Department of Electronics, Government of India and United Nations Development Programme to extend technical assistance to the developing nations. Many scientists and technologists have been benefited with access to the Education and Research in Computer Networks project abbreviated as ERNET with international facility in essence. The Videsh Sanchar Nigam Limited, India's international telecom carrier has contributed its mite to the development of internet technology in India which is called as Gateway of Internet Access Network (GIAN). A commercial network was launched on August 15, 1995 and set its nodes at Ahmedabad, Bangalore, Chennai, Delhi, Mumbai, Kolkata and Pune.

Network, in computer parlance, means a series of interconnected channels communicating the intended information to perform the functions of a business organization within and outside the business premises. The integration of operating system with the sum total of channels is called **network**. Computer with modem can send and receive information from one place to another place within the organization, between its branches, distributors, factory, salesmen, warehouses, dealers and record instantly without delay.

Modern business organizations are getting bigger in size and becoming the phenomena production and supply of goods; and having many departments/ divisions with inventory management, planning, purchasing, manufacturing, engineering, research and development, warehousing, sales services, accounting, marketing and so forth. Towards this end, one service that could play a greater role in fostering with cooperation, coherence and coordination to bring together is network communication.

A social network is an online service, platform or website. It is focused largely around uniting individuals, allowing them to communicate and interact. Facebook is currently the world's largest popular social networking platform, having supplanted previous champions like MySpace and Friendster. This list includes social networking sites which have achieved great popularity and utility among Indian users. The top social networks in India are as;

facebookhttp; //

www.facebook.com

googlehttp://

www.google.co.in

twitterhttp://

Twitter.com

YouTube
Bharat student.com
Indian.friendfinder.com
India forumshttp://
www.india.forum.com

4. **Utility of Network:** Business organizations with more complexes at new heights started to encounter a severe paper work crunch. In business arena, a significant change initiative is Web Information Technology (WIT) which found itself to be popularly known as information explosion. The efficiency, quality, better services and safety are important benefits of computer. Network is grouped into six types as mentioned below.
   (a) Wide Area Network (WAN) is located over nation or worldwide basis through optical fiber cables and satellite transmission for transmission of messages
   (b) Local Area Network (LAN) is a group of microcomputers or terminals located within the same building or a group of buildings close each other with a common cable
   (c) Metropolitan Area Network (MAN) is linked with a single microcomputer in a metropolitan area
   (d) Business Area Network (BAN) is interconnection within a multi-tenants building
   (e) Campus Area Network (CAN) is located in a campus/education institution with computer equipment
   (f) Backbone Network (BN) is a single business unit being connected to terminals, micro-computers and main frames

9.2.4 Electronic Mail

Transportation of information via electronic message from one computer to another computer with a communication network is called **electronic-mail** abbreviated as **e-mail**. In business, it is largely replaced by print hard copy for external (outside the company) correspondence and taking the place of memos for internal (within the company) communication. E-mail is very useful for sending messages and is still the best suited for messages that are fairly brief in nature. For instance, the manager can contact the persons at various levels through e-mailing and internet chatting. Across the globe, e-mails are emerging as the means of the fastest communication system. Today, communication through e-mail is an effective way for the corporate management to share its thoughts and persuade employees:

- To follow business messages
- To provide guidance and direction
- To keep abreast of the change by obtaining feedback

1. **Essentials of E-mail:** Business uses automated e-mails to acknowledge the communications received from the public or to remind the associates on the periodic reports or payments due. Tips for effective business e-mails are:

- Demonstration of proper salutations and avoid mix-up in case a message is accidentally sent to the wrong recipient.
- Subject lines are clear, brief and specific. It helps the recipient to understand the essence of message.
- Close with a signature identifying you by creating a signature block which automatically contains name and business contacts information.
- Avoid abbreviation and all caps.
- Omit unnecessary words and keep the message brief.
- Use a good format for ease of reading and getting to the point.
- Reread, revise and review. Catch and correct spelling and grammar mistakes before pressing 'send'.
- Reply promptly and watch for an emotional response.
- Use 'Reply all' sparingly.
- Give feedback or follow up.

2. **Easy and Instantaneous Sending:** Sending of messages is easy and instantaneous. Along with the message, a whole document prepared on computer can be sent as an attachment. Prepare the message on word processing programme, log onto the internet, copy and paste the prepared message on the 'compose' frame and send it by clicking the 'send' button. The message first goes to the mail server of Internet Service Providers (ISP) and then sends it to the mail server of the recipient. Until the receiver checks the 'mail', it remains with the receiver of computer. The receiver can read or delete it at any time. An important feature of e-mail is the physical transfer and movement of messages. The companies and job advertisers insist those who are interested to send their letters and resume only through the specified e-mail address. Having an e-mail ID and familiarity with the medium of communication is not only useful but also an essential tool in modern days.

   All the interested people worldwide can 'meet' on a topic of interest (say globalization, economic crisis, market crisis, human resource development practices, women's studies, Mahatma Gandhi's peace movement, effective corporate governance, Trump administration, green environment, disturbances among the countries of globe and alike to hear new ideas or innovative thoughts or find solutions discussing them in a group through an e-mail conferencing. Someone or some organization with a computer network can set up 'theme of meet' and puts it up on the internet with list. Those who are interested can participate and subscribe to the conference and send their contribution to the discussion. It is automatically distributed to all the participants through the e-mail. Send response through e-mail at a convenient time. Submission of response is left to the interest of participants. The e-mail also provides other ways to interact with the writers of research papers or books. Every website provides an e-mail address for any visitor or reader to send back comments and reactions.

3. **Creation of an E-mail ID:** Name, i.e., computer ID and address of the recipient is essential to send an e-mail. It is like this: someone@someplace – (i) someone could be person's real name like rasri, sujela or a word/letters chosen by the person, like

crama or abc2 or anything else; and (ii) someplace is the address of computer and network on which the person has an account like yahoo.com, gmail.com, hotmail.com, vsnl.com., etc. Any error in a single letter or number or punctuation or space in e-mail account will prevent the message from being sent. In such a case, the message will be flashed on the screen stating that the address could not be found and the sent information will come back into sender's own mailbox.

A person wanting to send an e-mail is required to have an e-mail account with any website which provides an e-mail service. The e-mail ID is similar to the postal address; a person must have it to receive mail or couriers. For creation of an e-mail ID, see Exhibit 9.1.

Exhibit 9.1 How to Create an e-mail ID

Choose a website which provides the facility for sending and receiving e-mails (hotmail, rediffmail and yahoo are the most commonly used e-mail websites). Then, connect the computer to the internet and log on to the internet, type the address of website in the address space provided.

Address: http://www.gmail.com

Hit the Enter key and download the homepage of website. The homepage gmail provides a list of facilities available (news, mail, movies, entertainment, etc.) By clicking on the mail icon, select the mail which provides a mail page of gmail:
Username: dr.reddycr
Password: India
Sign in:

Sign up for new account

On clicking the Sign Up for New Account, a page will appear in which type all the details like Username, Password and other personal details such as name, date of birth, occupation, etc. Usually, the username is the name of the person wishing to create an e-mail ID and chooses a Password in such a way that it can be remembered easily. Then, click on "Finish" or "Done" button. An e-mail ID is, thus, created. A confirmation to this effect is received stating that the request for an e-mail ID has been accepted.

4. **Use of E-Mail:** The issue of confidentiality and security is a dual problem posing both risk and abuse. Because of this, many organizations restrict their access to the e-mail and the internet. Another problem is what kind of messages should not go by e-mail. For example, the message carrying a scolding or warning from the boss to the subordinates; neither is good by e-mail and alike. Except these, the e-mail provides certain advantages. The utility of an e-mail is that it:
   - Is swift
   - Provides immediate access to worldwide contacts
   - Has a large global reach and access
   - Is extremely economical
   - Enables the business to run efficiently and profitably

- Helps to implement marketing programme with greater accuracy
- Increases efficiency and effectiveness of public relations programme
- Is largely reliable and the sender can know the message reached
- Can be readily acknowledged by the receiver
- Uses normally the telegraphic language and salutation
- Can be stored and retrieved as and when required
- Sends copies of message to many others instantaneously
- Ensures the security of delivery postal mail avoiding delays and loss of mail
- Helps lawyers, doctors, consultants and government departments to keep in touch with intended services
- Sends copies by journalists across globe

Exhibit 9.2 **Smart Shopping on the Rise**

A steep upward trend in e-commerce propelled by expediency has seen the purchase online made double in India through mobile phones in the last two years. An Online Shopping Survey 2014 by MasterCard, covering 14 countries across Asia-Pacific, showed that China continued to lead with 70.1 per cent of the polled respondents having used their device to make online purchase followed by India at 62.9 per cent. The report on online shopping habits of respondents includes interviews with 7000 respondents from 14 markets and aged between 18 and 64 years. The MasterCard Survey found that 95 per cent of Indian respondents with a mobile phone have access to Internet through it. Through an online transaction, the new mobile technologies are gaining transaction in the region. Digital payment solutions like mobile banking apps and digital wallets made a long way to further enriching purchase experience for ever-evolving consumer. [*Source:* MasterCard Online Shopping Study – India]

5. **E-mail differs from Fax:** Fax was popular to send letters and documents without delay in 1980s. Even today, it is in operation for sending messages, but nearing down its closure. E-mail sets up a temporary circuit between the origin and the destination of the call for which to be paid regular or STD or ISD phone rates accordingly. It has immediacy of fax; makes efficient use of network on permanent, open lines without incurring any additional cost in sending e-mail to any place in the world even long distances with no need of STD or ISD facility. It is much faster and can reach its destination with document of many pages; during that a single page of fax is still transmitting. E-mail, today thus, is more efficient, effective and economical.

   (i) ***Voice mail:*** Voice mail or v-mail is a form of e-mail. It is used to send the voice of the sender instead of sending written message to the receiver. The mechanism of sending message is almost the same as in case of e-mail. It is useful to communicate with the original voice tone of the sender.

   (ii) ***Audio-Video teleconferencing:*** Audio-video teleconferencing brings people together without having to spend time and money. It is an interactive

conversation often used as the most productive and inexpensive medium by using an ordinary telephone. The widespread use of audio-conferencing is because of the following reasons:

- Everyone can use a telephone
- Telephone is available anywhere
- Easy to participate from any telephone in the world
- Takes only a few minutes to complete a conference call
- Costs very little

In video-teleconferencing, people can see and hear each other at the time of conversation and interaction. A variety of complex technologies such as advanced network, transmission services and compression of digital signals are involved in the system of videoconferencing to 'talk' with one another. Monitor, camera, microphone, speaker, code (compressor-decompressor), equipment control pad at each location and network services to connect the locations are the basic components of video conferencing. In this video-conferencing, communication allows people face-to-face conversation, makes the facility fruitful for discussion, saves time and travelling cost and participating people feel that they are connected. All these go a long-way in building up good relationship and benefit each other. For instance, the manager wants to call a sudden meeting with his colleagues and subordinates and goes through the traditional proceedings, then, will first arrange the place and the hospitality for delegates, which involves more time, more energy and more money. But through proper use of video-conferencing, the meeting can be arranged proficiently and fruitfully within a short span of time. Video-teleconferencing costs high and hence, only a few organizations have their own stations.

6. **Telephone:** The most commonly and widely used electronic device of communication is telephone. By telephone, people can transmit information orally within a minute. Recently developed satellite telephoning system has added new dimension to telecommunication system. In most of the cases, it is the easiest and less expensive way of communicating with distant people. Nowadays, the development and diffuse of cellular or mobile phone has been an expected euphoria to all of us. Definitely it is becoming extremely popular.
7. **Telex:** Telex is an important device of modern **communication technology**. In it, a teleprinter is used by which information can be communicated from one place to another with the help of a machine. The teleprinter consists of two parts, namely, keyboard transmitter and receiver. When a message is to be sent, the typist presses a button, waits for the dial tone, dials the number desired and types the message. The message is typed on a small strip of paper at the receiver's end like that typed in the originating office. This is one of the quickest and most accurate methods of exchanging written messages.
8. **Fax:** The use of fax or facsimile is gradually increasing for transmitting visual materials such as picture, diagrams, illustrations, etc., through the fax

machine connected with a telephone. Feed the document to be transmitted through the machine and then scan electronically and send. Then, the signals are transmitted to the receiving end, where an identical copy of the document is reproduced on a blank sheet of paper by the receiving machine. The fax machine makes it possible to send copies of important documents including certificates, testimonials, degrees, agreement, contracts, etc., from one place to another at the speed of a telephone call. For this reason, it is a universally used method of communication.

9. **Internet:** Conveying data through satellite links and telephone wires by using the computer networks is called **internet** also simply called **net**. The concept, internet has brought in a revolution in communication; wherein everything seems to be e-enable right from the operational level to the strategic level in every sphere of organizational activity with the means of digitalization. This is necessitated in the context where the local market is moving globally bringing in new markets, new products and new players. Today, internet is a boon to the whole world.

   Advancement in information technology and telecommunication in addition to the cable and satellite related changes have resulted in a rapid growth of internet use. As per National Readership Survey (2002), the growth of internet has stabilized at two million per annum: half of it using internet services from cyber cafes. The convenience of cyber cafes, growth of ownership of personal computers and decline in surfing cost are affecting growth of internet's usage. Internet is a multi-data system allowing the users to access a variety of services. The most important are:

   - Internet Relay Chat (IRC) to send messages in real time (appears on the recipient's computer screen as soon as typed)
   - Pooling of UseNet news to the groups and answering messages on public bulletin board
   - File Transfer Protocol (FTP) to store and retrieve data files on large computer system
   - CU-See Me, a video conferencing system wherein users send and receive both sound and picture simultaneously
   - Exchange of electronic mail

   Today, internet has become a popular channel in communication network throughout the world as good medium of advertising. Corporate sector even making consumer goods have so far limited their advertisement spending on the internet but the situation may be fast changing. In 2015, advertisers spent ₹ 8000 crore on other media such as print and television; the internet's share was ₹ 900 crore. Regular internet users in the 25 plus age category are close to 3.20 crores. Among the reasons favoured, the internet is that the advertisers could reach the specific target groups like cricket fans or those interested in personal care products or those who are conscious of fitness. Internet is recognized by the sector of banks, insurance providers and car makers. The internet enables the users to:

- Connect through personal computer and local telephone line
- Exchange e-mails with all those who have an internet account
- Share business and research data among colleagues
- Post information to the concerned people who need it
- Gather valuable feedback and suggestions
- Provide help with the questions and problems
- Publicize and market goods and services
- Access to multimedia information
- Subscribe to mail lists on the topic of interest

9.2.5 Word Processor

Processing is a manipulation of words. Input occurs through a keyboard. Keyboard is the input component, the processing unit receives instructions and coordinates the entire system. Typing skills, basic computer literacy and word processor software are essentials for using a word processor. The operator of a word processor can easily edit the text, give it in a desired format and insert or delete words, phrases or sentences wherever he likes. The storage is receiver's memory component and stores data for manipulation. The output may be obtained either by display on the screen of video or on a printer.

The role of word processor in today's business communication needs no emphasis. Word processing of software application of Ms-word, Word Star, Lotus, WordPro, etc., add elegance and convenience to the written communication covering business letters, memos, reports and others. Till achieving the desired level of effectiveness and design, it is possible to erase, reword, edit, retrieve, regroup and restructure the written text several times. To ensure elegance and effectiveness of written business communication, one must become familiar with a word processor and the options it offers in terms of fonts, letter size, colour, pagination, margin, etc. In brief, the word processor is a new dimension which has an added feature to the elegance of written communication. The merits of word processing are:

- Easy correction
- Easy revision
- Easy storage of message
- Easy creation of new documents from the stored data
- No erasures and overtyping
- Easy print of charts and figures

9.2.6 Multimedia

Multimedia is an excellent invention for upgrading the **communication system**. It is a combination of many media brought together to transfer messages. This media includes graphics, photo, music, voice, text and animation. When all of these are placed together before the computer screen, then they become multimedia. It can be effectively used for advertising and publicity campaigns. It is a powerful means of communication.

9.2.7 M-Commerce

Transaction having a monetary value that can be conducted through mobile communication network or Wi-Fi network is m-commerce. According to Keen and Mackintosh, m-commerce is extension of e-commerce from wired to wireless computers and telecommunications and from fixed locations to anytime, to anywhere and to anyone. As per Durlacher, any transaction with a monetary value is conducted via a mobile telecommunication network. Clear benefits, including high response rate and low costs are rapidly turning email marketing into an invaluable tool said by Peppers and Rodgers.

M-commerce is buying and selling of goods and services through wireless handheld devices such as cellular phone and personal digital assistants. In the era of networked society, sending, spending and receiving money with a mobile phone is essentially fast becoming a part of life for billions of people. A right plan could lead into business in billions. This rapid business requires a change essentially involving payment by network, making mobile commerce as easy as cash. A mobile device is a small smart device and can provide information anytime and anywhere (ubiquity). Ubiquitous interactivity is what makes mobile devices unique. Wireless devices enable users to send, receive and act on information in real-time. Thus, m-commerce has been likened to having 'your best salesman in the pocket of your best customer'. Morgan Stanley released a report in which they expected India's e-commerce market to grow from $2.9 billion dollars in 2013 to over $100 billion by 2020, making it the fastest growing e-commerce market in the world. All this is because of the adoption of 4G penetration and availability of mobile internet.

E-commerce and m-commerce are major progressive segments of business which support to boost up the economy of nation. With the fundamental business principles, m-commerce could act as another channel through which value can be added to e-commerce process. Specifically, the e-commerce and m-commerce involve transactions via a computer and mobile devices respectively. The wireless environment is sometimes described as m-commerce or m-internet but it is broader than e-commerce. M-commerce ensures consumer as more time conscious than money and improves personalization, i.e., carry mobiles, everywhere and anytime. But, the operators can detect a user's exact location, and the operators are able to determine the identity of the users unlike e-commerce.

Benefits of M-commerce

- Websites search option helps consumers to find easily and rapidly a particular product with different classification variety.
- Confirmation of code is sent to the email and mobile phone of consumer for the transaction undertaken.
- Easy hold of mobile device helps to avoid going physically to the shop.
- E-commerce and mobile-commerce are the frontiers in global business and trade.

Demonetization is good for the m-commerce in India as it is adopted widely by the merchants because the customers are claiming for the convenience to reduce customers' friction and sell more through the mobile channels. Data (in $) on retail sales in India is presented in Table 9.1.

Table 9.1 Retail Sales In India

Year	Total retail sales	% of change	Retail e-commerce sales	% of change	% of total retail sales
2013	635.25	10.0	3.59	55.60	0.60
2014	717.83	13.0	5.30	47.60	0.70
2015	818.33	14.0	7.69	45.20	0.90
2016	941.08	15.0	10.68	38.90	1.10
2017	1082.24	15.0	14.18	32.80	1.30
2018	1244	15.0	17.52	23.50	1.40

Source: www.e-marketer.com

The growth in m-commerce has been fuelled by the availability of affordable smart phones and mobile data plans. Mobile internet users' base in India has increased to 371 million in 2016 and the user base is expected to annually grow by 50 million till 2019. The current online shoppers range from 80-100 million and are expected to increase to 175 – 200 million by 2020.

9.2.8 Governance and E-Communication

Origin of Indian e-governance goes to 1970s with focus on development of in-house government applications in the areas of defense, economic monitoring, planning and the deployment of information technology to manage data on intensive functions related to elections, census, tax administration, etc. The efforts of the National Informatics Center (NIC) connecting all the district headquarters is a significant development. Emphasis has been primarily on automation and computerization; the state governments use ICT tools into connectivity, networking, setting up systems for processing information and delivering services. The ICT tools, at a micro level, range from IT automation in individual departments, electronic file handling and workflow system, access to entitlement, public grievance system, service delivery of high volume routine transactions like payment of bills, tax dues to poverty alleviation goals through the promotion of entrepreneurial models and provision of market information.

Indian planners tend to justify adoption and expansion of government's governance through e-communication on the ground of less costing, reduction of waste, promoting transparency, eliminating corruption, generating possibilities to resolve rural poverty and inequality, and guaranteeing a better future for people. E-governance is a big challenge and also a big opportunity to bring services to the satisfaction of people. The most significant characteristic of it is its 'quality' and 'accessibility' for the good progress of the society.

1. **Electronic governance** or e-governance is the application of information and communication technology to deliver government services, exchange of transactions, and integration of various stand-alone systems with *efficiency, effectiveness, transparency and accountability of informational and transactional exchanges*. This e-governance service is between Government-to-Customer (G2C), Government-to-Business (G2B), Government-to-Government (G2G) and Government-to-Employee (G2E) as well as back office processes and interactions within the entire government framework. The e-governance is abounded and there is no distinct geographical boundary hindrance. The government has launched Common Service Centres (CSCs) with optical fibre network to provide services in rural areas to generate Aadhaar cards, e-tickets booking and alike. As of May 2016, there where 170000 CSCs. E-governance ensures efficiency as the motto of e-government, being abbreviated as SMART. The abbreviated word SMART spells out e-governance as:
   (a) Simple (S) - getting easy access to electronic documents through communication
   (b) Moral (M) – value in good governance without delay
   (c) Accountability (A) – provide citizens definite information with accountability
   (d) Responsive (R) – get an intended piece of information speedily
   (e) Transparency (T) – governing values, no disclose, no delay and keeping government information close to the needy citizens

   Growth of e-governance fully with functionality depends on technical, organizational and managerial feasibilities. The e-governance for good governance is broadly categorized into four stages.
2. **Cataloguing** is the first stage in e-governance to create and administer a website with non-transactional information for which people need to have an online presence and access to information on government services with least cost function for users. Here, the government departments have home pages with description followed by reorganization of information services with different actions or events. With official websites including emails, all the government departments and the states address questions from the website users. In most cases, the government websites are unable to give replies on time to the queries but the websites managed by private sectors handle the customer queries very quickly and effectively.
3. **Interactive,** two-way communication is the second stage in the structure of e-governance. Citizens' move from a passive to active role to transact with the government online, the latter ought to respond with confirmation, receipt, etc. Citizens can renew their licences and pay fines or taxes or obtain birth or death registration through an online transaction. E-transaction ensures an improved efficiency to the customer and the government. Now, it is possible to get reservation (rail or airlines) online, transact money or fill forms for most of the departments. By rendering services, be it Election Commission or bank, income tax or insurance, colleges or railway, the Indian Government can reach the second stage successfully.
4. **Transaction:** In this third stage, a complete transaction can be made on internet. This interaction in turn results in vertical and horizontal integration which changes

the way services are delivered, but the effort is made for completion of transaction through internet with the help of back-end integration.

5. **Network:** This fourth stage comprises the services of (i) telecommunication, train, bus, flight, driving licences from Government to Citizen (G2C), (ii) e-democracy, e-bank from Citizens to Government, (iii) e-administration, e-police and e-judgment from Government to Government, and (iv) e-taxation, e-licensing, e-tendering, etc., from Government to Business are made available on an integrated online network. Communication and sharing information through all the level of functions, then the shared information propagates immediately helping citizens to access the services and works across a wide variety. Inclusion of all is a key hallmark. The Seventh Central Pay Commissions used the online portal for inviting feedback and consultation on various relevant aspects through the questionnaire and processing of the same electronically is an instance.
6. **Plan of E-governance:** The e-governance plan is grouped into national and state e-governance. With the inauguration of the National e-Governance Plan (NeGP) in 2006, the motto of national e-governance is to set up 100000 Common Service Centres (CSCs) across India, one for every six villages with 27 Mission Mode projects, largely for back-end computerization of different areas of governance activity and also national e-governance infrastructure of State Wide Area Networks, State Data Centres, and National Service Delivery Gateways. Under the NeGP, the Passport Seva is intended to transform the delivery of all passport-related services across the country with accent on process efficiency, citizens' focus, employee productivity and system transparency. It is expected to issue passports within 3 days and, in case it requires police verification for its completion, another 3 days. Therefore, it envisages 68 Passport Facilitation Centres all over the country. The other Mission Mode Projects (MMP) of the NeGP include:

(a) Banking: Core Banking Technology for online mass payment system electronically
(b) Central excise: Filing of service tax and excise returns
(c) Income Tax: Nineteen defined services including e-filing and online submission of forms and online payment of taxes are being covered. The MMP will include processing, correspondence, tax accounting and allocation of PAN
(d) National Portal of India being implemented to provide a single window access to the information and services of Indian Government at all levels from the Central government to the State Government to District administration and Panchayat for the citizens
(e) State Level Mission Model Projects work in areas of Agriculture, Commercial Taxes, Employment Exchange, Land Records, Municipalities, Panchayats, Police, Property Registration, Road Transport and Treasuries.

9.3 SOCIAL NETWORKING

The social networking service is an online service focusing on social networks among the people who share interests, events, activities, backgrounds or real-life connections. Web based social network services provide means for the users to interact over the internet, i.e., e-mail and instant messaging. The social media sites contain hundred or even millions of different peoples content. Social networks help keep the people connected with their friends and families in an easy way. The pros and cons of social networking are given below.

9.3.1 Pros of Social Networking

- Provides connectivity with friends and families in today's fast and ever-changing world. One is able to rekindle old friendship, share family photos and special events with everyone known at the same time.
- Traditional dating in today's world is quite common.
- Helps to reach an impossibly large and diverse population, i.e., artists, musicians, etc., and promote their products in the market.
- Updates breaking news and other important information through social media.
- Helps to catch and convict criminals.

9.3.2 Cons of Social Networking

- Anything false can spread to millions of people within hours or days through social media causing panic and severe misinformation in society.
- Communicated information is completely under wraps and hence thrust on social networking is limited causing major relationship problems in the society.
- Employers issue employment news looking for a certain criteria of qualified persons but cannot legally express that criteria by using social media prescreen applicants.
- Having access to people's lives at all times is not always good as the trend of cyber bullying causes havoc across the world.
- People become more and more addicted to social media which hampers their progress at the educational, professional and personal fronts.

9.3.3 Recent Trends in Communication

The aspects of communication have assumed great significance due to the following recent technology trends. These are discussed below.

1. **Pager:** Paging establishes contact between the organization and the personnel working away from the organization either locally or far away. It is a telecommunication device used for oral communication with the required personnel in an organization. A contact can be made with the person who has code. To receive the signal or the message transmitted, the personnel carries a device known as **beeper**. Paging can be operated by using the telephone exchanges or satellite links for the purpose of transmission. The pager system removes all the restrictions on the movement of personnel say doctors, police, travelling executives, defense, etc., who are on the move from one place to another by virtue of their positions

in discharging their duties. It can be localized or far-flung according to the needs of an organization. Localized paging facilities had started in India and begun with the state of Delhi, expanding to other major cities.

2. **Broadband:** Radio communication indicating a range of wavelengths within a specified limit is called **band.** An amount of data that can be transferred in a fixed time is called **broadband.** It is expressed in bytes per second in case of digital device and in cycles per second in analog device. It has thousand times faster interactions with services to the internet.
3. **Satellite:** Satellite communication is like radio relay station which uses electromagnetic propagation in open space covering larger geographical areas. It is placed in a stationary object about 22300 miles above the earth's surface to receive data and sends it to the earth station satellite antenna. Telephone and microwave signals are relayed to an earth station for transmission to the satellite communication. In global overseas communication system, satellites have become an integral part. As on today, a number of satellites are placed in the geo-orbit. Satellite communication like radio relay station solves the problems that arise in case of remote and isolated locations surrounded by oceans, mountains and other obstacles of nature. Today, satellite is a global communicating system covering long distance communications.
4. **Laser:** Laser as a communication device is used to generate an intense and highly controlled beam of light. This beam of light is received by the relay stations. The normal line of sight transmission is 15 miles.
5. **Radar:** Radar as an acronym of Radio Detecting and Ranging was first developed in 1942 during the Second World War by the US Navy. It is a device to gather information about a distant object. The electromagnetic waves are sent to the target object and analyze the scanned detected objects like pressure, pollution and movement of solid in the surrounding space. Both the transmission and reception of high frequency waves reflect in the radar apparatus.
6. **Television:** In transmission of mass information, television (TV) has become a popular medium of both audio and visual. Visual in combination of audio and video in motion is a distinct feature of television. As per the Grolier encyclopedia, experimental television broadcasting was started in the United States of America in the 1920s; electric television tube was invented in 1923; and then the picture tube, electronic camera and television home receivers came. Television stations were set up in New York and London in 1930s. The National Television Service of India first telecasted through Doordarshan from Akashvani Bhavan, New Delhi on September 15, 1959. Satellite technology in India is known as Satellite Instructional Television Experiment (SITE) which was conducted in 1976. In India, television has a three-tier structure viz., national, regional and local. Television, today, enjoys an unrivalled and unparallel status as a medium of mass communication worldwide.

Revolution in information technology has transformed communication into an information obsessed global village. On reexamination of the old concept of knowledge and information which made a slogan, called knowledge 'power.' Sitting in houses, people can join millions of spectators during the grand spectacle like Olympic Games, great functions like President of America swearing-in ceremony, Presidents of various countries and some other national and global events. In all cases, distance has been washed away. In one word, people from different parts of this planet can 'talk' and 'see' one another at a time, and millions of viewers can watch all over the world. On becoming more and more complex, the business organizations use computer to encounter the severe paper work crunch. (See Exhibit 9.3)

Exhibit 9.3 Use Computer to Reduce Paper Work

The Fast Food Company Limited is engaged in production and supply of foods having many departments/divisions like business planning, purchasing, manufacturing, engineering, research and development, warehousing, marketing, sales service, accounting and so forth in addition to several branches throughout the country. To make available the needed information and analysis, the entire data covering the said aspects are fed into the computer for storing. This computerized data as and when required, can be picked up, arranged suitably to get a solution. Computer, thus, is not merely a storehouse of classified information but also a problem-solving instrument.

Under the control of a set of instructions, computer accepts data as its raw material and converts this data into desired and classified form of information. Data process essentially involves manipulating and restructuring using techniques such as calculation, selection, sorting and summarization. Enormous data can be suitably placed and interacted to produce the desired solution. Thus, the computer does the job quickly and accurately. It renders services to the following tasks:

- Data base (data sorting, manipulating and printing and retrieval)
- Spread sheets (electronic ledgers)
- Financial analysis
- Accounting
- Graphics

Communication is an art that every Indian has mastered! Indians communicate in numerous ways. Every Indian loves to converse, mingle, network and socialize. In spite of being the most linguistically diverse country in the world, India has no barrier to communicate. For instance, Indians are taught to welcome others with warmth and affection, hospitality is unique reflecting the reverential culture beautifully spread across the country. Communication via media has been relentlessly evolving, giving people newer and wider options. They have been lucratively encouraging, emotionally engaging and precisely leveraging every media until today.

After 'tech savvy', it is the 'social media savvy' that has become synonymous with the generation of today. About two-thirds of Indians spend time online on different social networking sites like Facebook, Twitter, YouTube, Pinterest, etc. Even the trend of sending personal emails seems to have become outdated as compared to social media. Interaction, live chat, status updates, image and video-sharing are few major aspects that play a key role in popularizing social media. Social media's multiple roles played beyond its core role of merely communicating information is leading to its popularity.

The number of social media users in urban India, by December 2012, had touched 62 million. Sudden availability of smartphones and mobile internet has also led to a spurt in the use of social media. All the business units in India rely on social media to understand their consumer base, brand awareness and interaction. Indian netizens use social media to build virtual communities, groups to interact and chat. Undoubtedly, the information and technology is rapidly increasing the role of social media in shaping and fixing the customers' mind towards certain brand products and services. At the same time, it is also used for entertainment and leisure by most of the Indians online. Each day, about 100 million Indians are engaged in social media. Social media is defined as: Bringing people together through a network for communicating messages to each other. According to Merriam-Webster (2016), social media is defined as "Forms of electronic communication through which people create online communities to share information, ideas, personal messages, etc." The channels of social media and the purpose they serve are presented in Table 9.2.

Table 9.2 Channels and Purpose of Social Media

Social Media Channel	Purpose served	Tools
Blogs, Microblogs	Blogs are popularly known as online personal diaries. They help you share your thoughts in detail. Microblogging sites limit content sharing update. WordPress, Blogspot, Livejournal, and Typepad are examples of blogs while Twitter is a microblogging site.	Used for authoring
YouTube, Vimeo, Pinterest, Instagram, Slide Share	As hubs that host rich media content and play a vital role in creating the attractiveness and various forms of content on social media	Used for sharing
Facebook, Google+, Twitter	These hubs are responsible for networking. Be it appealing to mass or creating one-on-one buzz, they are the most used social networks in the world. The major chunk of the audience is found to reside	Used for social networking
LinkedIn, Xing	LinkedIn is designed to showcase the professional attributes of a person to the world more evidently. It does not indulge in sharing photographs or discussing petty issues.	Professional social networking

Wikipedia, Google Docs	Globally, people use this platform to share content/documents and collaborate with other people to work on the same content remotely at the same time. Officially, many project managers remote to each other use the tools to work on a common topic.	Collaboration platforms
Foursquare, Google Latitude	Allow people to check in a particular location online and find out nearby areas like different stores in the locality. One can also observe the reviews of a place and learn online from the other visitors of the place. These networks can be mainly accessed via smartphones.	Location-based social networking

9.4 CLASSIFICATION OF SOCIAL MEDIA

Social media technologies may take many different forms including business networks, enterprise social networks, forums, microblogging, photo sharing, product/service review, social bookmarking and social networks, video sharing and virtual worlds. The development of social media started with simple platforms like sixdegrees.com. Research shows that the audience spends 22 per cent of their time on social networking sites, proving how popular social media platforms have become. This is a result of the use of smartphones among the population. The statistics of social media in India in 2014 is presented in Table 11.2. The term social media is usually used to describe the social networking sites as:

- Facebook allows users to create their personal profiles, share photos and videos, and communicate with others.
- Twitter allows users to post tweets for their followers to see updates in real-time through an internet service.
- LinkedIn allows users to create professional profiles, post-resumes and communicate with other professionals and job-seekers.
- Pinterest allows users to display photos of items found on the web by pinning them and sharing ideas with others.
- Snapchat allows users to send and share photos of their daily activities.

Table 9.3 Social Media Statistics in India

Channel	No. of users/ viewers	Global Users	Position of India
Facebook	72 million+	1.11 billion+	Use of 5% of total population comprises highly affluent, educated, English speaking individuals. India is third largest Facebook user in the world
Twitter	33 million+	More than 517 million	Sixth largest Twitter using in the world. Indian users account for 2.87% of total global users and 29% Indian netizens

Contd.

LinkedIn	20 million+	225 million+	Second largest LinkedIn user in the world
YouTube	55.80 million	1 billion users each month	Each month more than 400 million people access it. YouTube is accounted for a major share of the time spent online with 1250 Indians visiting every month. About 25% of viewer share comes from mobile devices. Largest number of content uploaders in Asia for YouTube.
Google+	50 million	More than 500 million	About 14% of global Google + users are from India. About 3.86% of Google+ users are from Bangalore, the highest in the world.
Pinterest	10.4 million	48.7 million	Natural fit for retail business to gain transaction through social network in front of potential customers. Pinterest is to roll out its 'buy' button for purchases of product they find on the site.
Foursquare	0.33 million	More than 25 million	About 5% of global Foursquare users live in India

Source: Facebook facts taken from Facebook Ads platform, June 2013
LinkedIn facts taken from LinkedIn Blog, May 2013
Active Twitter users in India
Forbes: http://www.forbes.com/sites/victorlipman/2013/05/01/

9.4.1 Web and Social Media

Social media is the collection of different types of online communication channels dedicated to the social community based on inputs, interactions, contents-sharing and collaboration, Websites and application dedicated to the forums, microblogging, social networking, social bookmarking and wikis. It affects the way youth communicate with new forms of language. Abbreviations are introduced to cut down the time it takes to respond online. The commonly known 'Laugh out Loud' (LOL) has become globally recognized. Each year, new catchphrases and neologisms such as 'You Only Live Once' (YOLO) and 'Before Anyone Else' (BAE) arise and start trending around the world.

Social media alters the way we understand each other and allows for mass cultural exchange and intercultural communication. People from different regions or even different countries can discuss current issues on Facebook. Different cultures have different value systems, cultural themes, grammar and worldviews that they communicate differently. The emergence of social media platforms collide different cultures and different communication methods together, forcing people to realign in order to communicate with ease with other cultures. Different cultures continue to connect through social media platforms, so that the thinking pattern, expression style and cultural content influence cultural values to chip away.

India's 65 per cent of people are still far from getting on the internet but racing to catch up. As per Report on Social Marketing Agency, "India is among the top five countries in the globe in terms of growth of internet users." Here are the major milestones in usage of web, mobile and social media in India. India's:

- Active Internet users are 462 million, out of a global total of 3.63 billion
- Internet usage is growing at a rate of 90 per cent while the global average is just 19 per cent
- Web users have 153 million active social media accounts from a global tally of 2.43 billion
- Mobile connections are 10.1 million
- Social media users are 153 million, of which 130 million use it on mobile
- Active social media users are up by 23 per cent since March 2015, compared to 26 per cent global rise
- Mobile subscriptions in India grew only by 7 per cent

India's population represents a much smaller share of social network users accounting to 17 per cent and just 8.8 per cent of internet users. Across India, there are 143 million users of social media and urban areas witnessed 83 per cent of it as of April 2015. On the other hand, the number for rural India stood at 25 million, up from close to 12 million last year, showing a growth by 100 per cent. Though, Facebook emerged as a leading social media website with 96 per cent of urban users followed by Google Plus 61 per cent, Twitter 43 per cent and LinkedIn 24 per cent of their respective total. The largest segment of users was college-going students with 34 per cent followed by young men, 27 per cent.

India may have the world's second largest internet user base, but connectivity remains out of reach for nearly 950 million citizens. Even with the internet data plans, India being among the cheapest in the world with the average retail price of smartphones steadily declining, connectivity is still out of reach of nearly 950 million Indians (as per the Assocham-Deloitte Joint Study). India currently has about 350 million Internet users, second only to China.

9.4.2 Popular Social Networks

The compilation of statistics of most popular social networks worldwide prepared gives a clear picture of Facebook ruling supreme. This would not be a shock to anyone! With over 1590 million active users, it holds a 19 per cent market share, 7 per cent more so than its closest competitor, WhatsApp. The social network worldwide, as of April 2016, ranked by number of active users (in millions) is presented in Table 9.4.

Table 9.4 Network User Accounts

Networks	Users (in Millions)
Facebook	1590
WhatsApp	1000
QQ	900
WeChat	697
QZone	640

Contd.

Tumblr	555
Instagram	500
Twitter	320
Baidu Tieba	300
Skype	300
Viber	249
Sina Weibo	222
Line	215
Snapchat	200
YY	122
VKontakte	100
Pinterest	100
MMB	100
LinkedIn	100
Telegram	100
Total	8310

Some important social media networks are explained below.

1. Facebook is an online social networking site allowing its users to create their personal profiles, share photos and videos, and communicate with other users. As the most browsed social network on social media with a large base of 1590 million users, it clearly shows unfading away anytime soon in India. More than 80 per cent of those users have access to Facebook via their mobile phone.

   Using Facebook allows for both asynchronous and synchronous, open speech via a familiar and regularly accessed medium with the support if integration of multimodal content such as student-created photographs and video in a platform wherein many students are already familiar with. It also allows the students to ask many minor questions that they might not otherwise feel motivated to visit a professor in person during the office hours to ask. Facebook is one alternative means for shy students to be able to collect and articulate their thoughts in and outside the classroom. The level of informality to Facebook can also aid students in self-expression and encourage more frequent student-and-instructor and student-and-student communication. It is observed that the informality actually may drive many educators and students away from using Facebook for educational purposes.

   Familiarity and comfortability with Facebook is often determined with the socio-economic class. Instructors ought to seriously consider and respect these hesitancies, and refrain from forcing Facebook on their students for academic purposes.

2. Twitter is an internet service allowing the users to post tweets for their followers to see updates in real-time. It has 33 million users in India accounting to 76 per cent. This group has access to the used social media via their mobile phone.
3. LinkedIn is a networking website for the business community allowing the users to create professional profiles; post resumes and communicate with other professionals and job-seekers.
4. Pinterest is a social curative website for sharing and categorizing found images online. Pinterest requires brief descriptions but the main focus of site is visual. Clicking on an image will take you to the original source. For example, if you click on a picture of a pair of shoes, you might be taken to a site where you can purchase them. An image of blueberry pancakes might take you to the recipe; a picture of a whimsical birdhouse might take you to the instructions. Of the total chunk of 70 million users among the world; India's Pinterest is accounted for 5.50 million.
5. Utilization of Instagram is dominated by men in comparison to women with ratio being 75:25. In others words, it shows only one-fourth of women population in India is on Instagram while live selfies are more appreciated by men than women!
6. Snapchat is an app on mobile devices allowing the users to send and share photos of them doing their daily activities. It has 26.50 million Indian users.
7. Internet users are 24.30 crore. This figure will go to 50 crore by 2020.
8. In mobile usage, there has been a surge due to the emergence of Smartphone generation on account of major chunk of people that have access to internet and social media from their mobile phones. The mobile penetration of active internet users is 22 crore; but a total of 10.50 plus crore active social media users via their mobile is accounted for 41 per cent of total mobile internet users.
9. Digital media has changed its traditional meaning to advertising and selling. Following it, India has proved that it is going to get bigger and better! Digital advertising has been witnessing a steady growth. Indian online advertising market has touched Rs 2938 crore. E-commerce in India is expected to reach Rs. 10,12,800 crore by 2020. This explains what significance is being attached to e-retail stores like Flipkart, Myntra, etc.
10. Wikipedia is an online user-edited encyclopedia and its users can register as editors to create a user profile. For example, a professor at a University encouraged 600 students to enroll in his introductory management course to add to Wikipedia pages featuring contents related to the course. Like other educators, the university students argued that the assignment would not only strengthen the site's management-related content, but also provide an opportunity for them to engage in critical reflection about the negotiations involved in collaborative productive knowledge. However, Wikipedia's all-volunteer editorial staff complained that the students' contribution resulted in an overwhelming number of additions to the site, and some of the contributions were inaccurate. Wikipedia was founded in January, 2001.

11. YouTube is a frequently used social media tool in the classroom (also the second most visited website in the world). Students can watch videos, answer questions, and discuss the content. Additionally, students can create videos to share with others. Sherer and Shea (2011) claimed that YouTube increases participation, personalization (customization), and productivity. It also improves the digital skills of students and provides an opportunity for peer learning and problem solving.
12. LinkedIn is now the world's largest professional social network with over 300 million members in over 200 countries. The mission of LinkedIn is to connect the world's professionals to make them more productive economically. Many people describe LinkedIn as a professional Facebook, but it is important to remember that LinkedIn is not Facebook. Users tend to use a standard headshot as a profile picture and keep the contents and information as professional and career-focused as possible. Most LinkedIn users put their Curriculum Vitae online. Users can also post articles that they have written or published, which enables prospective employers to see their written work.

    There are over 39 million college graduates on LinkedIn, it has become the fastest-growing demographic on the site. In many ways LinkedIn uses and encourages the students to have a professional online social presence which comfortably helps them in searching for a job or an internship. The key to making LinkedIn encourages learners to build credibility through their profiles, dedicate class time solely for the purpose, how to navigate it and build their profile for success in future. Professors can also create assignments that involve using LinkedIn as a research tool.
13. Google+ (pronounced Google plus) is Google's social networking project, designed to replicate the way people interact offline more closely than is the case in other social networking services.
14. Reddit is a social news website and forum where stories are socially curetted and promoted by site members. The site is composed of hundreds of sub-communities, known as subreddits. Each subreddit has a specific topic such as technology, politics or music. Reddit site members are called redditors who submit the contents and are then voted upon by other members. Sending well-regarded stories to the top of the site's main thread page is the goal.
15. Mobile Use Mobile is used as social media. It is a mobile marketing application which allows creation, exchange and circulation of users generated content. Due to the fact that mobile social media run on mobile devices and differ from traditional social media by incorporating new factors such as the current location of the user (location-sensitivity) or the time delay between sending and receiving messages (time-sensitivity). According to Andreas Kaplan, mobile social media applications can be differentiated into four types.

    - Space-timers (location and time sensitive): Exchange of messages with relevance to mostly one specific location at one specific point in time (e.g. Facebook; Foursquare)

- Space-locators (only location sensitive): Exchange of messages with relevance to one specific location. It is tagged to a certain place and read later by others (e.g., Yelp; Qype, Tumblr)
- Quick-timers (only time sensitive): Transfer of traditional social media applications to mobile devices to increase immediacy (e.g., posting Twitter messages or Facebook status updates)
- Slow-timers (neither location, nor time sensitive): Transfer of traditional social media applications to mobile devices. Example such as watching a YouTube video or reading/editing a Wikipedia article)

9.4.3 Role of Social Media

Social media is becoming an integral part of human life. Most traditional online social media include social components such as comment fields for users. In business, it is used for marketing of products, promoting brands and connecting the current customers fostering new business. The role of social media is explained hereunder. The social media:

- Allows creation and sharing of information, ideas, career interests and other forms of expression via virtual communities and networks and operate in a dialogic transmission system. Social media are interactive web internet based applications. It is user generated content with text-posts or comments, digital photos or videos, and data generated through all online interactions. It facilitates the development of online social networks by connecting the user's profile with those of other individuals or groups.
- Uses the web-based technologies, desktop computers and mobile technologies to create substantially high interactive platforms and pervasively changes to communication between the businesses, organizations, communalities and the individuals through which shared, co-created, discussed, and modified user-generated contents or pre-made contents are posted online. It changes focus on the emerging field of techno-self studies. Internet users continue to spend more time on social media sites than on any other type of site.
- Can help to improve individuals' sense of connectedness with real or online communities. It is an effective communication or marketing tool for corporations, entrepreneurs, non-profit organizations, support groups, political parties and governments. Social media differs from traditional electronic media such as TV broadcasting in many ways including quality, reach, frequency, usability, immediacy, and permanence.
- As brand usage is much aware of its potential value in delivery to the satisfaction of consumers as compared to other channels. But for this, India is one of the major consumers in terms of social media utilization Statistics for 2016.
- Allows technologies to take many different forms including business networks, enterprise social networks, forums, photo sharing, products/services, social gaming, video sharing and virtual world. The social network revolution has led

to the rise of networking sites. This increase is because of the smartphones that are now in the daily lives of most humans.

9.4.4 Comparison Between Social and Traditional Media

Social media has a strong influence on business activities and business performance. The companies and other organizations can adopt social media tools and approaches to improve their business capacity and performance in terms of customer relationship management, innovation, training and knowledge management. The capability approaches engage experts, customers, suppliers, and employees in the development of products and services using social media. The channels of social media transformed into business performance capabilities of:

- Social capital
- Revealed preferences
- Social marketing
- Social corporate networking

Social media are distinct from traditional media to that of industrial media (such as newspapers, magazines, television and film). The former is comparatively inexpensive and accessible upon computer acquisition while industrial media requires significant resources to publish information as in most cases the articles that go through many revisions before being published. This process adds to the cost pushing up the market price. Originally, social media was used by individuals only but now it is used by businesses, charities, government and politics. One characteristic shared by both the social media and industrial media is the capability to reach audiences small or large. For example, a television show may reach nobody or millions of people. Some of the properties that help describe the differences between social and industrial media are quality, reach, frequency, accessibility, usability, immediacy and performance. The differences are presented in Table 9.5.

Table 9.5 Comparison between Traditional and Social Media

Aspect	Traditional Media	Social Media
Quality	Publisher is a typical range of quality substantially narrower than niche and unmediated market.	Quality varies from very high to low. Sometimes, even abusive or inappropriate content is telecasted.
Reach	Typically use a centralized framework for organization, production and dissemination.	By its very nature, more decentralized, less hierarchical and distinguished with points of production and utility.
Frequency	Users access number of times per day.	Numerous times throughout the day.

Accessibility	Low income people may have more access to TV, radio, etc., on account of being inexpensive and tune in free over air programming.	Available to public at little or no cost and supported by advertising revenue that have access to internet and computer or mobile device. Poor people lack access to internet and computer due to expensive computer or mobile device.
Usability	Naturally, requires skills and training. For example, to record a pop song, an aspiring singer would have to rent time in an expensive professional recording studio and also hire an audio-engineer.	Anyone with access to internet can operate the means of social media production and post digital pictures, videos or tests online. Singing a song requires only modest reinterpretation of existing skills.
Immediacy	On account of review by various editors and checkers due to instantaneous responses, time log is long.	Enable regular people to instantly communicate their opinions and information as a strength point. Lack of checking facilitates circulation of hoaxes.
Performance	Once created cannot be altered. For example, book printed and distributed, changes cannot be made.	Can alter almost instantaneously when the user decides to edit or due to comments from readers.

The community media constitute a hybrid of industrial and social media. Example: community radio, TV, and newspapers are run by professionals and some by amateurs which use both social and industrial media frameworks. Social media is recognized for the way how they have changed public relations professionals in conducting their jobs. They have provided an open arena where people are free to exchange ideas on companies, brands, and products. Social media provides an environment where users and public relation professionals can converse and promote their brand and improve their company's image by listening and responding to, what the public is saying about their products.

9.4.5 Social Media and Business Performance

The social media channels transform business resources into business performance capabilities. These are:

1. **Social Capital:** Share capital represents the extent to which social media affects the relationship of firm and organization with society; the way with which the organization of social media increases corporate social performance capabilities.
2. **Social Marketing:** It represents firm's social marketing resources. The examples of online conversations, sharing links, online presence, sending text messages are used to increase a firm's financial capabilities which increase in terms of sales and acquisition of new customers.

3. **Social Corporate Networking:** Social corporate networking refers to the informal ties and linkages of corporate/organizational staff with other people from their field or industry, clients, customers, and other members of the public formed through social networks. It can increase the operational performance capabilities in many ways. It can enable: (i) sales staff to find new clients, (b) marketing staff to learn about client/customer needs and demand; and (c) management can learn about the public perception of their strategy or approach.
4. **Customer Relationship Management:** Customer relationship management (CRM) is an approach to the interaction of the management of company with the current and potential future customers that tries to analyze data about customers' history with a company and to improve business relationships with customers, specifically focusing on customer retention and ultimately driving sales growth. One important aspect of the CRM approach is compilation data from a range of different communication channels including a company's website, telephone, email, live chat, marketing materials, and social media. Through the CRM approach, the systems are used to facilitate CRM; businesses learn more about their target audiences and how best it caters to their needs. However, adopting the CRM approach may also occasionally lead to favouritism among consumers, resulting in dissatisfaction among them and defeating the purpose of CRM.

   Innovation can be defined as a new idea, device or method or the application of better solution to meet new requirement, unarticulated need, or existing market need. This is accomplished through more-effective products, processes, services, technologies, or business models that are readily available to markets, governments and society. Innovation is generally considered to be the result of a process that brings together various novel ideas in a way that affect society. Innovation is often manifested via the process of engineering. In industrial economics, innovations are created and found empirically from services to meet the growing consumers demands.
5. **Monitoring, Tracking and Analysis:** Companies are increasingly using social media monitoring tools to monitor, track, and analyze online conversations on the Web about their brand products or related topics of interest. This can be useful in public relations management and advertising campaign tracking, allowing the companies to measure return on investment (ROI) for the amount spent on social media advertisement, auditing and public engagement. Tools range from free basis of applications to subscription-based with more in-depth tools.

   Social media tracking also enables the companies to respond quickly to online posts for criticism products or services. This helps the company to lessen the negative effect of online complaints pertaining to company's product or service sales. For example, if a customer criticizes a major hotel's cleanliness or service standards on a social media website, the management may get an alert quickly on the critical situation online and express concern for the sub-par service. Further, offer to the complaining person a coupon or discount on his/her next service-use plus a forward promise so that the problem will not be repeated.

6. **Data Mining:** Data mining is a technique to analyze data to detect patterns. It is a process of representing, analyzing and extracting actionable patterns from collected data of the activities of people on social media. Social media mining introduces the basic concepts and principal algorithms suitable for investigating the massive social media data. It discusses theories and methodologies from different disciplines such as computer science, data mining, machine learning, social network analysis, network science, sociology, ethnography, statistics, optimization and mathematics. It encompasses the tools to represent formally, measure and model patterns meaningful from large-scale social media data. Detecting the patterns in social media use by data mining is of particular interest to advertisers, major corporations and brands, governments and political parties, among others.
7. **Business:** Role of social media in business and consumer market in India cannot be undermined. It brings changes in consumers' behaviour that is the changing role of social media in India. With time, use of social media has seen a drastic change from just use for fun to fun plus knowledge and marketing. For business purposes, Facebook is the most important social media platform as there is customers' engagement, followed by Twitter, YouTube and blogging.

   So, not only individuals but every organization, be it big or small, has an online presence on Facebook, Twitter, Pinterest, YouTube channels and other related social media platforms. Organizations in India use 95.70 per cent social media to build communities, 76.10 per cent to highlight brand news, platform specific parameters such as number of likes, share, and comments. As far as the budget is concerned, most organizations set budget below 10 million on their social media spending to make 1-5 per cent of their total marketing budget. Social media interaction provides useful information about the behaviour of the customers to the organization on regular basis.
8. **Recruitment:** Social media and recruitment go hand in hand with social media which is, now, becoming an integral part of recruiting firms. The firms using LinkedIn, Facebook and Twitter find new employees and skills. So, gone are the days when employment recruiters and employees used to rely on employment exchange and classified advertisements in the newspapers. Hiring through traditional media is based on gut feeling whereas social media is based on interaction, communication and direct response. Most organizations have well planned strategies for talent acquisition through social media.
9. **Indian Premier League:** Social media is also playing an active role in the Indian Premier League (IPL) by providing up to date and live information on sites like Facebook, Twitter, Google+ and YouTube. Teams are in constant touch with their fans through social media and have great interaction. For the IPL sponsors and brands, interaction and reach of social media is a boon. Thus, there is no way to ignore social media for business and entertainment purposes.

   Criticism of social media ranges from the use of specific platforms and capabilities, disparity of information available, issues with trustworthiness and reliability of information presented the impact of social media use on an individual's concentration, ownership of media content, and the meaning of interactions created by social media. Some social media platforms offer users the opportunity to cross-post simultaneously while some social network platforms have been criticized for poor interoperability between the platforms. This leads to creation of information silos, viz. isolated pockets of data contained in one social media platform. Again, social media have positive effects like allowing democratization of the Internet as allowing individuals to advertise themselves and form friendships. Others have noted that the term, social cannot account for technological features of a platform alone. Hence, the level of sociability should be determined by the actual performances of its users. There has been a dramatic decrease in face-to-face interactions on account of more and more introduction of social media platforms with the presumptive threat of cyber-bullying and online sexual predators being more prevalent.

10. **Social Media and Politics:** Social media has become so integrated into peoples' daily life as everyone is already having a public profile. A recent survey showed that every Indian spends 5-6 hours on social media. Still a lot is needed to access it but most youth are accessing it from everywhere. We know 65 per cent of the population is under the age of 35 years.

    Traditional campaigning is mandatory up to 48 hours before closing the polls. Unlike this, the Election Commission cannot put a ban on use of social networking website campaign in elections. The campaign makes communication and intervention with everyone directly without any interference and involvement. According to Facebook CEO, only one-third Indians use Facebook. In Facebook, growth is fourfold.

Social media is also accessed by politicians. Politicians through different activities of politics have brought social media into the limelight. Today, it plays a huge role and influences the general elections to a great extent. The study by IRIS Knowledge Foundation and supported by the internet and Mobile Association of India (IAMAI) has indicated this fact. Social media will be real game changer with the political leaders having millions of fans on Twitter and supporters on Facebook and Google+. Most of the politicians in order to build a certain image also have their own websites.

Dr. Abdul Kalam as President of India had a page on Facebook, Social Media Campaign against corruption in India by Anna Hazare. Many researchers have indicated that social media would become stronger and more persuasive than television in influencing people.

9.4.6 Social Media Analytics

Social media analytics is the practice of gathering data from blogs and social media websites; analyzing the data to make business decisions. The most common use of social media analytics is customer sentiment to support the activities of marketing and customer service. Social media marketing takes the advantage of social networking to help increase a company brand exposure and broaden customer reach. The goal is usually to create enough content compelling those users who will share it with their social networks.

Marketing of social customer relationship can be a powerful tool in business. For example, establishing a Facebook page that provides people a venue for communication, marketing and networking.

From the perspective of customers, social media makes a company and everyone else take about their experiences, whether such experiences are good or bad. The business can also respond quickly to both positive and negative feedback, attend to the problems of customers and maintain, regain or rebuild customer confidence. The enterprise social networking allows a company to connect individuals who share similar business interests or activities. Internally, social tools can help employees' access information and resources they need to work together effectively and solve business problems. Externally, the public social media platforms help an organization to stay close to their customers and make it easier to conduct research that can be used to improve business processes and operations.

QUESTIONS

1. Explain the evolutionary process of e-communication.
2. Discuss the new concepts of e-communication.
3. What is e-mail? Explain the procedure of creating an e-mail and sending message.
4. What is e-commerce? Explain the facets and future of it.
5. What is internet? State its utility.
6. What is social networking? Explain its operations.
7. What is social media? Explain its working with web.
8. Discuss the importance of social media networks.
9. Explain the role of social media.
10. Distinguish between social media and traditional media.
11. Write a note on social media analytics.
12. Explain the following:
    (a) Electronic communication
    (b) Web life
    (c) Audio-video teleconferencing
    (d) Word processor
    (e) Pager
    (f) Broadband
    (g) Satellite
    (h) Social media and politics

10 CHAPTER

Resume Writing and Career Opportunity

"When work is a pleasure, life is joy. When work is a duty, life is slavery."

— **Maxim Gorky**

LEARNING OBJECTIVES

This chapter will enable you to

- know the basics of a job and how to prepare a resume, and
- understand approach and style of discussion in a group.

INTRODUCTION

Man is a member of a family, profession or occupation and society in which he interacts in one form or another with one person or another. After acquiring education, including skills, everyone tries to get an opportunity to provide services to mankind and also to get employment for living and good economic progression. An important segment of man's life is that of finding a career; for which a strong domain of knowledge with soft (communication) skills is a must.

10.1 BASICS IN CAREER PLANNING

An application seeking for a job is, perhaps, the most difficult task. It is like a sales letter in which the applicant sells his services to the market for the best price available. There is no shortcut to success and 'no-gain without-pain.' Therefore, the students should build up four qualities, namely, 'sankalpam' (strong will), 'shrama' (hard work), 'shraddha' (faith) and 'sahanam' (patience) to climb the ladder of success. Therefore, devote for a while your time and thought on communication skills in career planning.

After acquiring the right education qualifications, every student wants to jump into the workplace. Here, one should know that translating the ambition into reality calls for fine-tuning of his abilities. This is because that every recruiter thinks and rethinks when employing a person without hurry to grab the first guy who walks in for the interview. In this context, every applicant who desires to enter the workplace needs to assess himself first on the aspects: (1) Take stock of plus and minus points. An applicant may feel that he has no minus points. (2) Look carefully at habits and realize the after-effects of college life. (3) Get rid of such minus points; if you fail to overcome these, you may find a job but it may not last long. If one becomes a master in the following issues beforehand, he will find a job without much difficulty. These are discussed below.

1. **Strong in Subject:** Be thorough in the subject. This would need regular brush up on the fundamentals not letting books gather cobwebs and gathering additional information on the latest concepts in the subject area. For instance, in an interview for an IT company, a fresher was asked, 'What is the function of a cursor?' The candidate a B.Tech. in Computer Science fumbled to give an answer. So remember, the recruiter is going to test the candidate's knowledge that he has gained through the particular course he has undergone. If he fails to answer in the area of his specialization, he will put up a poor show in the interview and may not get beyond the first round.
2. **Strong Skills Set:** The applicant needs to polish communication and interpersonal skills. Communication is just not only the ability to talk but also involves body language, pronunciation, gestures and ability to listen and answer. Interpersonal skills refer to the way one talks to others, listens and holds on to his emotions in the right manner. Communication and interpersonal skills reflect one's personality.
3. **Strong Time Sense:** Existence of business organizations and making profit always depends on the principle of timeliness in the delivery of goods and services to the market. Failure to meet deadlines will certainly show the door sooner than later. Hence, it is essential to practise the habit of doing work in a defined time bracket. Punctuality will put an employee in good stead when he enters a job.
4. **Simple Mindset:** Shed the habit of complicated thinking and keep up objective of business in mind and work towards that direction. Be a doer rather than a thinker which would ensure obedience, quotient and recognize you as a person of performance.
5. **Sure and Steady:** Consistency is the hallmark of a great mind. Perform well on a regular basis; this does not mean a need to improve performance. If an employee allows himself to be right one day and dull the next day, he will not find the person to appreciate him for the good work done; rather pointed out for the shoddy performance.

10.2 CURRICULUM VITAE

Curriculum vitae (CV) means 'course of life' in Latin. The curriculum vitae is a concise document summarizing one's past, professional skills, proficiency and experience. The purpose is to demonstrate that he has the necessary skills and also some complementary ones to do the job for which he is applying. The curriculum vitae also called vitas and resume have similar purposes as the jobseeker's marketing documents which provide key information about skills, experience, education and personal qualities to prove an individual as an ideal candidate for the job in an easy-to-digest format.

The CV is formatted to A4 paper whereas resume to letter-sized 8″ x 11.5″. It includes personal information like sex, nationality, date of birth, marital status, etc. Resume does not usually include interests or hobbies unless they are relevant to the position an individual is applying for while it is acceptable to include the additional information in a curriculum vitae. Whereas a resume does not typically include a headshot and a photo as is acceptable on CV, and international resumes. An individual resume sometimes called his CV, is the most important tool when applying for a job. It does not matter how qualified he is or how much experience he has. If his resume is poorly presented or badly written, the chances of getting a job on even cracking an interview are less. Taking time to work on the resume is really important. The following is necessary:

- Write a resume that generates purposive results
- How to know the socks off a prospective employer
- A few guidelines for a better presentation
- I am not sure the job that I am looking for is the right one for me
- Add power to your resume with power words

Writing a great resume does not necessarily mean one should follow the rules he hears through the grapevine – a page or specific resume format. Every resume is a one-of-a-kind marketing communication. It should be appropriate to the situation and do exactly what one wants it to do. Instead of a bunch of rules and tips, it is better to chase in brief and offer the most basic principles of writing an effective resume.

Creation of a resume with a little extra effort makes an individual stand out. Even if the candidate faces fierce competition with a well written resume, he interviewed more often than many people more qualified than him. The applicant will have to learn how to think and write in a style that will be completely new to him. Let us take a look at the purpose of resume.

Resume is a tool with one specific purpose to win an interview. If it doesn't, it isn't an effective resume. A resume is an advertisement, nothing more, nothing less. If you buy this product, you will get these specific, direct benefits. It presents you in the best light. In the same way, it is so pleasing to the eye that the reader is enticed to pick it up and read it. It whets the appetite, stimulates interest in meeting the candidate and learning more about him/her. It inspires the prospective employer to pick up the phone and ask you to come in for an interview.

10.3 PREPARATION OF JOB APPLICATION

Communication of written or oral information with regards to employment is the first communication to an individual who has education qualifications and is seeking a career opportunity. Find out what the candidate is good at and what he/she likes to do; taking into stock his/her achievements and abilities. Preparation of a job application requires the following:

1. **Identify Job Opportunity:** Saying goes that professional life is eventful in one's life. Hence, professional life is as important as family life, if not more. The job has a profound impact on one's life because a career often extends a period about 30 to 35 years. Due care must be taken in applying for a job and seeking a career as 'good fit' to the qualifications, talent, skills, temperament, aspirations and

potential. While seeking a job, one should remember that there is sufficient scope for self-development as well as advancement in the career. In other words, long-term potential of job and organization should be kept in mind while applying for a job.

Ensuring an appropriate job is a two-way process. First, it involves selecting the right candidate by the organization and the interview panel. Second, the job-seeker has to ensure the keenness to pursue the offer. A desk-oriented person with no desire to take up a field level travelling job, an accountant by qualification who has no interest for a sales job and a computer engineer who has no temperament for modules development are some examples of seeking a job wherein the 'heart' is not really there. The job seekers should have on-the-job temperament; otherwise it would lead to unavoidable mismatch. Therefore, the candidate should make conscious decision when applying to a job of his liking especially when a reasonable choice is available. In brief, take up a job where your heart is or if the choice is limited, accept the reality and adapt to the job environment.

2. **Submission of Application:** Submission of an application is the next step in the process of seeking a job after having identified it. An organization receives hundreds of applications from various parts of the country and even abroad. The candidate while submitting the application letter should be conscious of its contents in response to the organization's request sought and package offered. A good quality paper, attractive presentation, neat and error-free typing, good folding (if any), forceful sentences, correct spelling of the name of addressee or organization, etc., though little but make a noticeable positive difference.

   Submitting an application letter for seeking a job is of two types, namely: (a) sue-motto and (b) in response. The former refers to sending a letter by the aspirant himself after making enquiry besides homework thus: Is the organization taking up new projects? Is the organization looking for candidates in specific functional and geographical areas? Is the organization looking for or in need of candidates? Is the candidate equipped with necessary qualifications and experience to fill the post? The submission of letter refers to sending letter as a response to the advertisement or announcement or invitation in which the details of job offer, required qualifications and experience, position in the hierarchy, emoluments, posting place, selection method, etc., are sought. See Exhibit 10.1 for the approach of preparing a resume.

Exhibit 10.1 **Resume Builder**

The chairman of Microsoft, Bill Gates makes the following observation about the resumes the company receives. "We receive 600 to 900 resumes from job applicants every day by postal mail or via our resume builder on the Microsoft Website. Seventy percent of the resumes arrive electronically via e-mail or the web. A paper resume is scanned and converted into text that goes into database. All resumes are electronically matched with the job position within 24 to 28 hours of receipt."

3. **Covering Letter:** The applicant has to state clearly how he is suitable for the post advertised covering all the relevant details in his application. The details to be covered are as: (i) bring out your strengths, highlight your distinguishing features and underline all those qualities which make you suitable for the job and (ii) appraise yourself as a right candidate for the job. This letter is often accompanied by a covering letter with the contents as short and sharp as possible making it more appealing and elegant.

   Address the letter to the right person. (say post-box number, recruitment agency, selection board, etc). In case of submission of application letter on sue-motto, care is to be taken to address the application/covering letter to the appropriate authority. If it goes to the wrong person or department, there is possibility of it being lying there without getting redirected to the appropriate person or department.

   If the letter is to be addressed to a company; the salutation is 'Sirs'. If it is to be addressed to an individual like the personnel manager, the salutation is 'Sir'. The complimentary close for an application letter is 'yours faithfully'. Letter that opens with a statement of the best qualification is more attractive, such opening sentences are becoming more popular. See Exhibit 10.2 for preparing a covering letter.

Exhibit 10.2 Preparing Cover

My three years experience as counter salesman in a children's garments shop has given me good knowledge of customers, which will be useful in your newly opened shop. I request you to consider my candidature for the post of a senior salesman.

10.4 PREPARATION OF RESUME

Though the terms biodata, curriculum vitae and resume can be used interchangeably. The term bio-data consists of biographical data of a person like the date and place of birth, sex, height and so on. It is suitable for applying to a government job. The term resume, on the other hand, is a summary document of one's skill set, professional/educational qualifications, work experience and achievements/accomplishments. Ideally, it is meant for the middle/senior-level executives, and the contents here are limited to one or two pages only.

The short documentary account of a fresher's career, qualifications and employment history typically prepared for a position is called resume, it is also called curriculum vitae (CV). It is a personal data-sheet containing academic qualifications, job related experience, skills and strong points of a person. In other words, the curriculum vitae is an appropriate document for fresher which basically reveals one's academic achievements, personal information, technical skills, volunteer or part time work experience, memberships and can be two or three pages long. Preparation of curriculum vitae is an art. It should reflect the following aspects positively:

- Does the job one seeks need those skills?
- If the organization does not require those skills will he/she be refused the job?
- Does the candidate really possess strong communication and organization skills which can be used?

The employer will decide whether to interview the candidate depending on the contents of his curriculum vitae. The curriculum vitae, thus, is not just a documentary record of the candidate's career to date but also a chance to sell himself. Spending a little time in preparing the curriculum vitae appropriately, therefore, is well worth effort involved.

A good resume helps in bringing out the basic strengths of an individual in terms of academic achievement, job related skills, attitude and aptitude and other relevant details. This holds up the attention of the employer and also helps in getting an interview call which is nothing but a move closer to getting the job. The resume should be:

1. **Neat and Legible:** Presentation of resume in details in an organized and orderly manner is the first and foremost essential aspect. For this purpose, prepare a neat format on good paper and avoid mistakes.
2. **Optimum Length:** Resume is the first opportunity to impress the employer. It should contain details in brief leaving out trivial or minute achievements. It should be of optimum length, neither too long nor too short.
3. **Accurate and Up-to-date:** An important feature of a good resume is accuracy of the updated facts and figures. Honesty and sincerity are the ingredients of a resume which ensure truthfulness about qualifications and achievements. In simple words, projecting one's natural self along with the strengths of the applicant. A resume should not contain at any cost wrong information. An opinion about the contents of resume is spelled out in Exhibit 10.3.

Exhibit 10.3 **Good Resume**

London based Risk Advisory Group (RAG), the largest employee screening firm in Europe said that in the screening in the last quarter of 2001, 54 per cent of the resumes showed some type of discrepancy. Previous employment details and academic qualifications were areas most frequently fudged by desperate job hunters.

4. **Build Focus on Employer Needs:** Keeping in view the job profile with the underlying needs, the resume should highlight the positive points, skills and attitudes so that it can add value to the job. Every employer is keen on getting the right candidate. Right fit for the post obviously shows on the response to a question like: Are you Mr. Right or Ms. Right? If so, try to highlight it without making it very obvious.
5. **Appealing and Distinctive:** Fine-tune a resume with key words which will go well with job description and a personal touch. In other words, gather and present all the relevant details in a clear, correct, honest and visually appealing and distinctive manner.

6. **Right Format:** The format is not common; personal details and academic qualifications are common to most of the resumes and the other headings may or may not be relevant depending upon the age and experience. Hence, choose an appropriate format covering the headings or captions for furnishing the data. The suggestive list of captions or headings appropriate for a resume is presented in Table 10.1.

Table 10.1 Components of Resume

Heading	Coverage
1. Personal details	Name, age, date of birth, present position or designation, nationality, address and phone/fax/e-mail
2. Academic qualifications/distinction	Mention in chronological order, medals won, merit scholarships conferred, etc.
3. Work experience	Present effectively: range and period, functional designation, duties and responsibilities, present position and positions held earlier
4. Areas of specialization	(a) Specific functional areas: personal banking, labour law, (b) specific industries: mutual funds, information technology, (c) specific regions: South India, South-east Asian Markets (d) Specialized training: advanced training in financing services, etc.
5. Career related achievements	
6. Seminar and workshops attended	
7. Papers and publications	
8. Membership of Boards and Committees	
9. Guest faculty/consultancy	
10. Other relevant information	
11. Languages known	
12. Marital status	
13. Hobbies and interests	
14. References	Referees hold important positions like teachers, supervisors, heads of department or institutions who know the candidate well enough to give their opinion on the skills and aptitude of the candidate
15. Testimonials	Letter of open acknowledgement of candidate's character and abilities

10.5 SPECIMEN

In the following pages, the specimen with regards to resume, application letter, selection and recruitment, appointment letter, promotional letter, etc., are described. These are:

10.5.1 Resume

Name	: Sai Ram					
Address	: Sai Orchid, 25, Ram Nagar, Anantapur - 515004					
Telephone	: 0891-245568					
Date of birth	: 10-01-1990					
Marital status	: Single					
Education:						
Year	**Degree**	**College**	**University/ Board**	**Special Subjects**	**Marks (%)**	**Class**
May 2013	M.Com	University Department	S.K. University	Finance	66.00	I
May 2011	B.Com	Arts College	S.K. University	Taxation	69.00	I
April 2008	Inter-mediate	St. Augustine Junior College	Board of A.P.		86.00	I
April 2006	S S C	St. Augustine High School	Board of A.P.		86.00	I
Scholarship and awards		Open merit State Govt. Scholarship at Intermediate level for 2 years Femina scholarship at B.Com level for 3 years				
Cocurricular activities		Completed a diploma course in e-commerce				
Languages known		English : can read, write and speak well Telugu : can read, write and speak well Hindi : can speak				
Work experience		Worked as Accountant in Rural Development Trust				
References		1. Sri Durga Prasad, C.A., Income Tax Practitioner, 18/c, Cooperative Colony, Hyderabad. Cell No. .... 2. Prof. C R Reddy, Dept. of Commerce, S. K. University Anantapur-515 003. Cell No.				

10.5.2 Conventional Application Letter

Sir, Date: ....

Would you consider my candidature for the post of Accountant, advertised in today's Financial Express? I am enclosing my resume.

I am seeking new employment in order to improve my prospects. My present salary is 12,000 per month and expecting a reasonable increment in the grade which applies to the post of Manager in your firm. I have enclosed copies of my certificates and shall produce the originals at the time of interview.

May I have an interview so that I could answer questions you may wish to ask me?

Yours faithfully,

(SAI RAM)

Encl: Copies of requisite certificates

The process of selection and recruitment is as:

10.5.3 Calling Letter

The received applications are scrutinized by the Personnel Department or by Head of the Department concerned. Applicants are selected for an interview on the basis of the presentation of the application, qualifications and qualities. The selected applicants are sent an interview call. The letter calling applicants for interview mentions the application, the name of the post, and the place, date and time of the interview. The calling letter is as follows.

Dear, Date: ....

With reference to your application for the post of Accountant; please be present for an interview on (day, date and time) at (place and address). Please bring your certificates with you.

Yours sincerely,

10.5.4 Appointment Letter

After the interview, the selected candidate is informed by a letter and asked to report at the office.

Dear Ms Nirvi, Date: ....

I am happy to inform you that you have been selected for the post of Accountant for which you were interviewed on the 15th last month. Please call at our office between 11.00 a.m. and 1.00 p.m. on any week day by the 20th and meet Mr ABC, Personnel Manager. He will give the appointment letter and also introduce you to your officer.

Yours sincerely,

10.5.5 Letter to Non-Selected Candidates

The other candidates who were interviewed and not selected are sent a letter informing them that the post has been filled.

Dear, Date: ....

Thank you for coming for an interview on...... The post has been filled by a candidate whose qualifications were more suitable for our job requirement. We wish you the best in your efforts to find a suitable post.

Yours sincerely,

10.5.6 Confirmation Letter

At the end of probation period if the person's work is found satisfactory or even earlier if the person is found efficient, the firm issues confirmation letter. This confirmation letter is important because certain benefits like leave, provident fund, pension, etc., become applicable only after confirmation. Once confirmed, the appointment cannot be terminated by either side unless the required notice is given.

Dear Ms Date: ....

In application of your good service during the last one year, your appointment as Accountant is being confirmed from 1st May after completion of two years probation period. You will be eligible for provident fund and other benefits of the post from the date of confirmation.

Please sign and return the attached copy in acceptance of the confirmation.

Yours sincerely,
Manager

10.5.7 Warning Letter

If an employee's work is unsatisfactory or violates rules and regulations or behaves in an undisciplined manner, the firm will issue a warning memo in confidence after being given an opportunity warning. A warning letter contains clear and exact details of faults committed by the employee with documentary evidence as support. Otherwise, the management will be in trouble with employees' union or in the court of law. It is not a threat of dismissal from service but it is only to state firmly that better work or behaviour is expected; unless there is an improvement, confirmation or increments or promotions may be withheld.

Dear Mr. L, Date: ....

It has been brought to my notice that your attendance or behaviour in the office has not been proper. You have reported late by more than half an hour, eight times during this quarter despite warning by your supervisor.

Further, there are several mistakes in your work which were pointed out to you by your supervisor on each occasion, yet you have not shown any concern to perform better.

You are expected to be regular and punctual in attendance with good behaviour and to be attentive in your work. If you do not improve your conduct and work, disciplinary action in the form of withholding increments may be initiated.

Yours sincerely,
Manager

10.5.8 Appreciation Letter

A team leader appreciating others is a major function. It motivates employees to reach their best potential in achieving their own and the organization's goal. The manager congratulating personally is ranked first among 67 possible incentives. Firms also realized that their workforce is an asset; appreciating this asset leads to growth. Good wishes should be in brief, direct and concise with natural expression.

Dear M, Date: ....

The display you have created for the 'window with wall' is just beautiful. Several persons in the sales staff have told me that they have received numerous compliments from customers.

Congratulations on a job well done.

Yours sincerely,
Manager

10.6 GROUP DISCUSSION

A number of persons engaged in interaction with one another is called **group discussion**. Group communication takes place in a meeting which may be formal (the statutory and conventional meetings like Annual General Body Meetings or Board of Directors Meeting, selection of students for admission, etc., held at fixed interval with fixed agenda) or informal (committees often meet to transact the assigned specific tasks) conducted in different ways depending upon its purpose and the size.

Working in a group can provide opportunities which, as an individual learner, are not so readily available. In other words, the knowledge or experience of a member of the group may help other member(s). A sense of responsibility to fellow students can provide good motivation and encouragement either in preparation of work schedule or its implementation. A number of skills can be developed in working as part of a team. These are:

- Interpersonal skills: assertiveness, oral communication skills
- Self-appraisal: thinking about performance or contribution to the group
- The organization calls for interview of those applicants who submitted their resume and were considered for scrutiny. These candidates are required to participate in the group discussion
- Specific skills: critical reading, time management, negotiation and decision-making

1. **Discussion Topics:** The topics selected for group discussion are such that they are possible to argue both for and against. Such topics sometimes may lead to heated and animated discussion leading to confusion and chaos. Candidates possessing strong interactive skills can intervene effectively and turn chaos into order. Neither too much aggression and domination nor too much hesitation and dillydallying is desirable. What is important for the candidate is to support personal view by analytical approach and logical reasoning. Personal attachment, intimidation, submissiveness, etc., should be avoided. At the same time, confidence, wit, humour, respect for fellow participation, accommodation, etc., should be used advantageously.
2. **Screening:** After screening the resumes based on knowledge, experience, skills and accommodating nature would help to weed out the superfluity from the candidate pool and narrow down to promising ones; and then call for group discussion. To evaluate the performance of the candidates, the seasoned observers

thoroughly observe the each candidate and take notes. At the end of the group discussion, these observers evaluate each participant in terms of well-defined parameters and prepare a score sheet. Candidates who communicate effectively, respect group discussion and distinguish themselves in thoughts and expressions tend to score more. In a group of 8 to 10 members, probably 3 to 4 may qualify for the personal interview.

3. **Interview:** Interview is conversation with a purpose. The first few minutes in the interview are the most important because the interview starts when the candidate walks through the door. The interviewer will notice how the candidate walks, shakes hands, sits down and answers the preliminary questions.

   Instead of random questions, it is always advisable to ask questions to determine the candidate's essential skills, qualifications, likes and dislikes and preferred communication methods as well as determining the acceptable answers for the same. This would help shed light on the candidate's work style, motivation and key on-the-job along with ability to meet the expectations and achieve goals.

   For instance, the panel may ask you about some historic value of your native place or even the meaning of your name. These small things also matter. Besides being clear, logical and communicative, the content is important both in group discussion and personal interview.

   No point in looking at half-a-dozen newspapers or memorizing old magazines. There are some aspects that need to be kept in mind, in order of importance. These are (i) effective communication, (ii) team skill and (3) leadership. While content has to do with providing perspective direction and depth, communication as an abused term does not mean fluency or flamboyance. English language skills are critical, of course, but then they are not on the lookout for an orator. So, even if your accent is dented and vocabulary limited, if you think logically and speak clearly, you will make the cut.

   In terms of team skills, selectors are closely watch your interaction, body language and etiquette. Do you get agitated when others contradict you, are you magnanimous enough to appreciate a sound argument? Similarly, leadership does not mean U-turn into a traffic policeman. Can your thoughts give direction to a discussion and lead them to a deeper level of debate? In corporate culture, leadership is not about power or authority but direction.

   What the experts expected from the interviewee is the response to the basics. For instance, if you are an electrical engineer, the panel may ask you why a fan has three blades. Sometimes, students dig their own grave by claiming to be interested in marketing or finance which leads to further questions.

   With permission after completion of interview, ask for feedback at a later date. This provides you with a valuable 'hook' for future contact and ensures you leave the door open even if you are rejected.

Exhibit 10.4 Conversation Flow

Conversation flow volunteering information is a must. The candidate is ought to prepare and respond to the following ten questions:

Tell me about yourself

Q: Can you sell yourself?

A: Give a quick snapshot of your background, skills and personality but do not ramble.

Why did you apply for the job?

Q: How motivated are you?

A: Research the job beforehand; state the benefits you expect to gain and those you can offer. Say why you want this job.

Tell me what you do in your spare time?

Q: Are you a rounded person and could your hobbies interfere with work?

A: Express your interests quickly, emphasizing any work related skills they give you.

When have you been involved in teamwork?

Q: Are you a team player?

A: Highlight any team role of promoter, developer, organizer, producer, showing creativity, etc., and try to link answers to the job.

What are your main strengths and weaknesses?

Q: Are you self-aware and capable of developing?

A: Link your strengths to the job. Select positive weakness and turn it into your strength. For example, I am a bit of a perfectionist but that is good for quality.

Why should we employ you?

Q: Can you add value to the company?

A: Briefly state how you can, also give a comparison between the job description and your skills and back up anything you say with facts.

When did you last work under pressure or deal with conflict and how did you cope?

Q: Can you cope with problems efficiently?

A: Think of an example and explain how you dealt with it. Be truthful but avoid appearing negative if you are asked directly anything that made you annoyed or frustrated.

Where would you like to be in the next five or ten years?

Q: How committed and motivated will you be?

A: If you do have some insight into where you are heading, think of some functions and responsibilities you would hope to have.

So sell me this product?

Q: Can you think on your feet?

A: Do your homework and prepare to demonstrate your skills in action!

What salary do you expect?

Q: How do you rate yourself?

A: Do not undersell or oversell yourself. Workout a salary you consider reasonable. Give a range to show that you are prepared to negotiate.

10.6.1 Do's and Don'ts

During the meeting each member should have an opportunity to give and receive feedback on the group worked together. Be positive, but consider how you would improve things the next time. Think about what worked well with this group and write down one suggestion for working in a group the next time. Ten do's and don'ts for members working in a group are given in Table 10.2.

Table 10.2 Do's and Don'ts

Do's	Don'ts
Contribute to the group by putting forward ideas and getting involved in discussion	Sit back and do nothing
Cooperate with others in the group	Think that others will do the work
Select specific roles for every member (leader, time-keeper, scribe, spokesperson, etc.)	Take lead and ignore others
Take given role within the group	Afraid to speak
Organize the meeting in time and stick to its duration	Expect all your own ideas to be used
Share the workload equally	Leave people out of discussion
Respect the values and opinions of others	Become distracted from the subject
Communicate and share ideas with each other	Aggressive, interruptive or criticizing
Encourage others to speak	Ignore other members of the group
Value diversity	Allow one person to dominate

10.6.2 Reasoning Skills

Reasoning skills are a part of intelligence. Intelligence depends upon five characteristics: (i) perception, (ii) learning, (iii) process and reasoning, (iv) memory, and (v) behaviour. Perception is the primary ability to observe the complexities of the real world, learning is developing new skills through knowledge, processing includes reasoning, transforming and keeping information in memory. On the other hand, memory is the capability to store and recall the information whenever required. Finally, behaviour is the response and ability to answer to suit the situation. Samuel Butter has beautifully described reasoning skills thus: "Life is the art of drawing sufficient conclusions from insufficient premises." See exhibit 10.5 for how to draw reasoning logically.

Exhibit 10.5 Apply Reasoning to Find Logical Answers

Dear students let us take a free-flowing debate on the budget-2014. Did budget-2009 address the problems of global recession?

Weighing pros and cons of the topic, the students were divided into two groups in the issue. One group opined that the budget was growth-oriented and the Finance Minister focused on the core areas like power, defense, health, agriculture and infrastructure development. Further, the group argued that the budget was pro-farmer, as over 30000 million rupees were allocated for agriculture and for people living below the poverty line. This group, thus, suggested that agriculture is the backbone of the country's economy and the Finance Minster had done the right thing by giving priority to it. It is too early to predict the budget effects but long-term investment in agriculture and core industries will eventually do a lot of good to the country. Finally, the group viewed that the problems associated with global recession will bail out the country in the long run.

The budget-2014 had very little for the middle class and argued a steep rise in the commodity prices and fuel prices. Though agriculture has been given major thrust, but at the same time corporate sector has been neglected. Budget focused nothing about the National Rural Employment Guarantee Avenues (NREGA) scheme as it would benefit millions of poor families and very little has been done to solve the problem of unemployment among the qualified youth especially post-recession. If rural growth is the mantra, then primary education should have been given more importance which was not so. And the best way to beat the recession was to increase the purchasing power of the people and accordingly the Finance Minister should have raised the taxable limit significantly to some cushioning to the salaried class.

To sum up the success of budget depends upon its implementation and how the allocated funds are judiciously utilized. Honesty and transparency are the key factors.

Various reasoning skills that help the students to crack an interview are highlighted below.

1. **Evaluation:** A typical interview increases the likelihood of selecting the best candidate. It is illustrated as: If you toss a coin you would be correct 50 per cent of the times getting head or tail. If you added an interview you would only be right 52 per cent. This is because shrewd candidates can manipulate interview conversations to show that they perfectly match the job requirements. So, design the assessment questionnaire to gather skills, strengths and weaknesses for the specific positions. Never forget to gauge personality factors to check if the candidate can fit with the company culture.
2. **Reference Check:** Diligent reference and background checks are again crucial as candidates are not beyond falsifying information on their resumes. Wary about possible misrepresentations hence thoroughly probe qualifications and past employers. This will help to ascertain the candidate's work ethics, management style, team orientation, values and past performance. In effect, selecting the right candidate is the result of careful planning and informed decisions. Only then, it

is possible to select a compatible candidate who can effectively contribute to the job and organization.

3. **Co-curricular Activities:** The following nine traits are more relevant in an effective group discussion: (a) Taking initiative, (b) grasp of the subject, (c) active listening, (d) seizing the opportunity, (e) appropriate body language, (f) concern for time management, (g) organizing thoughts and ideas, (h) logical reasoning, and (i) analytical ability, being brief and focused, and summarizing.

10.6.3 Role Play

Role play is a teaching strategy which allows the candidate to practice a variety of communication skills by enacting the real-life situations in a safe environment like a classroom or youth group. Various role plays are as follows:

1. **Scripted role play:** Each role play sets a character or role through which the story will be developed exploring control over the exact language of the speech. Role plays and subsequent feedback sessions encourage friendship and cooperation.
2. **Simulation based role play:** A group of people receive a set of inputs which they analyze and prepare their inputs in a model and tabulate the results. This approach sharpens decision making skills of candidate or use for experimenting with concepts taught in a subject.
3. **Talk:** When an opportunity strikes to meet a stranger, increase your network by starting with (a) introduction of yourself in a memorable fashion, (b) emphasize the benefits you provide, (c) showcase your uniqueness, (d) get asked questions, (e) set yourself apart from the competition, and (g) begin to build your new relationship. If you craft and deliver an effective and meaningful speech, the doors to success will open.
4. **Elocution:** A prepared flow of expressive delivery of speech without interruptions is called elocution. Attitude, eye contact, speech patterns (modulate your voice, pick words you can pronounce, punctuate for a purpose, raise your tone slightly) and posture and hand gestures constitute the contributing factors of elocution.
5. **Impromptu Speech:** An instant response to a given topic is referred to as impromptu speech. One may not have enough time to give full expressions to the cultivated delivery skills (thoughts) as in elocution. A creative mind will do well. Do not speak out of context to lose your audiences' interest and attention. Channelize ideas, plan and design, and check facts as well as acquiring information.
6. **Recitation:** It is citing to repeat and tell again and again. Poem recitation involves a live performance. Demonstrate critical skills in selecting an apt segment of a poem and recite with purpose and dramatize in your body language the meaning of the poem. Prose can also be selected for recitation.
7. **Quiz:** By participating in quiz, one can remain updated on the current issues, past events and their dates, people with important achievements and contextual guessing skills. It improves the speed of recall system.

10.6.4 Conscious Learning

Learning is a journey from incompetence to competence. There are 'known knows' and 'known unknowns'. It is important to know the stages and change of approach accordingly. Knowing about how to learn can improve learning ability; help to stick at it when confidence is low and to improve skills more efficiently.

Remember that we plodded around a keyboard using one or two fingers on the laptop. Frustrated with the time to write a simple email, we even progressed to use more fingers to prepare a lengthy note of pages, which may be by taking a class or online tutorial. We may make plenty of mistakes but eventually we can type freely, only looking at the screen, never at our fingers. Four stages of conscious competence learning matrix are shown below.

Conscious Competence Learning Matrix

	Competence	Incompetence
Conscious	We know, We Know (3)	We don't know, we know (2)
Unconscious	We don't know, we know (4)	We don't know, we don't know (1)

1. **We Don't Know, We Don't Know:** In this first stage, we are blissfully, sometimes, ignorant about the existence or relevance of a skill or behaviour, and we go about our business happily. Then, a shocking thing happens. We get some feedback from a colleague or friend telling us that we are lousy at something important to them. Or we are told that business re-engineering requires us to learn some new skills. At this point, we are painfully aware of our deficiencies and we move onto the second stage. Encourage feedback to make people aware of their improved opportunities and kick start their learning and developing journey.
2. **We Know, We Don't Know:** In the second stage, we are highly motivated to improve skills either through fear or desire. By 'having a go' at the new skill, we find out exactly how far we have to go before we are reliably proficient at this skill. If competence is a long way off, it is important to create smaller, more achievable learning goals to maintain enthusiasm and energy. In this second stage, we have a light moment when all becomes clear and enlightenment allows us to move onto the third stage. Here, create a safe learning environment for education, training and practice which will certainly help build competency in the new skill.
3. **We Know, We Know:** We can now reliably perform the new skill. But, we are consciously aware that we are doing it and still have to make a mental effort. We can teach someone else but will probably feel awkward or make mistakes while doing so. The more we practice, the more automatically we learn.
4. **We Don't Know, We Know:** Eventually skills become instinctive and competently performed with no thought whatsoever. It is so effortless to do this once difficult task and we no longer notice we are doing it. It may become so deeply embedded and become difficult to explain exactly how to do it.

People need to develop the practice of learning by creating their own personal development plans and regularly review their progress. This builds up a smooth and conscious learning process. The participants can serve as a place where the community can gather and learn through organized and informal activities like festivals, picnics, sports, etc. "We remember only 20 per cent of what we hear, 50 per cent of what we see, but 80 per cent of what we do."

10.7 JOB INTERVIEWS

For building a knowledge society, there is need for empowering students with the developmental and operational skills in addition to the behavioural, communicative and entrepreneurial skills. Equally important is the promotion of holistic development of students through participation, involvement and promotion of social consciousness.

Entrepreneurship is all about doing new things or doing the same things in a new way, and taking risk of succeeding. The spirit of entrepreneurship or enterprise, today, has set its roots in India. The arrival of challenges in business led to a rethinking of business model recently in India. This necessitates following a dream, the path of change and innovation which would contribute potentially to grow into a much bigger success.

For instance, Infosys has been one of the best known success stories. On the eve of India's 62nd year of Independence, the Chairman of Infosys said this: "I believe that we can make India's image better only by aspirations, achievements through hard work, smartness, honesty, sincerity and discipline. In recent times, China's hard-power global expansion has been the result of premeditated and orchestrated State policy while India's influence in the world has largely been achieved through soft-power. Success of entrepreneurs invariably depends upon the following aspects:

1. **Communication:** The message should be clear, concise and respectable internally and externally.
2. **Team Building:** Pay attention to all the players and improve cohesiveness by leading from the front. Once they know you truly, a team can change and adapt no matter where you drive the bus.
3. **Interpersonal Skills:** Use phrases like "I need you to include me more when disseminating information" instead of "you did not tell me" while interacting.
4. **Composure:** Do not react but weigh the situation and postpone in an emotional response. Leave hastily composed e-mails in draft mode for an hour or two, mull over them, before hitting 'send'.
5. **Writing Skills:** Writing skills encompass text messages and e-mails. All forms of messaging should be treated as business communication. Paying careful attention to the correspondence would lead to many top-persons, seemingly out-of-reach leaders. It does nothing extraordinary, just writing sincerely and takes care to compose the message.
6. **Global Mindset:** Understand, strategize and act knowing yourself, knowing the other side, adapting as the situation demands. See how it impacts the world and open up your mind to include the global village. Make the internet your teacher.

7. **Changing Times:** The student's landscape is definitely changing – away from the marked tendency to keep the professionally qualified, ever-innovative and brave new business India.

10.8 MOVING TOWARDS A CAREER

Your career is like your work which requires careful planning. There is a stark difference between work and career. While in the former, one can delegate certain responsibilities to others but in the latter one cannot entrust one's career progress to anyone else. To reach career aspiration, a person must actively manage it on his own. Some suggestions to set on the right course are as follows.

1. **Daily Record:** At the end of a period say, week or month make note of at least one accomplishment which the employee has achieved to his credit even a small win. The basic idea of writing down accomplishment is to get an idea of the value he adds to his company. When he identifies the significance of the work he does either in terms of increased productivity or reduced cost or meeting milestones which can be presented during the performance reviews. Increasing visibility for an employee's work among superiors is the first step that provides the perfect launching pad for your career to take off.
2. **Update Resume:** Continue adding your latest accomplishments to the basic content in your resume. This can customize to match the specific requirements of any good job opening that you come across. Citing the specific examples adds weight to you credentials.
3. **Professional Certification:** Acquiring professional certification adds expertise and helps keep pace with the latest developments taking place in the field. This would help one to get an excellent opportunity to associate with successful professionals in his domain, seek their advice, learn about available opportunities and also understand how to face challenges and uncertainties.
4. **Coach Yourself:** Continue to adapt yourself to new roles. To become a better performer, you must make necessary changes to your behaviour, attitude and approach towards work. Even an external indication say feedback from your boss might point towards a need for personal change. If you do not know what exactly to change, find a mentor who can guide you appropriately. If this is not possible, follow self-coaching. In self-coaching, honestly make a list of what exactly is going wrong in situations that you cannot handle very well. For example, if you shout at subordinates with short temperedness, they mess-up things further. Create your goal to change your behaviour which rewards success.
5. **Overcome Setbacks:** Things will not happen according to the expectations in an uncertain world. Accept setbacks and maintain your self-confidence by rating your progress. When you acknowledge success, it provides you the motivation to move forward.

For moulding your career, you must know your strengths and weaknesses well. Always promote your strengths and make sincere efforts to overcome weaknesses. More importantly, you must develop a determination to move ahead in spite of stumbling blocks being present at every turn in your journey.

QUESTIONS

1. Discuss how you prepare a resume.
2. Explain group discussion. What are the traits for effective group discussion?

11 CHAPTER

Analysis of Case Studies

11.1 EFFECTIVE TOP-DOWN COMMUNICATION

Ms. Rhina was in-charge of administrative branch of ABC Company. Many typists were women and they were efficient in their jobs, and completed the work assigned to them for that day before leaving office. No overtime duty was allowed in the section.

One day, the Managing Director of the company sent for Mr. Kutty, the Manager of Administration Department and informed him that persons in his department have started taking liberty in regard to punctuality in the office. He said that when he was coming to office some day at 9.40 a.m., he found two typists coming late and that it was not the first time that he had seen this. He wanted Ms. Rhina to take note of this. Mr. Kutty listened to the instructions of the Managing Director and promised him to ensure punctuality.

Mr. Kutty called Ms. Rhina and told her about the incident of two late comers and the Managing Director's observations. He also stated that punctuality should be observed at all cost. Mr. Rhina replied that she was aware of the situation and did not feel the necessity of taking any action. She said that the typists are very hard working and they do not mind even sitting late for an hour or so in the office if there is pressure of work. They were keen in finishing the day's work before leaving the office and usually observe punctuality and were not habitual late comers. She also pleaded that probably due to some personal reasons, one or two typists may be late by ten or fifteen minutes which should not be taken seriously in the interest of good working. Mr. Kutty, however, insisted that she should act according to the instructions of the Managing Director.

Ms. Rhina got perplexed and went back to her section and communicated the entire story to her typists. Also she told them that the Managing Director wanted them to come to office in time and that he is against any relaxation in this matter. Further, she told that action will be taken against the late comers.

Ms. Rarla and Ms. Parla who came late that day discussed this matter during lunch. Ms. Rarla said 'It is very strange things have been taken too far. I have now decided that if I am asked to sit late, I won't and I shall leave the office at 5.30 P.M. leaving the work where it is.'

Just after two days, the private secretary to the Managing Director sent some urgent typing work to Ms. Rarla at 5.15 P.M. Two typists would require at least one hour typing the entire material. The Managing Director was to see the Chairman in the evening with these important papers. He wanted the typed matter back to him in any case by 6.30 p.m.

Ms. Rhina assigned the work to Ms. Rarla and Ms. Parla, but both of them expressed their inability to undertake the job as it would take an hour whereas they could stay in the office at the most for 15 minutes. The office closes at 5.30 p.m. Both typists did not fail to remark that if the officers sometimes wanted them to sit late, why such hue and cry should have been made when someone was late by a few minutes that took on a few occasions?

It became a problem for Ms. Rhina to get the papers typed. She was afraid that the other typist may also give the same reply. Then, she went back to the private secretary to the Managing Director stating that the private secretary and she may have to share the work and do it, though the private secretary had some other work of priority.

Analyze the case and answer the following questions:

1. What is your opinion about the behaviour of Ms. Rhina, Ms. Rarla and Ms. Parla?
2. How do you feel about the Managing Director's attitude?
3. What do you feel about Mr. Kutty?
4. What is your advice to improve the situation?

11.2 CLARITY OF THOUGHT

All human beings are bestowed with thinking power which is the secret of their strength. Whenever necessary, the situation is analyzed and a right decision is taken. In practice, people confuse at one time and clear at another time. Due to lack of clarity in thinking, even top intellectuals take wrong decisions at some point of time. It is understood that the biggest obstacle in the way of success is lack of clear thinking. A man with clear plans and thoughts is always a champion and achieves his goals.

Thinking leads to right decision, right path and correct action due to mental exercise as the brain needs regular exercise. So, thinking is a vital element for success and happiness. It is bedrock on which joy and flow of good things of life depend. To utter surprise, there was an incident wherein a girl refused to get married to a boy simply because he did not know how to ride a motorbike. This fact indicated poor thinking due to her interest in riding bikes.

Unfortunately, only a little room is allotted in educational institutions to promote thinking. One can enhance one's thinking caliber by cultivating good habits, reading good books and consulting academicians, etc. Without clarity in thinking, success becomes dubious. Hence, people miserably fail in achieving their desired goals. Many hard workers and dedicated people fail due to lack of clarity in their thinking. Mere hard labour is not sufficient but it should be supported by clear thinking. Otherwise, all the sheer efforts will be futile and reading good books and going to holy places will certainly help a lot to enrich thinking power, which plays a key base role for success. Wise people never take decisions on the spur of the moment. Even for petty issues, they clearly analyze the problem and later take an appropriate decision.

Many people particularly students blindly follow the footsteps of their friends and do not take their own decisions. If their friends select a particular group, they will join the same course unwisely. This type of practice makes aspirants very lazy and gives a chance to lose their thinking abilities. Consulting others and exchange of ideas are always welcome.

The students are not supposed to rely entirely upon other's choices. They should collect the necessary information before they choose a course or a college. Everyone has their own ambitions and life goals. So, a person has to fix his goal first and then think clearly to reach his destination. Remember that success is not an accident but it is the result of right ways of thinking.

Analyze the above case and answer the following questions.

1. What do you understand from this case?
2. What is required to take a right decision?

11.3 CAREER RECOGNITION

Recognition of talents motivates to do still better which, in turn, helps in career progress. It is fact. Generally, happens that many times the best efforts will go almost unnoticed. This is because talent alone is not enough to get recognized, a subtle promotion is necessary too. Recognition is honest efforts being noticed by others about your skills and abilities. In the fiercely competitive world, it is necessary to make visible your achievements.

It is known that packaging plays a key role in marketing of any product. Companies vie with each other to package their products attractively to grab the attention of potential buyers. In a similar vein, your ability to influence others, to large extent, rests on the way you present yourself. Focus on the professional appearance and good manners to make a favourable first impression. Walk, talk and work within self-assurance that compel others to pay attention. Take a little time to assess how your management notices about what you are and what you do. Instead, start building your image informing your boss about the significant achievements by making a copy to his bosses. This will prevent your boss from usurping the credit which rightfully belongs to you. When your talents become known to your immediate superiors, the chances of getting selected for key assignment improve.

Publish your special achievements, say explain the roadblocks encountered and solutions developed to surpass them, through the company's newsletter, house journal, web forum or internet so that everyone sees it. Become an expert in a niche area from the crowd and sharpen an area of strength to such level of finesse which helps to be known as a genius in the field. Acquire professional certification and seek opportunity to present your expertise.

Volunteer to work on boards or committees to put your special abilities. This provides an opportunity to move closely with some big shots of the company and develop a good network of contact which gives a chance to expose talents and come out and participate in seminars, workshops and public forums to present your skills. Use these events to cultivate friendship within and outside the organization and develop alliances with people who make vital decisions. All these make perfect sense against tough competition.

Question: Analyze the case and write a note on the ingredients in career development.

11.4 SOCIAL ADVERTISING

Advertising can be used to promote a cause say 'don't waste water', or 'don't waste fuel' or 'don't kill animals'. It is necessary to use strong appeals to break our stupor or indifference. The advertiser asks you a straight question. "Would you murder a woman just because you liked her skin?" The denial is linked to a plea for not murdering animals for their hide. The tagline is also very effective – 'Be human. Let Animals be."

Answer the following questions.

1. Can we use communication to promote social causes?
2. What are your comments on the straight question appearing in advertisement?

11.5 EFFECTIVE LISTENING

To be a good teacher, you need some of the skills of a good actor. You must be able to hold the attention and interest of your audience. You must be a clear speaker with a strong pleasant voice with which you can. You must be able to convey full meaning of what you are teaching in order to keep your audiences' attention intact.

Watch a good teacher and you will see that he does not sit motionless before the class. He stands most of the time, walks about, uses arms, hands and fingers to help in explanations, and face to express feeling. Listen carefully, and you will hear the quality, the tone and the rhythm of the voice changing according to what he is speaking about.

Though the teacher needs some of the gifts of to be a good actor, it does not follow that the teacher can necessarily perform well on the stage. There are some important differences between the teacher's work and the actor's work. The latter has to speak words which he has learnt by heart and repeat exactly the same words every time he plays his part. Even his movements, actions and expressions are fixed. What he has to do is to make these previously learnt words and actions appear natural on the stage.

A good teacher works quite differently. His audience has to take an active part in the play; they ask questions if they do not understand. So, the teacher has to act suitably to the needs of the audience which is his class. He cannot learn his part by heart; he has to invent as he goes along.

Many teachers who do a fine job in the classroom cannot act on the stage because their brains refuse to be limited to the words written by someone else and learnt by heart.

After understanding this in the classroom, answer the following questions:

1. What skills of the actor does a teacher need?
2. How does a good teacher use his voice while teaching?
3. What does an actor have to do with his part when he is on the stage?

11.6 EFFECT OF UNDERSTANDING

If man began with speech; and civilization with agriculture and industry began with fire. Man did not invent fire; probably nature produced the marvel for him by the friction of leaves or twigs, a stroke of lightening; he merely had the saving wit to imitate Nature and to improve upon her. He put the wonder to a thousand uses. First, perhaps he made it to serve as a torch to conquer his fearsome enemy, the darkness; then he used it for warmth and moved about freely from his naïve tropics to less enervating zones, slowly making the planet human; then he applied it to metals, softening them, tempering them and combing them into stronger and more supple forms than those in which they had come to his hand. It was fire that created the old and honourable art of cooking; extending the diet of man to a thousand foods that could not be eaten before. So, beneficent and strange was it that fire always remained a miracle to primitive man, fit to be worshipped as God; he offered it countless ceremonies of devotion and made it the focus of his life and home. He carried it carefully with him as he moved from place to place in his wanderings and would not willingly let it die. Even the Romans punished with death the careless virgins of the temple vista who allowed the sacred fire to be extinguished.

Answer the following questions:

1. To what uses did man put fire?
2. Why did primitive man worship fire?
3. How did fire create the art of cooking?
4. What was the attitude of the Romans to fire?

11.7 UNDERSTANDING MESSAGE

Machines were made to be man's servants. Yet man has grown so dependent on them that they are in a fair way to become his masters. Already men spend most of their lives looking after machines. The machines are very strict masters. They must be fed with coal and given petrol to drink and oil to wash with; and they must be kept at the right temperature. If they do not get their meals, they refuse to work, or burst with anger and spread destruction all a round them. This brings us to the questions, what do we do with all the time which machines have saved for us and the new energy they have given us?

For the most part, we use our time and energy to make more and efficient machines; but more machines will only give us still more time and still more energy, and what are we to do with them?

The answer is that we should try to become more civilized. For the machines themselves and the power which machines have given us are not themselves civilization; they only make civilization possible. Being civilized means making and liking beautiful things, thinking freely and living rightly, and maintaining justice equally between man and man. Man has a better chance today to do these things than he ever had before. He has more time, more energy, less to fear and less to fight against. If he gives this time and energy which his machines have won for him to making more beautiful things, to finding out more and more about the universe, to removing the causes of quarrels between nations, to discovering how to prevent poverty, then our civilization would certainly be the greatest, as it would be the most lasting that there has ever been.

Answer the following:

1. What were the machines intended to do?
2. What are the two things that machines have given us?
3. What use does man make of these two things?

11.8 EFFECTS OF TELEVISION

Although television has reached to more remote areas, but it is imperative to recognize the great divide which exists between the urban and rural lifestyles in India. Indiscriminate consumerism promoted over this powerful medium, because Doordarshan depends on industrial sponsors for revenues, can be a dangerous development. Eighty per cent of our population is rural. It does not need the bulk of advertised consumer goods. So, there is a grave necessity that television should not be used to increase disparities, and discontent because industries only think of markets and profits, not what happens to people. If we are concerned with rural communities, we must also concentrate on what happens to children.

Promoting glittering perspectives of affluence by marketing consumer goods over television will do irreparable harm in rural economy if the country's economy cannot keep pace with people's new demands.

In developed countries like Japan and America, television commercials are geared increasingly to children who harass their parents for more and more possessions. It is easy to see what damage such commercials could do in India. Any planning for television outreach, therefore, has to take this reality of adult and even parental indifference into consideration. A children's hour serves little purpose today when a child of three knows how to switch on a television set.

Answer the following questions:

1. What is the effect of television in rural areas?
2. Does television programs harm children?
3. Does television commercials damage childrens' progress?

11.9 OPEN-DOOR POLICY

Richi, the new Human Resource Manager for Saptagiri Limited was just getting settled in his office. He had recently moved from another company to take over his new job. He had been selected over several in-house candidates and many other applicants because of his record for getting things done efficiently. He had a good reputation for working with people to get the job accomplished.

Just then there was a phone call. The person at the other end of the line said "Mr. Richi could I get an appointment to meet you?" "Certainly", said Richi. "When do you want to meet me"? "How about today after working hours? It might be bad if certain people saw me speaking to any one in the management", the other person said.

Richi was a little puzzled but he set up an appointment for 5.45 P.M., when nearly everyone would have gone. At the designated time, there was a knock on his door. It was Liril, a senior maintenance worker who had been with the firm for more than 15 years.

After the initial welcome, Liril began talking. "Mr. Richi, several of the workers asked me to talk to you the grapevine that you are a fair person. The company says it has an open-door policy. We are afraid to use it. Miril, one of the best maintenance men in our section, tried it several months ago. They harassed him so much that he quit recently. We just don't know what to do to get any problem settled. There have been discussions of organizing a union. We really don't want that, but something has to be done."

Richi thanked Liril for his honesty and promised not to reveal the conversation. In the following weeks, Richi was able to verify that the situation was just as Liril had described. There was considerable mistrust between the managers and workers.

Answer the following questions:

1. What type of communication breakdown had occurred in the company?
2. Discuss the impact of grapevine on resolving this problem.

11.10 MEMO PREPARATION

The Board of a courier decided to do away with lengthy reports, memos and other materials by way of hard copy. The entire network of courier was connected through a website and all important functionaries were given e-mail IDs to communicate through it. All memos and intimations would be sent by e-mail to all the concerned and there would be no hard copies made. This system took some time to get into the groove of everyone and worked with a purpose. Via e-mail all the information was traded and feedback to queries was received. No paper was traded between the officers anymore in the office.

Various branches of mailbox particularly hub-centres began to rise more, then some data is deleted to store data. It has become normal practice for the branches which had mail-traffic.

The Income Tax Department wanted to record its clients' data for the last three years and so made a request to the Head Office of Courier Company about how packets of letters were couriered from the clients' offices to certain places and addresses.

The courier company had records for the last three years and asked all the officers to give the record relating to the particular customer. Some officers sent very quickly and others were having certain problems which could not be envisaged earlier. Some officers had already eased records of the period six months prior to the date when the request was made. Since then the officers were fully computerized and they had made their own norms regarding retention of old records. The head office had a lot of explaining to do for this lapse on the part of their offices.

Some offices had failure in their back-up power system and their data had been lost. This had led to serious problems in reconstructing the courier records of the client in question. Only records they had were the records of booking made at their office. This is what saved the day for them. All officers' work in records were handy in this situation.

It is noted that the back-up data on electronic media or as hard copy for use when urgently required in the future is necessary. It is also important to define retention time for business records. A lot is communicated by records and records can also help a courier company review its own performance. Hence, a record can be replayed at will only if it is preserved:

Answer the following question:

1. Assume that you are technical officer; prepare a memo on the above case addressing to the President (Information Technology Company).

11.11 ADVERTISEMENT

Some people argue that advertising influences them to buy goods and services they do not need through exaggeration of product or service benefits. Others argue that without advertising and promotion, there would be no mechanism to inform consumers about the alternatives that exist.

New ventures will often find it necessary to develop promotional strategies that may use newspapers, magazines or direct mail. The real issue involves a determination of what is truth, exaggeration or deception. At one extreme, we have the advertisement that offers a product that can extend your lifespan. Is this exaggeration or deception? Advertisements that suggest a new venture's product can outperform a competitor's product without any substantiation. Is this exaggeration or deception? In some cases, there may not be any question of ethical integrity of the advertisement. However, there are many cases where companies insist that their claims are true, although there is no real proof to the integrity of information.

Answer the following questions:

1. What is involved in determination of truth, deception or exaggeration?
2. What factor should an entrepreneur consider in designing an advertisement to promote his venture?

11.12 UNDERSTANDING OF COMMUNICATION

The repayment of every loan can only come from the borrower's future earnings. When an individual wishes to borrow by way of a personal loan, perhaps in order to buy a car, repayment must come each month from his wage or salary. In order to know his proposition, the manager asks for details of his earnings and normal expenditures including any existing mortgage and hire purchase repayments. This information is required because often a borrower asks for a loan without having calculated whether or not he can make the repayment.

In business too, the loan can only be repaid from future profits unless the business is to cease trading and sell off assets to pay its creditors. Therefore, the manager needs to ensure that lending money will increase the profits of business, after allowing for the interest and charges to be made on the loan. Nowadays, a bank manager is trained to consider the future profitability of business and it is usual for him to ask the borrower for his business cash budget and projected profit and loss account and balance sheet for the forthcoming year. A cash budget gives a month-by-month estimate of future receipts and payments; and shows the estimated closing bank balance at each month-end for the period for which it is prepared. Thus, this assessment provides a guide to the maximum overdraft that is likely to be needed. It relies for its accuracy on the estimates made by the business itself. The longer period of the budget, the less accurate it will be in the more distant months. A manager soon comes to know those borrowers that stick to their forecasts and those that produce a budget simply to keep him happy. The projected profit and loss account and balance sheet for a future accounting period incorporate much of the information contained in the cash budget and also shows the estimates of gross and net profits which may also be used to assess the future profitability of the business.

Answer the following questions:

1. As a communication receiver, spell out what you understand from this.
2. What is the principle of lender of loan?

11.13 FINANCIAL AID FOR PEACE PROGRESS

India's financial resources and capacity to save for investment in economic development is proportionate to her low productivity. Indian industrialists and businessmen diligently thought that in order to double within 15 years the standard of living in the country, an investment of over thirty million dollars was necessary, at the then rate of exchange. Allowing for the depreciation in the value of money and the increase in the population which has taken place since then, the investment required would now be in the neighbourhood of 80 billion dollars. This might seem an exceptionally high figure to a country like India where her national income is about 20 billion dollars and capacity to save is less than two billion. Even if the whole of such savings could be invested in projects of economic development, it would take 40 years to achieve the results required within fifteen years. In the mean time, the population would have more than doubled and the average standard of life would therefore be no higher than at the beginning.

This explains the key issues of findings and some means to control population growth until productivity caught up with the existing population. It also shows that if India is to succeed in her fearful task, her own internal resources must be supplemented by foreign investments, loan and possibly temporary financial aid to enable her to force the pace progress in the initial years.

Answer the following questions:

1. What central focus could you understand from this case?
2. What are your specific suggestions?

11.14 KNOWLEDGE MANAGEMENT

Knowledge management is repository of relevant information for a service engineer in the modern day's corporate sector. It helps desk systems and supporting cost associated with them would be impossible to implement without this technology. Knowledge management shares information between departments and individuals in an enterprise or between enterprises even beyond the boundaries of a nation through an integrated e-commerce strategy and system.

Accessing your 'corporate memory bank' to check how a particular crisis was handled in the past; identifying who all among your employees possesses the required specific skill; knowing 'people profile' by simply calling; and what IBM is developing in a new product or service called knowledge utility; retrieving or mining data using special text search engines. In brief, knowledge management is the use of technology to make information relevant and accessible wherever it may reside.

Firms have long known about the increasing role of knowledge along with traditional resources of land, labour and capital in the process of economy. But for this, knowledge has become a key while determining a firm's competitive edge. As response, firms have been oriented towards accumulating and applying knowledge to organization processes as a distinct factor of production for creating economic value and competitive opportunity. An automatic increase in knowledge and an incentive to search for new knowledge are built into the very nature of firm's strategic competitiveness. Recently, there is an upsurge of interest in the management of knowledge. More and more organizations, today, are talking about building up strengths in knowledge management practices as a powerful tool to work and learn together. Perhaps, such shift towards the development and deployment of Information Technology has been the strongest immediate source responsible. When one expands the coverage of knowledge to macro level, a nation can be considered to be a large enterprise with broader interests in economic health, growth rate, global competitiveness and welfare of people, global competitiveness and exploitation of resources. Most concepts of knowledge management thus become applicable equally well at the enterprise level and national level. Thus, knowledge management has emerged as a powerful corporate resource, and works around establishing the policies and practices for creating and employing firm's intellectual assets.

An organization in this information age must optimally deploy its most valuable asset, knowledge available with people and database. Management is all about locating and using such information to create value and add value. The new name of the game is knowledge management.

QUESTIONS

1. What is knowledge management?
2. What are the broad areas in which knowledge management plays a significant role?

Objective Questions

Fill in the blanks with correct answers

1. A firm handshake, as non-verbal communication, indicates __________ and __________.
2. All living beings connect with __________.
3. Audio-visual communication involves demonstration and __________.
4. __________ communication occurs among all the stakeholders in business organization.
5. Non-verbal aspects of the spoken word are known as __________.
6. __________ allows the users to create their personal profiles, share photos and videos and communicate with others.
7. __________ is a networking website that allows users to create professional profile, post resume and communicate with other professionals and job-seekers.
8. A letter of acknowledgement of a person's character and abilities is known as __________ letter.
9. A set of principles or morals in conduct of business is referred to as __________.
10. Accompaniment of added idea to every expressed idea is called __________ communication.
11. Activity of making available goods produced by business units to the consumers at right place, right time, right quantity and right price in right manner is known as __________.
12. All education and training takes place by means of __________.
13. An electronic machine device using the language of strings of binary numbers with set rules to store, process, analyze and retrieve information is called __________.
14. An obstacle or difficulty in transmitting information is known as __________.
15. An official report and published news on topical interest is called __________.
16. Application of information and communication technology through computer to deliver the government services, exchange of transactions and integration of various standalone systems with efficiency, effectiveness, transparency and

accountability of informational and transactional exchange to the people is called __________.

17. Aspect of voices of people who know but do not speak and those who speak but do not know is called __________.
18. Bringing people together through an interactive conversation for most productive and inexpensive medium using a telephone is known as __________.
19. Build-up and development of managerial effectiveness __________ and __________ are essential as twins.
20. Buyer and seller transactions of goods and services through internet is known as __________.
21. Carrying out activities and communications for purpose of promoting good will with the community is known as __________.
22. Collection and integration of organization data into a single system is known as __________.
23. Communicating data through the satellite links and telephone wires using computer network is called __________.
24. Communicating message to a large number of people for promoting public progress is called __________ communication.
25. Communication between two or more persons who are neither in the same section nor on the same hierarchical level of organizations in different section is called __________ communication.
26. Communication is __________ while language is __________.
27. Communication is both __________ and __________.
28. Communication through words is called __________ communication
29. Communication using the symbols like pictures, colours, signs and signals, body language and so on is known as __________ communication.
30. Computer mediated communication with internet is called __________.
31. Concise document summarizing individual's past, existing professional skills, proficiency and experiences is __________.
32. Conscious and attentive listening of messages is known as __________ listening.
33. Considering other people's feelings is called __________.
34. Conversation, face-to-face between two persons is known as __________.
35. Conveying message through the cultural background of people's dress is known as __________.
36. Discovery of symbolic communication is called __________.
37. Eliciting the relevant information and calibre to assess, appraise and evaluate suitability of the candidate to offer a position is called __________.
38. Green colour in communication conveys __________.
39. Presentation of gathered facts and information logically on an issue is known as __________.

40. Facial expressions, gestures and postures, attire, voice, sign and signals and other body movements are called __________.
41. Firm's message about its employees or members in printed form is referred to as __________.
42. Forming a word from the initial letters of words in a set is called __________.
43. Getting full meaning of speaker's words is called __________ communication.
44. Hallmark of any good communication is __________.
45. Healthy communication trend with a balanced flow of information is __________ approach.
46. Placing the initials of dictator and typist of the letter below notation is called __________.
47. If the message conforms the purpose of it to the sender in addition to precise, accurate and up-to-date information is known as __________.
48. If the receiver receives the message with purpose of it being sent, then it is called __________ communication.
49. Information that moves from superiors to subordinates is known as __________ communication.
50. In a system, showing periodical reporting information upward is known as __________ communication.
51. In acronym of ABCD, the letter 'D' stands for __________.
52. Information put forth in speech form, writing and body movements like gesture, facial expression, silence, etc., is referred to as __________.
53. Informing or spreading information with meaning is __________.
54. Integration of computer and network components for communicating messages is __________.
55. Integration of operating system with the sum total of channels is called __________.
56. Japanese saying 'yes' means 'yes' while Americans saying 'yes' means 'agree' is an example for __________ barrier.
57. Without thought is labour lost, thought without learning is __________.
58. List of items to be discussed at the meeting of an organization is called __________.
59. Listening is active but hearing is __________.
60. Often use of word with no meaning is called __________.
61. Orderly arrangement and presentation of data through rows and columns is called __________.
62. Organization of thoughts sequentially to convey meaning is called __________.
63. Payment of amount electronically over internet is __________.
64. People talking and listening simultaneously is called __________.
65. Prepared flow of expressive speech delivery uninterruptedly is called __________.

66. Process of representing, analyzing and extracting from people data on social media is __________ communication.
67. Production of goods or supply of services for wants satisfying human beings with little profit is called __________.
68. Putting a candidate in difficult situation to test his reaction is known as __________.
69. Reading makes a full man, conference a ready-man and writing a __________.
70. Science of meaning and sounds are __________ and __________.
71. Study of body motion as related to speech is called __________.
72. Sending back the information about the message to the message sender is called __________.
73. Sending messages to all the stakeholders in business organization is called __________ communication.
74. Sending messages with and without expecting receiver's feedback are __________ and __________ communication.
75. Shopping through use of credit or debit card without moving is called __________.
76. Speech given instantly on a given topic is called __________ speech.
77. Spreading or telling information with its meaning is __________.
78. The 80% of unfocussed effort generates only 20% of results and the remaining 80% of results are achieved with only 20% of the effort which is called 80/20 rule. This is called __________ principle.
79. The channel through which the message moves from the sender to the receiver is called __________.
80. The letters 'A' and 'A' in acronym stands for __________ and __________.
81. The management of knowledge is __________ and not __________.
82. The nature of writing scientific report with offshoot of knowledge on business transactions is called __________ report.
83. The person who uses mixed language in communication is referred to as __________.
84. The process of oration giving a performance with focus around an individual's direct speech to live audience is called __________.
85. The process of putting thoughts into symbolic form is __________.
86. The second letter 'S' in acronym SKILLS stand for __________.
87. The state of wordlessness and communication with less verbal words is called __________.
88. The use of identifiable mark by the firm for goods or services say, a word, name, symbol, device or number or combination thereof, in the market is called __________.
89. The way by which a message flows from the sender to the recipient is known as __________.
90. The words that have opposite meaning are known as __________.

91. Transparent paper at the central front of the envelope to read inside address is called __________ envelope.
92. Transportation of messages electronically from one computer to another through network is called __________.
93. Transmission of information and reception of feedback exists in __________ communication.
94. Unclear and confused messages often transmitted and passed on by word-of-mouth are known as __________.
95. Use of a device for transmitting copies of print/images over telephone line are called __________.
96. Written record of decisions passed at the meeting is called __________.
97. __________ with words like Sirs, Ms, etc., to the receiver of letter are two spaces below the inside address.
98. Collection and integration of organization's data into a single being is known as __________.
99. To sustain high visibility in a competitive environment on publicity campaigns __________ is out of sight.
100. Never write a letter when you are __________.
101. A document with detailed information to employees on a specific matter is called __________.
102. In this busy world, communication is __________ for teachers, lawyers, auditors, politicians, consultants, business executives, parents and children.
103. The eminent person(s) called interviewer asking questions to the other person called interviewee with a specific purpose is known as __________.
104. Allowing communication through an internal telephone system between the persons in different parts of a building or campus is called __________.
105. Paper containing daily news and opinions on current events coming from the nation's four sides of north, east, west and south is called __________.
106. ISI mark is the symbol of __________.
107. All living beings are connected by __________.
108. First essential quality of good communication is __________ of message.
109. __________ speaks the language of love, compassion, sincerity, courtesy, confidence and dependability.
110. Language is a vehicle of __________.
111. Hearing is __________ while listening is __________ involving both the body and mind.
112. Written messages read on mobile phone are known as __________.
113. A good __________ rivets the attention and gets registered in the mind of the reader.
114. An effective __________ presentation of data makes the reader remember much better.

ANSWER KEY

Q. No.	Answer	Q. No	Answer	Q. No	Answer
1.	Confidence and keenness	39.	Report	77.	Communication
2.	Communication	40.	Body language	78.	Pareto
3.	Presentation	41.	House journal	79.	Media
4.	Corporate	42.	Acronym	80.	Attention, action
5.	Body language	43.	Effective	81.	Brain, brawn
6.	Facebook	44.	Simplicity	82.	Documentation
7.	LinkedIn	45.	Passive	83.	Pidgin
8.	Testimonial	46.	Identification notion	84.	Public speaking
9.	Ethics	47.	Correctness	85.	Encoding
10.	Meta	48.	Effective	86.	Living
11.	Commerce	49.	Downward	87.	Silence
12.	Communication	50.	Upward	88.	Trademark
13.	Computer	51.	Dignity	89.	Channel
14.	Barrier	52.	Body language	90.	Antonyms
15.	Bulletin	53.	Communication	91.	Window
16.	e-governance	54.	Network system	92.	email
17.	Paralanguage	55.	Network	93.	Two-way
18.	Audio-video teleconferencing	56.	Cross-cultural	94.	Grapevine
19.	Human relation, communication	57.	Perilous	95.	Fax
20.	e-commerce	58.	Agenda	96.	Minutes
21.	Database	59.	Passive	97.	Salutation
22.	Public relations	60.	Cliché	98.	Database
23.	Internet	61.	Table	99.	Mind
24.	Mass	62.	Message	100.	Angry
25.	Diagonal	63.	Digital money	101.	Circular
26.	An art, a tool	64.	Full duplex	102.	Valuable asset
27.	Unifying link, binding force	65.	Elocution	103.	Interview
28.	Verbal	66.	Mass	104.	Intercom
29.	Non-verbal	67.	Business	105.	Newspaper
30.	e-communication	68.	Stress interview	106.	Quality
31.	Curriculum vitae	69.	Exact man	107.	Communication
32.	Active	70.	Semantics, Phonetics	108.	Clarity
33.	Courtesy	71.	Kinesics	109.	Smile
34.	Dialogue	72.	Feedback	110.	Thought
35.	Attire	73.	Corporate	111.	Physical, intellectual
36.	Language	74.	Two-way, one-way	112.	SMS
37.	Interview	75.	Online shopping	113.	Table
38.	Growth and brightness	76.	Elocution	114.	Pictorial

Glossary

Acknowledgement: A mark of courtesy expression for benefit received

Acronym: Forming a word from the initial letters of a word in a set phrase

Active (Emphatic) Listening: Listening to a message attentively and consciously

Agenda: List of items to be discussed at the meeting of an organization

Aide-memoir: Informing message easily and forcefully with a purpose with the help of visual messages and material prepared beforehand

Audio Teleconferencing: Interactive conversation through telephone

Automated Teller Machine: A special purpose with mechanism of transaction terminal used to provide remote banking service

Backbone Network: A large central network which connects all the terminals, micro-computers, main frames, local area networks and other communication equipment on a single company or university site. Backbone network is also called a campus area network (CAN)

Barrier: Blockade or barricade that may arise in the process

Bibliography: List of classification of literature used from available books, documents and reports

Body Language: Body movements expressed in the form of facial expression, gesture and posture, appearance, voice and alike with meaning without using words

Booklet: A small thin book containing information about organization's performance to be issued to the visitors, prospective customers, executives, trainees, newly recruited employees and other audiences

Bulletin: Report of official and published news of topical interest

Business to Business: Business to business is the portion of internet market which effects transactions between business operations and their partners in marketing sales, development, manufacturing and support

Cell (Mobile) Phone: Operation phone through airways within the jurisdiction of network of signals

Channel: The medium used for sending a message

Chart: A device portraying an organization's managerial position and relationships in carrying out business transactions

Circular: A document detailing information (orders or instructions) on a specific matter

Communication: To inform or spread information with meaning. If the sender gets his intended response from the receiver, it is effective communication. The receiver correctly understands the sender's message what he means, is good communication. Sending message in white and black record form and in oral is written communication and oral communication respectively. Passing of information between two or more persons who are neither in the same section nor on the same hierarchical level of organization is diagonal communication.

Condolence: Meeting for a solemn occasion

Conference: Meeting of long duration and larger participation of people for the purpose of discussing the theme of a common problem or issue

Corporate Communication: Passing of generated information by an organization to its stakeholders within and outside premises

Courier: A modernized and sophisticated form of private service delivery of messages at the door step of the recipient

Chart: Device showing non-numerical information

Crisis Management: Managing or finding solution for the un-conducive environment or problem/situation in the functional activity of an organization without loss of time

Culture: A shared set of values and attributes of a person or a group of persons

Dialogue: A conversation between two or more persons. In business, it means an exchange of ideas and opinions between two persons or groups or countries on a particular issue with a view reaching a friendly and amicable agreement.

Digital Money: Payment of amount electronically over internet

Electronic Business: The conduct of business using the internet and other electronic modes

Electronic Commerce: Buying and selling of goods and services over the internet for business purpose

Electronic Communication: Conveying information through the use of information technology devices

Electronic Mail: Transportation of information through electronic messages from one computer to another with communication network. It also covers data files, software and multimedia messages and documents as attachments

Electronic Payment System: A method for payment of cash or credit using electronic technology for the products and services in electronic commerce

Enterprise Resource Planning: Integrated software in which all the processes of operations of the enterprise affect the use of resource management.

Emphatic: Understanding the feeling

Fax: A device for transmitting copies of printed matter/images over telephone

Feedback: Reaction or response of the receiver to the sender or receiver's response to a message

Facial Expression: Emotional feelings being expressed through face without the use of words

Grapevine: Spread of unclear and confused messages being the result of gossip and rumours

Group Communication: Communication of people taking place in a group meeting

Handbook: Usual form of written information pertaining to policies, rules, procedures, practices, etc., of an organization protecting its image and impression

House Journal: A document containing information about firm's image and goodwill as messages among its own employees

Impromptu Speech: Instance responses to a given topic

Intercom: Internal telephone system allowing communication between the persons in different parts of building or campus

Internet: A connection of networks usually connected through routers

Interview: A meeting at which one person or an expert of the committee called interviewer asks questions on the subject matter to the applicant called interviewee

Knowledge Management: A practice that blends management and techniques to achieve results

Language: Symbolic communication

Leaflet: A small printed document used for informing people outside business premises about the product or service, its features, uses, durability, etc.

Local Area Network: A group of micro-computers or terminals located in the same area or a building situated close to each other and connected by a communication circuit for exchange of information

Magazine: A periodical publication containing information on opinions, findings of studies, articles, etc.

Manual: A small book containing all the information pertaining to organizational structure and responsibilities of each position, job, description, salaries, prevailing relationships among members including organization procedure.

M-commerce: Buying and selling of goods and services through wireless handheld devices

Meeting: Involving all the concerned people on the specific issues of fixed agenda with a person (usually executive) on the chair to administer and maintain orderly arriving decisions with consensus

Memorandum: A brief note on a particular issue to all the concerned ones in an organization. It is a one-way and good communication tool internally.

Message: Thought or idea being informed to the intended ones either in writing or body language or face-to-face

Meta-communication: Additional of new ideas to every expressed idea

Minutes: Written record of decisions taken at the official meeting of an organization

Miscommunication: Undesirable changes or contrary to the sender's expectation in the receiver's action and attitude

Motivation: Actuating behaviour or energizing an individual towards a goal

Network: A series of computers connected together in a way to allow sending information electronically

Networking System: Integration of computer and network components for communicating messages

Newspaper: A paper containing daily news and opinion of current events. The term news stands for north, east, west and south sides; and news and opinions coming from these sides is called a newspaper

Noise: A barrier to communication

Non-verbal Communication: Communication through symbols such as pictures, colours, signs and signals, body language and so on.

Notice (Bulletin) Board: A commonly used method to display an issue being discussed

Organization: Assembly of various need inputs or services for accomplishment of objectives

Paralanguage: Aspects of the voice. Say, people who know do not speak and those who speak do not know.

Passive Listening: Receiving and absorbing message with inert or no conscious effort

Pidgin: A person who uses mixed language

Phonetics: The science of sounds

Postscript: Additional information after the completion of document fully

Public Relations: Carrying out activities and communications for promoting goodwill with the community

Reference Initials: Initials of letter dictator and typist

Report: Document on the entrusted task in a given subject for taking decision

Resume: A brief account of one's career, qualifications and employment history typically prepared for achieving a position.

Semantics: The science of meaning

Short Messaging Service: Messages transmitting through cellular mobile phone

Smart Card: A portable service which contains some non-volatile memory and a microprocessor. It has a password or encryption key and furnishes it directly to the computer for the log-on procedure

Smile: A very potent form of facial expression

Silence: The state of wordlessness

Social Networking: Online service facilitating the social networks among people who share interests, events, activities or real-life connections

Soft Skills: Personal qualities and attitudes that are compatible as employee resource

Stakeholders: Individuals or group of persons who have some interest or stake in business and work for its success

Statutory Report: A report prepared u/s 165 of Companies Act containing the auditors' and Board's report and Annual account

Stress Interview: An interview which puts the candidate in difficult situation in order to know his or her reaction to stress

Table: Orderly arrangement of data in rows and columns

Tête-à-tête: Private and confidential conversation between two individuals

Trademark: An organization's identifiable mark, say a word, name, symbol, number or device or any combination thereof governing under legal protection

Verbal Communication: Communication through words

Video Teleconferencing: Inactive conversation between sender and receiver seeing each other through the network

Wide Area Network: A network used for transmitting data, voice, image and video information by interconnecting computers and other data transmission facilities on a countrywide or worldwide basis

Window Envelope: A transparent paper on the centre of cover through which one can read the inside address

World Wide Web (WWW): A repository of information spread all over the world and linked together

Bibliography

Gates, B. (2011). Business at the Speed of Thought. Penguin Books.

International Institute of Management Sciences (1994). Business Communication. 2nd Ed. Kolkata.

Kushner, M. (2011). The Light Touch — How to use Humor for Business Success. New York: Simon and Schuster.

Madhukar, R.K. (2010). Business Communication. New Delhi: Vikas Publishing House Pvt. Ltd.

Murphy, H.A., Hildebrandt, H.W. and Thomas, J.P. (2006). Effective Business Communication. New Delhi: McGraw-Hill Private Limited.

Pal, R. and Koriahalli, J.S. (2011). Essentials of Business Communication. Delhi: Sultan Chand and Co.

Reddy, A., Nagaraj and Rao, R. (2010). Essentials of Business Communication. Mumbai: Himalaya Publishing House.

Index

A

Active listening 203
Advertisement 273
Advertising message, aspects of 188
Agenda 77
    conduct of 78
    minutes of 79
    record of 79
Anonymous communication 117
Application-oriented knowledge 1
Appointment letter 254
Appreciation letter 255

B

Body language 96
Business communication 149
    and management 36
    classification of 53
Business correspondence 45, 146
    operational approach in 47
    persuasive approach in 46
    problem solving approach in 47
Business letter 125
    appearance of 134
    essentials of 126
    layout of 139
    parts of 135
    punctuation of 129
    types of 141
Business report 162
Business, interface of 147

C

Calling letter 254
Candidate
    competencies of 94
Career planning 246
Career recognition 268
Commerce 37
Committee meeting 82
    demerits 83
    merits 83
Communication model 187
Communication skills 3, 87, 197
Communication technology
    classification of 214
    evolution of 213
    features of 212
Communication,
    and mankind 5
    as discipline 15
    as foundation 38
    as management tool 39
    barriers to 26-30
    basics of 1
    channels of 110
    cross-cultural barriers 28
    definition of 7
    determinants of 17

- effects of 11
- elements of 18
- essentials of 22
- evolution of 4
- features of 9
- flow of 112
- functions of 12
- governance and 50
- guidelines for 25
- importance of 12
- improvement of 16
- meaning of 6
- methods of 153
- nature and scope of 8
- objectives of 10
- physical/technical barriers 28
- policy of 25
- principles of 9
- process of 17
- recent trends in 229
- socio-psychological barriers 29
- strengths of
- time in 4
- types of 110
- ways of 20

Condolence meeting 86
Conference 73
Confirmation letter 255
Conscious competence learning matrix 262
Conscious learning 262
Consensus 118
Conventional application letter 253
Conventional media 149
Corporate communication 123
Corporate education 196
Cross-culture communication 185
Curriculum vitae (CV) 247

D

Diagonal communication 117
Diffusion 177
Downward communication 112
Downward communication channel 113

E

E-business 190
E-commerce 190
- interface of 191
- scope of 191

Effective listening 31, 269
Electronic communication 214
- demerits 215
- merits 215
- terms of 216
- types of 215

Electronic mail 218
E-marketing 188
Employer employee communication 47
External communication 35
External report 160

F

Face-to-face conversation 67
Farewell speech 85
Feedback 20
Formal communication 111, 122
- demerits 112
- features of 111
- merits 111

Functional report 163

G

Group discussion 256
- dos and don'ts 259

H

Hearing 203
Horizontal communication 116
- demerits 117
- features 116
- merits 116

I

Informal communication 118, 122
- demerits 119
- features of 120
- grapevine 119
- merits 119

Insufficient communication 11
Integrated marketing communication 179
Interactive communication 73
Internal communication 35
Internal report 161
Interpersonal communication 156
Interpersonal skills 4
Interviews
- process of 91
- types of 88

J

Job application 248
Job interviews 263

K

Knowledge management 2, 275

L

Language 5
Letter to non-selected candidates 254
Listening
- barriers to 204
- process of 202
- types of 203

Listening skills 200
- importance of 201
- improving of 205

M

Management, role of 48
Marketing communication process 178
Marketing communication-mix 179
Marketing ethics and communication 181
- rationale of 182

Mass communication 153
M-commerce 225
- governance and 226

Media
- choice of 148
- interface of 147

Meetings 76
- demerits 82
- merits 81
- types of 81

Memo, preparation of 272
Message development 187
Message, loss of 21
Meta-communication 87
Minutes book 79
- format of 80

Miscommunication 11
Modern mode 150
Multimedia 224

N

Non-statutory reports 163
Non-verbal communication,
- importance of 95
- skills of 96

O

One-way communication 20
Online shopping 192
Open-door policy 271
Oral communication 65, 86
- demerits 66
- features 65
- forms of 67
- merits 66
- principles of 66

P

Passive listening 203
Personal barriers 29
Personal communication 117

Pictorial communication 101
demerits 103
merits 102
utility of 102
Popular social networks 235
Productive meetings 84
Profession 37
Public speaking 205
strategies of 208
tools of 207

R

Reasoning skills 259
Report
body of 167
documentation of 168
functions of 160
meaning of 159
purpose of 159
qualities of 170
structure of 165
types of 160
Resume,
components of 252
preparation of 250
Role play 261
Routine report 161

S

Selective listening 203
Self-development 3
Semantic barriers 27
Social advertising 269
Social media analytics 244
Social media networks 236
Social media,
channels and purpose of 232, 240
classification of 233
role of 239
statistics in India 233
Social networking service 228
demerits 229
merits 229
Soft skills 198
Special report 161
Specimen reports 171
Statutory report 163
Study skills 3
Supply chain management 189

T

Telephone talk 85
Television, effects of 271
Thinking skills 3
Thought, clarity of 267
Three-phase communication 118
Top-down communication 112, 266
Traditional media 240
and business performance 241
Two-way communication 20

U

Upward communication 114
demerits 115
merits 115
Upward communication channel 115

V

Verbal communication 54
Visual communication 103

W

Warning letter 255
Web and social media 234
Word processor 224
Word-of-mouth 71
Writing skills 63
Written communication 54, 86
essentials of 55
features of 54
forms of 64
types of 56